BAROLO:
TAR AND ROSES

BAROLO:
TAR AND ROSES
A Study of the Wines of Alba

MICHAEL GARNER
&
PAUL MERRITT

A JILL NORMAN BOOK
CENTURY

First published in 1990 by Century, an imprint
of the Random Century Group Ltd,
20 Vauxhall Bridge Road, London SW1V 2SA

Random Century (Australia) Pty Ltd,
20 Alfred Street, Milsons Point, Sydney,
New South Wales 2061, Australia

Random Century New Zealand Ltd,
PO Box 40–086, Glenfield, Auckland 10, New Zealand

Random Century South Africa (Pty) Ltd,
PO Box 337, Bergvlei, 2012 South Africa

British cataloguing in Publication Data
Garner, Michael
  Barolo : a study of the wines of Alba
  1. Italian wines
  I. Title   II. Merritt, Paul
  641.220945

ISBN 0 7162 3942 X

Photoset by Speedset Ltd, Ellesmere Port, South Wirral
Printed and bound in Great Britain by
Mackays of Chatham Plc, Chatham, Kent

IN MEMORY OF RENATO RATTI

CONTENTS

ACKNOWLEDGEMENTS

Our most obvious debt is to the many producers who have opened their cellars to us, often with a candour that belies the Albese reputation of insularity. We apologize here to any of the smaller producers whom we have overlooked in our survey. We owe thanks for the support and encouragement of both the London office of the Istituto Commercio Estero and the Consorzio of Albese Wines, where Beppe Colla and Antonio Maggiore have given us much help. Dr Chiri of the Cuneo Chamber of Commerce has supplied much vital information for our maps. We are grateful to Professor Morando of the Alba Enological School for his guidance on the subject of viticulture. On a practical level, we are greatly indebted to our friend Luigi Bertini. In terms of inspiration we must not overlook the contributions of both Nicolas Belfrage and Renato Trestini. Finally we must thank Trudy Garner and Vicki Nobles, whose common sense and patience has with luck been reflected in these pages.

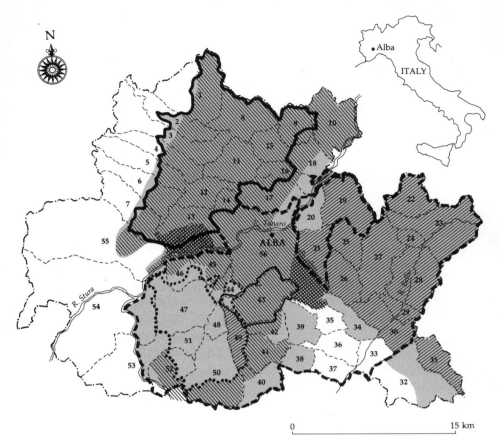

N

• Alba

ITALY

0   15 km

Barolo

Barbaresco

Barbera d'Alba

Moscato

Nebbiolo d'Alba

Roero

Dolcetto d'Alba

Dolcetto di Diano d'Alba

1 Montà	23 S. Stefano Belbo	45 Roddi
2 S. Stefano Roero	24 Camo	46 Verduno
3 Monteu Roero	25 Neviglie	47 La Morra
4 Montaldo Roero	26 Trezzo Tinella	48 Castiglione Falletto
5 Baldissero d'Alba	27 Mango	49 Serralunga d'Alba
6 Sommariva Perno	28 Cossano Belbo	50 Monforte d'Alba
7 Pocapaglia	29 Rocchetta Belbo	51 Barolo
8 Canale	30 Castino	52 Novello
9 Priocca	31 Perletto	53 Narzole
10 Govone	32 Cortemilia	54 Cherasco
11 Vezza D'Alba	33 Bosia	55 Bra
12 Corneliano d'Alba	34 Borgomale	56 Alba
13 Monticello	35 Benevello	57 S.Vittoria d'Alba
14 Piobesi d'Alba	36 Lequio Berria	
15 Castellinaldo	37 Arguello	
16 Castagnito	38 Albaretto Torre	
17 Guarene	39 Rodello	
18 Magliano Alfieri	40 Roddino	
19 Neive	41 Sinio	
20 Barbaresco	42 Montelupo	
21 Treiso	43 Diano d'Alba	
22 Castiglione Tinella	44 Grinzane Cavour	

PREFACE

A multitude of different wines are produced in the Langhe, too many to document fully here. While two of them, Barbaresco and Barolo, are known the world over, others are of purely local interest. We have therefore chosen to limit our study to the Barbera d'Alba zone and those wines from within its boundaries. This means that certain wines will be excluded which are usually considered to be Albese in origin – the Dolcetti* from Dogliani and the Langhe Monregalesi. In the case of the former, though some excellent wines are made, we feel that an examination of their production would contribute little of extra interest to the discussion of Dolcetto d'Alba and Dolcetto di Diano d'Alba (pp. 121–4). Dolcetto delle Langhe Monregalesi on the other hand is a relatively minor denomination.

Mention must here be made of Asti Spumante: a wine of such international significance deserves a book in its own right and is unfortunately beyond the confines of this one. There is the additional consideration that Asti Spumante is not regarded locally as an Albese wine: although in part produced in the Alba zone, at its eastern edge, this often excellent dessert wine really belongs to the province of Asti and those larger concerns which are frequently associated with vermouth as well as sparkling wine. The Langhe is a region of the small to medium-sized winery.

---

* We have followed the convention of using an upper case initial letter to distinguish a wine from a grape variety e.g. Dolcetto is the wine and dolcetto the grape variety.

But Alba is more than just an area that boasts a few names of international reputation: it represents in microcosm Italy's wine-making past, present and future. The major issues that confront Italian wine are all to be seen there: scandal, misunderstanding, misrepresentation, success and above all, potential.

INTRODUCTION

'Siamo sulla strada giusta': we are on the right track. What is nowadays a commonplace sentiment among the winemakers of Alba would just thirty years ago have been inconceivable. Until at least the middle of the sixties wine production was rooted, as elsewhere in Italy, in the viticultural dark ages. As Beppe Colla of the respected house of Prunotto and a recent president of the Consorzio of Albese Wines admits: 'If we, the Albesi, were still making wines the way we were thirty years ago, we wouldn't be selling a single bottle.'

A GLASS OF BAROLO

Every producer in Barolo and Barbaresco today has a different view about how to make wine. Sometimes the approaches vary slightly, sometimes enormously. While the wines' overall image is hampered by a lack of unity of style, these are fascinating times for the student of Albese wines. In one winery you can gaze on a possible blueprint for the future in the form of a wine made from low-yielding vines using the most up-to-date methods and equipment, while your next descent of cellar steps could lead to an authentic taste of what all the wines must have been like fifty years ago.

Despite the plethora of styles that make up Barolo at the beginning of the 1990s, certain general characteristics are apparent. First and foremost is sheer size. Even the intrepid Burton Anderson, probably the first outsider to attain the status of 'guru' of fine Italian wines, admits in his *Vino*: 'To be candid, the first Barolo I tried overwhelmed me; as I recall it took four or five experiences before I saw the light. And even now I approach the wine with a healthy measure of caution for it is not to be taken casually.'

In the glass, a distinctive 'autumnal' colour is the first of many surprises. The nebbiolo grape from which Barolo and Barbaresco are made does not contain strong colour pigments, so the wine can often look prematurely old. In some instances this may be a direct result of old-fashioned vinification methods which can cause much colouring material to be precipitated during the wine's lengthy spell in wooden barrels. However, while a young cask sample can sometimes show something of the deep, rich purple expected of a wine destined for long ageing, even a four- or five-year-old Barolo normally has more of a ruby/garnet colour – deep rather than dark – with tints that shade from mauve to rusty brown.

The initial sensations to the nose are often rather fleeting: fruit characters, mainly black cherries, raspberries and plums and sometimes, with some of the higher altitude wines, a pinot noir type note of strawberries. Flowers follow, often violets and the classic 'faded rose petals' intermingled with herbs like mint and camphor. Then the secondary aromas start to take over: it is here that the wine's extraordinary power begins to assert itself with scents of tar, licorice, truffles, bitter chocolate, ground coffee, tobacco, burnt toffee, aniseed and other spices; the list could go on and on.

For the uninitiated the palate can be a real struggle. Barolo's notorious vicelike grip of tannin can be enough to turn the lights out straight away. While the tannin content is an integral part of the structure which enables a wine to sustain many years of bottle age, for tasters it is rather like the wall marathon runners meet: some stop short, others break through to finish the course. It is what lies beyond the wall of tannin that counts. Renato Ratti (pp. 184–8) put the matter into its proper perspective: 'Some people taste a Barolo with a massive tannin content and say the wine has fantastic structure. What they often fail to realize is that the true structure of a wine depends on much more than that. The tannin must be balanced by, amongst other things, concentration of fruit, appropriate levels of acidity and alcohol. Only when its component parts are in harmony with each other can a wine be said to have fantastic structure.'

Off-putting though the tannins can be, they serve to promote one of Barolo's most prized features: its expansive and velvety texture. With age the tannins bond together to form longer molecular chains which transform that youthful, mouth-puckering severity into a silky and supple roundness, supported by the ever-present 'grace notes' of firmness and austerity. The technological advances of the last two decades have enabled more and more producers to effect a fine tuning, bringing richness and fruit flavours ever more into play.

Burton Anderson's choice of words must be applauded: 'overwhelming' is one of the few epithets that come close to conveying a classic Barolo's attack on the palate. Wave after wave of rich and concentrated flavours recalling the sensations apparent on the nose can leave the most experienced taster gasping. With every mouthful there is something new to be discovered; and that is one of the hallmarks of a great wine.

Barolo's real context is the laden table of Piemontese cooking; it excels with the region's plentiful game, roast and red meats, rich casseroles and pungent cheeses. In the vacuum of the 'show tasting', it will often appear savage and tongue-tied; so will the tasters!

Great Barolo is rightly seen as a *vino d'arrivo*, a wine to be arrived at, sometimes after lengthy experiment. Its uncompromising style leads those who cannot or will not see the light to insist that the wines are brutishly hard and severe. They continue to miss a rare enological treasure.

PIEMONTE, ALBA AND THE LANGHE

Piemonte is the northwestern outpost of modern Italy. It is an area of stark contrasts. Not much more than a century ago, the Piemontese played a leading role in the unification of their country and their principal city, Turin, became the new nation's first capital. At the beginning of the twentieth century Piemonte was in the vanguard of

Italy's move towards industrialization, leading the way in mechanical engineering and the textile and food industries. Turin and Ivrea (where Fiat and Olivetti are based) uphold that tradition today. Yet just twenty minutes' drive from these centres of industrial prosperity is a wholly different world where the country people have clung to their individual identity with an almost atavistic fervour. They keep themselves to themselves; some of the more remote villages can seem positively xenophobic. The commercialization of rural Piemonte is very much a postwar phenomenon.

Piemonte is divided into six provinces. The largest in terms of size and population, and by far the most rural, is Cuneo. A greater proportion of inhabitants live outside the provincial capital – the town of Cuneo – than in any of the other five. Second only to Cuneo in size, if not importance, is the small country market town of Alba (population 30,000) which stands on the southern bank of the river Tanaro. Alba is quintessentially Italian: the old centre is a labyrinth of narrow streets and alleyways which suddenly open onto small squares sometimes overlooked by noble houses. The many churches and the impressive cathedral date back to medieval times and their towers have yet to be dwarfed by modern office buildings. The town has the sort of quietly dignified atmosphere that time alone brings. Alba is comfortably prosperous today: it has a thriving clothes industry and the world-famous chocolate firm Ferrero is based there.

Ferrero's presence confirms something the locals (the Albesi) constantly remind you of: Alba's riches are traditionally those of the surrounding countryside. The green hills that flank the town on all sides are famous for their agricultural produce. Thanks to a particular local variety of hazelnut, Ferrero have made their fortune. Smaller fortunes change hands every autumn as gastronomes make a pilgrimage to Alba in search of the legendary white truffle, *tartufo bianco d'Alba*.

But the most vivid expression of the community is a range of extraordinarily characterful wines. Two made from the nebbiolo grape, Barolo and Barbaresco, are firmly established among the finest Italy has to offer, and are accorded the official status of DOC(G). The so-called lesser varietals Barbera and Dolcetto are, at their best, not too far behind. Nebbiolo d'Alba and the recently recognized Roero complete the picture of DOC reds. Of the two DOC whites, Moscato

4

d'Asti (a significant proportion is produced in the Alba zone) also enjoys a world-wide reputation, while Arneis di Roero may be set for a bright future. To these must be added an increasing number of high quality *vini da tavola* made according to the most up-to-date methods as well as a sprinkling of distinctive wines from rare local grape varieties.

By and large the vines are tended by smallholders who own, at most, a few hectares and often sell on their grapes to larger winemakers. Other small growers prefer the commercial security of belonging to a cooperative winery. Big landowners are few and far between in the Langhe hills. Even the biggest, such as Fontanafredda in Barolo's Serralunga, who own 110 hectares of vineyards, are small by international standards.

The inhabitants of the Langhe hills are the Langaroli, a proud and stubborn breed noted for their hard work, business cunning and reluctance to change their ways. In the past their insularity has too often been reflected in the style of their wines. Even at their best Barolo and Barbaresco are often easier to misunderstand than to appreciate. It is not difficult to have some sympathy with the wines' detractors: there are unfortunately still too many bad examples, a sorry fact which ultimately only the Albese winemakers can resolve.

LIFTING THE FOG

Rather than being 'on the right track', the Albesi stand at a crossroads. The way forward may be a lot clearer, but it is by no means certain that all producers will choose to follow in that direction. In terms of grape varieties, topography, soil types and climate, the Langaroli have the raw materials to take on the world; in terms of winemaking expertise, clonal selection, viticultural techniques and, above all, an unswerving commitment to quality, they still have a real tradition to build. A couple of dozen producers at most are consistently hitting the heights of excellence; the signs are that there are more to follow. Yet a fog of ignorance continues to shroud the wines of Alba: a closer examination of the viticulture, vinification, geography, history and, above all, some of the personalities behind the wines, can only help to clarify the picture.

I

THE GEOGRAPHICAL
BACKGROUND

Piemonte, the northwestern corner of Italy, borders on France to the west and Switzerland to the north. To the south it is separated from the Mediterranean by the narrow coastal strip of Liguria, while to the east in the province of Lombardia, the Po valley stretches from Lake Maggiore across the main body of the country to the Adriatic. Apart from this last natural boundary, Piemonte is ringed by Alpine mountain ranges. The name itself means 'foot of the mountain'.

Although its total annual wine production is outstripped in terms of volume by several other regions, Piemonte is a clear leader in winemaking prestige with no fewer than forty-two different DOC(G)s, significantly more than any of its rivals. When Luigi Veronelli devised the new 'super category' for his *Catalogo dei vini d'Italia*, four of the eight wines so designated were Piemontese (and all of them were red). Although there is a growing interest in white wines, and despite the presence of Asti Spumante, Piemonte remains at heart red wine country.

The traditional source of the finest red wines is the Langhe. This group of hills in central southern Piemonte has carried the reputation of great Piemontese, and to a certain extent great Italian red wine, from the start of the revival in Italy's winemaking fortunes. The zone is not a large one: the Langhe occupy no more than 2,000 square kilometres. These hills which cover the northeastern section of the province of Cuneo, are bordered by the plain of Turin to the north, the Monferrato hills to the east, the plain of Cuneo to the west and the

Maritime Alps of Liguria to the south. The area is traditionally subdivided into two distinct zones: the *alta* (upper) and *bassa* (lower) Langhe. The exploitation of the former is a relatively recent phenomenon. Large areas are still covered in forests of pine, fir, oak, elm, chestnut and beech, punctuated by the occasional patch of land cleared for agricultural purposes. The bassa Langa – the lower-lying northeastern section of the hills – has always been known for wine. The focal point of the bassa Langa is Alba, lying in an amphitheatre of hills with the river Tanaro closing the arc on the city's northwestern flank. Alba – apart from a brief period in the nineteenth century when nearby Bra assumed the mantle – has always been the distribution centre of those hills. They have a long, unbroken history of agricultural economy.

The region was formed during the Tertiary epoch, between the close of the Cretaceous and beginning of the Glacial periods. The Tertiary epoch is split into four subgroups: Eocene, Oligocene, Miocene and Pliocene; it is the last two, which occurred between 25 and 1 million years ago that concern us here. Though sometimes seen as a cadet branch of the Alps or Apennines, the Langhe are clearly of maritime origin. Their formation indicates a configuration of shallow seas and inlets, now identified as the Padano (Po) gulf. Sediments deposited at the bottom of the seas were compressed into conglomerate rocks like sandstone through the pressure of successive layers (in the Langhe these strata run from southeast to northwest at an average incline of approximately 15 per cent). The Tertiary crust movements, which thrust the Langhe up above the level of the sea, happened around the same time as the final elevation of the Alps. The climate then was warm and moist, gradually cooling to usher in the glacial period of the Pleistocene era about a million years ago.

THE MAJOR VITICULTURAL ZONES

To the north and west of the Langhe, the large plains of Turin and Cuneo extend at a gentle upward incline towards the encircling chain of Alpine foothills. These plains were gradually eroded through the action of rivers. As a result, a number of different territories were isolated, like the hilly table which once stretched in a northwesterly direction from the feet of the bassa Langa embracing the area now known as the Roero. At one time the river Stura flowed into the Tanaro as it headed northwards (through the Roero) towards Carmagnola. Between 150 and 200 thousand years ago the rivers changed course to the east (to join up with the Bormida and eventually the Po). The original course of the Tanaro is now visible as an almost continuous outcrop of rock (the Roero's famous *rocche*) stretching from just west of Pocapaglia up as far as Monta in a north-northeasterly direction. To the northwest of this great cut is the undulating plain of Turin and to the southeast lie the hills of the viticultural Roero and beyond them, the Langhe.

The Langhe

Nowadays, then, the Tanaro separates the bassa Langa from the Roero forming a neat, natural division between two very different terrains. On the lower (right) bank, south and east of the river, are the Langhe hills, formed during the Miocene era of the Tertiary epoch. They are long-ridged with rounded clay, sand and limestone outcrops and much subject to erosion – the mainly sedimentary accumulations that form the soil structure mean a lack of solid rock. The soil is basically neutral (sub-alkaline): the classic *terra bianca* (white earth) of the Langhe is a greyish-white, calcareous marl broken up with patches of yellow sand. There is generally a more compact sandstone on the lower ground while the higher ground gives way to clay rich in limestone and chalk. The soil is rich in mineral and trace elements: potassium, magnesium oxide, boron, iron, manganese, phosphorus and copper are present in significant amounts and the seemingly endless combinations result in wide soil variations between the different terrains.

For purposes of defence and drainage, habitation has tended to centre on the summits of the hills. The medieval castles and towers that dominate many of the hilltop villages are a constant reminder of the not so distant feudal past. The area is now crisscrossed with roads: these are often along the ridges, as at Castiglione Falletto and

Serralunga d'Alba. Until the eighteenth century at least, they were little more than tracks.

The Roero

The Roero occupies the left bank of the river Tanaro. The terrain is Pliocene in origin (the final phase of the Tertiary epoch) and is more closely tied to the final uplifting of the Alps. Stabilized in the climatic conditions of a later period, the hills of the Roero are characterized by the steep gradients and conical summits of its deep valleys and rocky outcrops, interspersed with more softly rolling land. The soil is typically friable, based on yellow sand with admixtures of limestone marl and marine-based sedimentary deposits (fossilized shells of small, prehistoric marine creatures are still to be found quite close to the surface). There are few of the elongated ridges that typify the bassa Langa and roads are thus often along the valley bottoms isolating the higher and steeper slopes where viticulture is traditionally strongest. The area is still quite widely forested with beech, chestnut, pine and in particular oak; the cultivation of the vine is correspondingly more sporadic than on the other side of the river.

Climate

Although benefiting from a classic continental climate, the area is far enough north to fall into Europe's temperate zone – the source of most of the 'old world's' premium red wines. It may come as something of a surprise to learn that Alba is on a similar latitude to Bordeaux. This is clearly not the sun-baked Italy of the tourist guides: the proximity of the Alps has a significant effect in maintaining reasonably cool and even temperatures throughout the year. Winters can be very long and cold with snow on the ground well into the late spring (this, incidentally, is an excellent time to spot the best vineyard sites: they are those where the snow melts first, indicating optimum exposure to the sun – a theory held by almost every grower you meet). Summers can occasionally be fairly hot and dry: in the *annus mirabilis* of 1985, following a wetter (103.6 centimetres of rain) and cooler (13.04 °C) than average May, there was hardly any rain at all until the late autumn, and July temperatures averaged out at 25 °C.

Generally there is much less fluctuation in temperatures between the months of May and October (roughly speaking the growing season of the vine). The following table, compiled from average monthly temperatures (measured in °C) over a period of 35 years, illustrates the point:

Table 1*

Jan	Feb	Mar	Apr	May	Jun	Jul	Aug	Sept	Oct	Nov	Dec
1.56	3.69	7.19	11.23	15.99	19.97	22.23	21.5	18.19	12.83	7.01	2.69

Rainfall is spread fairly evenly across the calendar, with peaks in late spring (April and May) and early to mid-autumn (October and November). The table of average monthly rainfall (measured in centimetres) is based on the same parameters as temperature:

Table 2*

Jan	Feb	Mar	Apr	May	Jun	Jul	Aug	Sept	Oct	Nov	Dec
31.53	42.17	52.83	72.24	84.77	44.87	26.47	44.93	38.78	72.83	59.19	40.78

Given the high average rainfall in October it is not difficult to sympathize with nebbiolo growers and their prayers that the rain will hold off until their crop is harvested. Vintages, particularly for the nebbiolo, are as reliable as in any other important wine-producing zone: there are on average two outstanding years a decade.

The exceptional natural feature however is the fog which blankets the landscape from autumn onwards, particularly at daybreak. Castiglione Falletto, right in the centre of the Barolo zone, is the perfect place from which to witness this remarkable phenomenon. If you're fortunate enough to be there on a cloudless and bright early morning, the view will root you to the spot. Beneath a brilliant blue sky, the shimmering white Alps ring the horizon providing a dazzling backdrop to the scene at your feet. The waves of vines that cover the Barolo basin are almost submerged in a dense, swirling mist; like Prufrock's 'cat', the fog twines itself around the occasional protruding green hillock. The scene is ever-changing: the fog rolls around the Barolo

*Source: Alba Endogical School/Instituto Tecnico Agrerio d'Alba

valleys as if searching for a way out. It is an unforgettable sight.

Other natural features are less friendly; because of the Langhe's location, hail is a great danger. Storms from the northwest (the Valle d'Aosta) pass over well-irrigated plains subject to strong evaporation and rise at the first physical obstacle – the Langhe, (because of the presence of the Monferrato hills storms from the east are much less of a problem). Hailstorms can have a devastating effect. In 1986 some Barolo producers reported a total loss of their nebbiolo crop owing to just twenty minutes' hail on 29 May. They will show you photographs of someone standing in a vineyard ankle-deep in hailstones, vines stripped of foliage and shoots. Not only is the size of the crop affected, but the quality of any subsequent fruit may result in off-flavours in the wine. The hail did more damage in some communes than others – there are even those who maintain that it had the effect of a natural selection process, resulting in a much reduced crop of high quality. Hail can strike at almost any time during the vines' growing season. We remember taking shelter from a brief storm in the middle of June 1988 in the winery of Fratelli Oddero at Santa Maria di La Morra when for a couple of minutes the hail cracked off the roof like gunshots. Meanwhile Luigi Oddero talked of the time that hailstones as big as golf balls fell on Monforte d'Alba!

The problem is a perennial one. Centuries ago cannons were trained on the skies from the hilltops in an attempt to break up the formation of hail clouds. Succeeding generations tried rockets and one modern response is to inject or 'seed' the clouds with sodium or silver oxides to try and prevent the ice forming. Protective plastic sheeting is impossible to fix as the ground can shift so easily, and it also cuts out essential light.   The topography of the area – spinelike ridges with a multitude of lateral spurs and valleys – creates a large number of individual microclimates, making generalizations on the nature of the climate as a whole more difficult. For example Olivio Cavallotto reported a crop loss of as little as 30 per cent in 1986: his estate at Bricco Boschis in Castiglione Falletto is a well-protected southwest-facing amphitheatre of vines where it is so mild he can even grow a few olive trees.

The climate of the viticultural Langhe can be summarized as cold winters (December–February), cool, wet springs (March–May), warm, fairly dry summers (June–September) and damp, foggy autumns (October and November). However, inconsistencies of the climate make every year different and the changing patterns of rain, sun, flood, drought, heat, cold, hail, snow and fog make up the addictive lottery upon which all producers gamble their livelihoods.

2

HISTORY

FROM EARLY RECORDS TO THE END OF THE NINETEENTH CENTURY

Piemonte's turbulent history, in combination with the Langhe's physical isolation, held the growth of the winemaking tradition in check for many centuries. Great wines are made not only in the vineyards and cellars but also by a receptive market.

Accessibility and ease of transport have a major role to play: Bordeaux and Oporto have the natural advantage of their ports while Burgundy and Champagne have long had good roads connecting them with the prosperous market of Paris. The winemakers of the Langhe had to remain content with serving local demand until the advent of improved roads and political stability in the nineteenth century.

The evidence of flints shows that the Langhe hills have been populated since the end of the Neolithic era. Systematic vine growing was probably introduced via Liguria by Greek merchants in the fourth and fifth centuries BC but Roman colonization in the first half of the second century BC gave greater shape to wine production. Roman viticulture favoured the high 'Etruscan' training system where vines were supported on low trees or by poles. The Romans built underground cellars for vinification, introduced wooden casks for storage and transportation and planted new vineyards on the clay slopes which also provided the raw materials for pottery and bricks.

Like the earlier Greek version, the Roman wine sold in the markets of Alba and Pollenza was sweet and sticky.

The first sign of the nebbiolo grape is a variety called 'allobrogica' by Pliny the Elder (AD 23–79) in his *Naturalis Historia*. It was grown by the Allobrogicans in northern Piemonte and Pliny describes the fruit as resistant to cold, late-ripening and deeply coloured. The wines were highly rated and even exported to Rome – doubtless the higher acid levels of nebbiolo grown at a northerly latitude gave a wine with exceptional keeping powers.

Roman rule represented one of the more peaceful interludes in the strife-ridden history of Alba. The town was accepted into the Municipal Federation in 89 BC and from the period when Consul Pompeo Strombone governed Piemonte became known as Alba Pompeia. The onset of Roman decadence was paralleled by the decline of viticulture in the region. Taxes on wine and vineyards were high and the countryside was gradually depopulated.

Between the fall of the Roman Empire and the arrival of Charlemagne and the Franks in the ninth century, the Langhe were laid waste and Alba destroyed by a series of incursions by temporary landlords such as Visigoths and Burgundians. During these so-called Dark Ages, monasteries were the sanctuary of wine culture. The rise of Christianity and the importance of wine as a sacrament saved vineyards from extinction. Under Charlemagne, Piemonte was for once allowed to choose its own form of government. This marked the beginning of a period of fragmentation and feudal rule which lasted longer than anywhere else in Italy, effectively until the French conquest in the eighteenth century. Under the share-cropping *mezzadria* system, half the wine made by the *contadino* would be given to his feudal lord.

During the tenth century, Hungarian and then Saracen marauders sacked, raped and pillaged their way across the Langhe from their strongholds at Frassinetto (La Garde Freinet near Toulon) and the Valle Bormida. The memory of these days is preserved in the hilltop towers (such as at Barbaresco), many of which date from this time, and in the Arabic words which still litter the Piemontese dialect.

In the medieval period, when Alba was occupied in turn by Provençales, Monferrini, Imperialists, Aigioni, Saluzzei and Visconti, both the evolution and documentation of viticulture are more in evidence. *Documents on Piemontese History* records the production figures and labour involved in the cultivation of 'nibiol' in Rivoli in 1268. Aromatic varieties such as malvasia and moscato were introduced and the move away from the Roman high training (*alteno*) to a shorter method of pruning supported by stakes, began. This new system was known as *a spanna*, a name which in Vercelli became confused with that of the nebbiolo grape – it is still known as *spanna* in much of northern Piemonte. Severe punishment for damaging vineyards indicates that these were times of petty vendettas, and the laws forbidding innkeepers to stock more than one red and one white wine and any water in their cellars suggest that falsification was not uncommon.

In the late medieval period the most powerful family in the Langhe was the Falletti, traders who made a rapid fortune and were admitted into the nobility (in the eighteenth century they were to be honoured as the Marchesi di Barolo). Their power was symbolized in a series of imposing castles built in the fourteenth and fifteenth centuries and which dominate most of the hilltop villages in the eleven communes of modern-day Barolo, including those at Serralunga, Castello della Volta in Barolo and, of course, Castiglione Falletto (the village was named after Manfredino Falletti in the fifteenth century). Across the river Tanaro, the largest landowners were the Roero family whose name is now used for the area.

In political terms, the most important noble dynasty in Piemonte was the Savoys. Their influence was first felt in the Langhe in 1531 when they acquired the Duchy of Asti and the Marquisate of Ceva and began to occupy and dispute many other territories. In 1713 Vittorio Amedeo II became king and the Turin-based court of Savoy brought about a period of relative stability until after the formation of the new Republic in 1861.

From the seventeenth century onwards the wines of the Langhe started to become a little more widely available. The nebbiolo, as it had now become known, was vinified into a fashionable pink *chiaretto* and lauded by the most respected wine authority of the day, Giovan Battista Croce (jeweller to the court of Turin), as the 'queen of black grapes'. Early the following century, while their country was at war with France, British wine merchants sought an alternative to red Bordeaux. The wines of Barolo were discovered and considered to fit the bill admirably but, because of poor or nonexistent roads and punitive frontier taxes, it proved impossible to transport the heavy casks of wine to Piemonte's port of Nice. It is tempting to speculate how different Barolo's history might have been with the British as clients. The French themselves were voicing a similar complaint: having recorded his pleasure at drinking wines from Alba at the French court, Colbert (minister to Louis XIV) lamented the fact that they were so difficult to obtain.

By the mid-eighteenth century the viticultural pattern evident today began to emerge in the Langhe. Until then a polycultural system had seen vines and other crops cultivated on the same plot. Vines were grown on the plain: without the demand for either quality or quantity there had been little incentive to deforest the hills and turn their more exacting slopes into vineyards. But under the greater commercial freedom of the unified Duchy of Savoy, the promise of new, quality-conscious markets like Turin gave rise to the planting of vineyards on the best south-facing hillsides. The vines were often planted in horizontal rows or terraces (rather than the earlier vertical rows or *ritocchini*) which were easier to work with oxen, and drainage ditches were cut into the hillside to lessen the effects of erosion. Where sixteenth-century records show 16 per cent of the bassa Langa under vine, by the mid-eighteenth century the figure had risen to 30 per cent.

In 1758 Alba issued an edict – the first attempt at DOC type legislation – prohibiting the import and blending of inferior wine from outside the area. Along with the establishment of a *banda di vendemmia* (an official date before which it was illegal to harvest grapes), this indicates a growing pride and seriousness in the Albese attitude to wine.

Winemaking techniques were also evolving. By the first half of the nineteenth century the first attempts were being made to vinify Barolo as a dry wine. Between 1832 and 1849 the young Count Camillo di Cavour, later Italy's first Prime Minister, researched and implemented new agricultural systems on the run-down farms around the family castle at Grinzane and gave local winemakers a spur by employing Louis Oudart, a French enologist from Reims. Cavour had doubts about the potential of nebbiolo, however, and planted 14 *giornate* (around 5 hectares) of pinot noir to try and emulate the great Burgundies that were still served at the Savoy court in Turin.

Oudart was also employed by the Marchesa Giulia Falletti to

improve the wine from the family estates in Barolo and Serralunga. King Carlo Alberto was so impressed with the results, the legend goes, that he ordered 325 *carrà* of wine (a *carrà* is a long, flat cask containing 476 litres), one for each day of the year (piously excluding Lent). Marchesi di Barolo were the first to bottle a wine labelled 'Barolo' rather than 'Nebbiolo' around this time (the exact year is unknown).

In the 1840s Carlo Alberto made his own contribution to the modernization of Barolo, setting up production facilities at his newly purchased Verduno estate under the control of General Staglieno, who had worked with Oudart at Grinzane. Staglieno made innovations in the cellar, introducing closed-vat fermentation and improving the use of sulphur dioxide. In the second half of the century most of the big companies involved with the production of vermouth and Asti Spumante grew up around Alba and Asti. Martini & Rossi, Gancia, Contratto, Cinzano, L. Bosca and Riccadonna were all established in a wave of prosperous industrialization stemming from Piemonte's (and especially Turin's) leading role in the new Italian Republic. By the turn of the century the main production centre for Barolo was the town of Bra.

In 1878 Count Emanuele Guerrieri di Mirafiore, son of King Vittorio Emanuele II and his official lover 'La Bela Rosin' (Rosa Vercellana) anticipated Villa Banfi in Toscana's Montalcino exactly 100 years later by redefining the landscape around his father's hunting lodge in Serralunga. Over a ten-year period he removed the dense woodland and planted nebbiolo and moscato vineyards: Mirafiore Vini Italiani was undoubtedly the most high-tech operation of the day.

The foundation of Alba's Enological School in 1881 met some of the needs of a rapidly expanding wine industry by providing an important link with other viticultural centres across Europe where rational systems of cultivation were already established. Its expertise was much in demand with the arrival of the triple plague from America: first oidium in the 1850s, then peronospera and at the turn of the century phylloxera. The school's first director, Domizio Cavazza, formed the Langhe's first cooperative at Barbaresco in 1894. Although he is also credited with pioneering dry Barbaresco, Oudart's earlier work for Count di Castelborgo in Neive probably laid the foundations for this style. The influence of the school also helped to establish the single Guyot training system as the norm in Alba.

THE POST-PHYLLOXERA PERIOD

In the nineteenth century vines such as freisa, grignolino, brachetto and malvasia were still much in evidence and vinified into sweet and sometimes sparkling wines. While the first two still have some following and brachetto is occasionally encountered, malvasia has all but disappeared from the zone. Following phylloxera, two major themes became apparent: the emergence of barbera as a strong and adaptable variety able to produce both quality and quantity; and the unequivocal confirmation of nebbiolo as the area's premium red grape. As elsewhere in Europe, traditions were reinforced in the face of adversity: though a clear identity for Barolo and Barbaresco had been realized only in the second half of the previous century, they quickly became the cornerstone of the new wine industry of the 1920s.

By now a new factor had severely dislocated the lifestyle of the Langaroli. In the early years of the twentieth century, Piemonte led the way in northern Italy's move towards industrialization and large numbers of the work force were lured away from the land by the promise of higher wages and less backbreaking toil in the factories not only of Alba but also further afield in Genoa, Milan and Turin. As in the period immediately following the Second World War there was widespread emigration particularly to the USA. This was also the time when many of today's larger negociant houses were established including Prunotto (1924) and Franco Fiorina (1925).

Inevitably, cultivation systems had to be adapted to a much-reduced work force. One of the first casualties was the labour-intensive practice of training the vines *a catene* (in chains) which had been losing favour since the second half of the nineteenth century. This method involved the retention of the productive shoots off the previous year's fruiting cane which were woven together to form a 'chain' of horizontal branches to support the new season's growth, sometimes with only one training wire 2 metres above the ground. Farming methods changed too and the 'circular' process of working the land began to disappear. Hitherto the life of the *contadini* had revolved around not only their grapes but also their animals. A proportion of the land had been given over to growing foodstuff for themselves and to feed their beasts which in turn ploughed and fertilized the fields. Grapes were only grown in the sites best suited to them. Here we see the origins of the so-called *cru storici* (see p. 139).

Ancient customs die hard in the fields: from their intimate knowledge of the land, the *contadini* had created a natural order which was almost mystic in conception. The timing of the various viticultural tasks such as pruning depended on the phases of the moon. These beliefs even extended into the sphere of vinification: new wine would only be racked during certain favourable lunar phases. The legacy continues to influence some of today's older generation of growers who insist, for example, that cuttings taken under the waning moon will break down to nourish the soil more quickly than those taken under the waxing moon. However, the lifestyle of the *contadino* was a punishing one: monotonous and exhausting physical toil brought scant rewards and new horizons seemed to offer the only way of escaping drudgery and poverty. The old ways are now perpetuated mainly in the terminology used to describe life in the vineyards. Thus many Langaroli continue to measure their land in *giornate* – a *giornata* is the amount of land one man can work in one day. There are approximately 2.66 *giornate* to a hectare and, typically, 1,500 vines in a *giornata*.

Concurrently with the drift away from the land, we see the beginnings of greater mechanization. Prior to the 1930s there was plentiful labour to crush the grapes by foot and, using long poles, to push down the floating cap of solids that rose to the top of the uncovered *tini* (barrels) used for fermentation. The supposedly traditional *cappello sommerso* (submerged cap) system of vinification dates back to this time. The introduction of a grille to keep the cap submerged throughout fermentation performed automatically a task once done manually.

During the first few decades of the twentieth century, mechanical efficiency was to replace cheap labour in much the same way as the tractor later replaced the ox (though not, in certain instances, until the 1970s). The new technology brought about many benefits. Beppe

Colla of Prunotto described how at one time cellar workers would 'rack' the wine by carrying it in *brente* (wooden buckets) strapped to their backs from the first barrel, across the cellar floor and up wooden ladders before stooping over to empty the contents into the new one. The arrival of the pump must have been greeted with great relief throughout the cellars of the Langhe.

By now a commercial structure had evolved which today still forms the basis of the wine trade in Alba. Negociant houses and the early cooperatives acted as the logical destination for the grapes of numerous smallholders who lacked the experience and resources to see the process through from bud to bottle. In 1934 the Consorzio for Barolo and Barbaresco was founded after decades of deliberation and, as a consequence, production rules were tightened up. With the face of their vineyards reshaped and cellar technology transformed, Albese winemakers were looking forward to a more stable future when the Second World War broke out.

The Langhe hills became a centre of the partisan resistance to the Nazi-Fascist alliance. The atmosphere of this time is vividly recreated in the novels of Cesare Pavese and Beppe Fenoglio. Many bloody battles were fought in the vineyards. Near Bricco di Neive seven young *partigiani* bravely but vainly took on a whole republican battalion while on 2 November 1944 at San Cassiano close to the Prunotto winery, a battle was fought for the city of Alba between 2,000 partisans and 10,000 fascist troops. Winemaker Luigi Oddero fought with the partisans as a fifteen-year-old. He remembers the murder of thirty-two partisans at Cerequio in La Morra on 29 August 1944: '. . . the blood poured down the hillside like rain'. During the war the wine trade in Alba ground to a halt and, once more, what wine was made was purely for local consumption. The cellars were so full, Oddero claims, that for six years after the war, Barolo was sold for the price of a one-year-old Barbera.

It took time for the trade to regroup when peace returned. The 1950s and 1960s were the era of the cooperatives: both the Terre del Barolo and Produttori di Barbaresco cooperatives were formed in 1958. Once more it became unfashionable to work in the fields and nearby factories continued to claim the descendants of the few *contadini* who had remained on the land. A temporary solution in the late 1960s was to draft a new labour force from southern Italy –

particularly Calabria. Since the 1970s the big negociant wineries have had their complacency shaken by the rash of small growers who have begun to vinify and bottle for themselves. In 1985 the notorious blenders of Narzole, a small town west of Alba, made their own tragic headlines when they poisoned a large quantity of Barbera del Piemonte with methanol. Newspapers reported the subsequent deaths of twenty old people, but in court it was later agreed impossible to attribute the fatalities directly to drinking the contaminated wine.

Alba's wealth has continued to grow. The town's major industrial success stories include Ferrero confectionery, Miroglio clothes and textiles and the evocatively named Mondo Rubber. Alba, 'city of 100 towers', retains an air of medieval mystery in its narrow alleyways, but the ugly new roads and ever-growing light industrial zones that surround it threaten to frighten the tourist away rather than lead him closer.

As a result of the new prosperity, road networks continue to develop. A virtual motorway takes you practically into the heart of Barolo. Sleepy little villages like Barolo itself are changing, awakening to the call of tourism. Barolo enthusiasts from Switzerland and Germany can now stay in a brand-new concrete Enomotel in the nearby village of Roddi. Local *hosterie* are lightening their robust, traditional fare and reducing the number of *antipasti* for clients whose day's labour has not been trudging up and down steep vineyards but cruising along the *autostrade* in the BMW.

The changes are painful for the few who remember traditions unaltered for centuries. There are those who doubt the value of the new outward-looking attitude in the Langhe, but the majority of wine lovers are not among them.

3

VITICULTURE AND
GRAPE VARIETIES

THE RELEVANCE OF THE VINTAGE

While a careless winemaker can turn excellent grapes into poor wine, no amount of technical wizardry can make a fine wine out of poor grapes. Nowhere is this more apparent than in a red wine region like Alba. As Alba has a relatively unreliable climate, winemakers are faced with the basic choice of whether to market their wines in favourable years only or to make the best of things when nature has been less kind to them. Even though economics dictate that the first option is unrealistic, with the agreement of growers in both zones, no DOC Barolo or Barbaresco was released from the abysmal 1972 vintage. Meanwhile perfectionists like Giovanni Conterno and Angelo Gaja prefer to bottle no wine under their own label when the harvest does not match up to their exacting individual standards (as happened in 1984). Others insist that it is essential to make wine every year and most dedicated producers manage to let their talents shine through in lesser vintages by performing a rigorous *scelta* (selection) in the vineyards, discarding any unripe or imperfect grapes. Quantities are thus sometimes drastically reduced, but by modifying vinification techniques – perhaps by reducing skin contact during fermentation and aiming for a fresher, fruitier style – a winemaker need not worry about compromising his reputation. Many delicious examples of the 1984 vintage were made by producers willing to adapt their techniques to the nature of the crop.

The idea of a *scelta* is nothing new: indeed at one time it was done as a matter of course. Sobrero, one of the masters of 'old school' Barolo, was last in line of several generations of winemakers and had no heir to carry on the tradition. He says:

> To make a great wine you have to start in winter when you prune. You must allow the vine to give what it can give and not a grape more. My brother was a master in the vineyards, he wouldn't allow me a single grape that wasn't ideal for making wine with. This is what I always say to people: I would like them to have seen how the nebbiolo harvest used to be. It was really something to see: they would take a bunch of grapes, turn it in their hands and pick off any grape that wasn't absolutely perfect. If there was a suggestion of humidity, nothing could persuade them to pick. In the evening when the sun went down, they picked the grapes, put them in wooden tubs and then in the morning before going out to pick again, they would clean the bunches. Probably if the merchants of that era were around today, they wouldn't buy any of the grapes on sale.

The Sobrero Barolo (which, incidentally, was made every year) bears testimony to the excellence of the winemaker and his raw material.

It is generally the final ten weeks before the harvest that determine the success or failure of a vintage. A spell of good weather at the end of the season can turn a previously unpromising vintage into something quite respectable (as happened in Barolo in 1984 for example). In Barbaresco in 1987, the poor spring and unreliable summer gave way to a period of warm, dry weather starting in late August and lasting just long enough for the grapes to be picked before heavy rains fell in the second week in October. But only grapes that are healthy to begin with can benefit from the effects of an indian summer: this is why the grower's work during the first half of the year is so vital.

THE CHOICE OF SITE

In addition to a suitably structured, well-drained soil and considerations of altitude and microclimate, there are three basic elements which enable a vine to function properly: sunlight, water and carbon dioxide.

Sunlight

The Langaroli categorize their vineyards in four main types according to the *sori'* or *sorito* – the lie of the land and its exposure to the sun. This will be a major determining factor in the choice of the right grape for a particular site. The east to southeast facing slopes have a *sori' della matina* (a morning exposure) in that they are directly facing the sun as it rises in the early part of the day. The most prized, south-southeast through to southwest facing hillsides have a *mezzogiorno* or noon aspect; they take the sun as it rises, are fully exposed in the middle of the day and continue to benefit from the sun's rays until they start to lose their power in the early evening. A mainly southwest to west facing vineyard is thus termed a *sori' della sera*, (an afternoon and evening exposure). The *mezzanotte* (midnight) exposures are primarily north facing and do not receive the sun directly at all. They are only of use for certain white grapes requiring a prolonged ripening season.

The hardier vines such as Barbera are preferred in the more exposed and windy positions, while the more sheltered *conca* (literally 'shell', or amphitheatre) sites are reserved for the most prized varieties.

Water

Although its leaves are capable of absorbing small amounts of moisture, a vine takes in most of its water supply through its roots. The 'day' roots close to the surface will absorb some rain but the base roots which anchor the plant by penetrating deep into the ground are of primary importance here. They locate the fine particles of moisture-retentive clay in the subsoil which sustain the plant during dry spells.

Carbon Dioxide

A vine's leaves are its lungs. During daylight hours they extract carbon dioxide from the air and release oxygen back into it; at night the process is reversed. The leaves manufacture the carbohydrate essential to fuel the plant's growth and which – as any excess is stored – will determine the amount of sugar present in the fully ripened grapes. These carbohydrates are formed by the process of photosynthesis: water and carbon dioxide are transformed in the presence of light into sugars through the agency of the chlorophyll present in the leaves. This 'assimilation' is clearly favoured in the earlier part of the day when the air is full of the carbon dioxide the vines have exhaled during the night: one very good reason why certain growers like Elio Altare of La Morra maintain that a south-southeast facing site is ideal for nebbiolo.

GRAPE VARIETIES

There are around 28,000 hectares of land under vine in the Alba zone yielding around 1.3 million hectolitres of wine each year, about 60 per cent of which is accounted for by DOCG wines. All but one of these are made from ancient and traditional indigenous varieties: the sole exception is one of the two DOC whites which comes from moscato, an ancient variety grown all over the world. Experiments with the various subvarieties of the pinot vine have been going on with varying enthusiasm since Cavour's time while the recent, fervent search for the way forward has prompted the rediscovery of rare native vines like favorita and pelaverga. Those ubiquitous standards cabernet and chardonnay are present but so far not in any great quantities: of the two, more interest is being shown in chardonnay – cabernet seems to be posing little, if any, threat to nebbiolo.

Nebbiolo

Alba's viticultural history has been dominated by the story of this noble grape. Although never the region's most widely planted variety, nebbiolo has consistently occupied centre stage in terms of prestige, with the other vines filling in as best they can. The name nebbiolo (nebbiö in Piemontese) almost certainly derives from *la nebbia* (fog): according to local custom, the grapes are not harvested until 'moistened' by the autumn fog.

If nebbiolo is so special, the fact that planting remains highly restricted must be explained. The reason is to be found in the variety's notoriously demanding nature: tradition dictates that nebbiolo will only give of its best in very particular locations. Professor M. Fregoni (*Carta dei vigneti di Barolo, Barbaresco e Nebbiolo d'Alba*) defines the ideal soil as subalkaline, rich in potassium, phosphorus, magnesium and calcium with a high proportion of other macro- and micro-elements including boron, manganese, copper, zinc and iron. This describes the basic formula of the limestone marl of Barolo and Barbaresco and the rather sandier soil of the Roero (the soils have an average pH, of 7.8–8.0 and 7.8–7.9 respectively). Nebbiolo also requires good drainage and will flourish on slopes up to 400 metres. As it is the first vine in the area to bud (normally in early April) and the last to be harvested (from early and mid-October onwards), its long ripening season customarily requires a *mezzogiorno* exposure. Indeed nebbiolo enjoys a virtually unchallenged monopoly of the 'golden triangle' between south-southeast and southwest in prime vineyard areas. It will always be planted on the most favourable part of a hillside: towards the top (*bricco*) where it will receive maximum exposure to the sun. Regarding the curve of the slope, some growers prefer a *conca* where the stiller air favours both higher temperatures and assimilation while others argue that a more exposed position with freer air circulation offsets the danger of cryptogamic diseases. Obviously the number of sites to which all these criteria apply is extremely limited.

Nebbiolo is, however, a hardy vine. Not only is it resistant to diseases but the thick-skinned fruit is able to withstand low temperatures. Some growers even maintain that nebbiolo actually benefits from a cold snap. Elio Altare provided the rational explanation for this unusual phenomenon: 'In a rainy vintage like 1980, the fruit tends to become swollen with water. The effect of the cold is to *apassire* [dry] the grapes.' The cold night temperatures partially freeze the fruit on the vine: as the day warms up the semi-frozen pulp begins to melt and some of the excess water evaporates through the skins. In exceptional years the nebbiolo harvest will not be completed until mid-November when the grapes are sometimes picked with snow on them. Similarly the cool night-time temperatures, which return to the Langhe from September onwards, slow down the ripening process ensuring that important aroma- and flavour-producing compounds are not burnt up overnight.

Nebbiolo is a robust vine in other ways too. Because of its strong vegetative growth, growers adopt a long pruning system with some ten to fifteen buds on the fruiting cane (the exact amount will vary according to the strength of the individual plant). Of these, around half will, in normal circumstances, produce fruit-bearing shoots (the first two shoots at the trunk end of the cane are never productive). Nebbiolo moreover will not produce high-quality grapes in large quantities and yields must be severely contained in order to arrive at well-balanced fruit.

The extreme vigour is a constant source of concern: with shorter pruning (e.g. six buds) the vine tends to concentrate all its energy into producing foliage and as few as two of those six may produce fruit. Extensive green pruning is essential although research is finally being carried out to find a compatible rootstock which will help to contain this tendency to abundant leaf production. For similar reasons the individual plant is allotted a large amount of space: the vines are commonly planted between 1 and 1.5 metres apart with up to 2 or even 2.5 metres between rows. The typical density of a nebbiolo vineyard is therefore usually around 4,000 plants per hectare. Many growers argue that the nebbiolo is not suited to more intensive planting (particularly in view of the fact that the Langhe's soil is very fertile).

As many as forty different clones have been identified and categorized by Alba's Enological School – they maintain a vineyard at La Morra where all forty can be found. Nowadays the law decrees that the two DOCG wines can only be made from the three clones that have been favoured over the course of the years, lampia, michet and rosé.

The great 'clone debate' has attracted much interest during the last decade. Michet is currently the most fashionable of the three. Its name comes from *micot*, a dialect word meaning 'little loaf', owing to the shape of its bunches. Michet's yields are said to be low and inconsistent though the quality of its grapes is often viewed as being superior. The michet vine has smaller than average five-lobed leaves and gives smallish, compact, cylindrical bunches of round, deeply coloured grapes. Those of its chief rival, lampia, are usually pyramid-shaped with the round, deep violet grapes clustered less closely together. Lampia's bunches often have lateral 'wings' at the top resulting in a bulbous T-shape (the local description is much more colourful!). Lampia usually has tri-lobed leaves and is generally more reliable in its fruiting patterns. The third clone, rosé, is a much rarer and more delicate species. Many growers have a few rosé vines in their vineyards but seldom more than a row or two. Rosé's distinguishing feature is clearly defined: the colour of its grapes is always relatively pale even when mature (if you hold a bunch up to the light, rosé grapes have a translucent rosy colour). Otherwise this clone's ampelographic characteristics resemble michet's.

Rosé is almost without exception regarded as an inferior clone producing a pale, light and comparatively feeble wine. In the glass it has a striking perfume notable more for its intensity of fragrance than its richness; the penetrating smell is sometimes compared to red-currants and has peppery, grenache-like tones. Perhaps because of its curiosity value, a number of growers have been carrying out experiments with rosé, amongst which Vietti's cru Briacca has attracted the most attention. Otherwise rosé will only play a more important role in exceptional circumstances, such as in the generally weak 1983 vintage when some growers found it their most successful variety. Despite the arresting perfume, the majestic richness which is the hallmark of great Barolo is lacking in rosé-based wines, the fruit being typically too slight to support the high levels of tannin and alcohol.

The fact that nebbiolo mutates very easily according to where it is planted has led several authorities to question the real differences between lampia and michet. Renato Ratti always maintained that the crucial factor about nebbiolo was its sensitivity to the soil. Michet, he insisted, performs best in sandier soil (such as is found in Monforte) yet if planted in ground with a higher clay content (certain parts of La Morra), the same vine could take on the characteristics of lampia. Professor Morando, a viticultural expert at Alba's Enological School, claims that a single plant may simultaneously show characteristics of both clones. He believes michet could be a form of lampia suffering a genetic mutation because of viral infection. In general lampia is rather more common than michet in Barolo and much more dominant in Barbaresco.

Michet followers, however, point to the fact that the buds on its fruiting cane are less regularly spaced than with lampia, that their preferred clone is a sturdier plant producing thicker wood growth and above all, that because of michet's higher skin-pulp ratio its extractable polyphenol content is naturally superior. Those who favour lampia argue that, unlike michet, it can be relied upon to fruit well and the quality of the wine it gives is similarly dependable. The more pragmatic growers suggest that few are aware exactly which clones their vineyards are planted to and that, in any case, the part of the slope on which nebbiolo is planted is far more important than the individual clone in determining the quality of the fruit. No conclusive research has yet been put forward to show who is right and the discussion continues unabated. The positive side is that in the many vineyards with a less homogeneous soil structure, the subtle variations from plant to plant can contribute almost infinite shadings to the final product.

The other nebbiolo clones have no real significant presence in the zone: bolla, rossi, san luigi and other obscure and localized variations are not considered fine enough for producing Barolo and Barbaresco. Although at one time more widely dispersed throughout northern Italy, nebbiolo is no longer frequently encountered beyond Piemonte.

Barbera

The rise and rise of barbera has been meteoric. Although there is scant historical reference to the vine (barbera is first mentioned in the seventeenth-century archives of Nizza Monferrato), it is now one of Italy's most widely planted varieties. Barbera's exact origins are unknown but historically it is the most favoured variety of the Monferrato hills just east of the Alba zone, so it generally qualifies as an honorary native. Its widespread presence was only established following phylloxera. The reasons for this are straightforward: barbera is a very vigorous variety, resistant to cryptogamic diseases, bears abundant fruit consistently and, unlike the other red grapes of the zone, is not particularly exacting as to the soil or location in which it is planted although this final factor does play a vital part in determining the quality of its fruit. It buds a week or so later than the nebbiolo and ripens at a very convenient time: from the end of September to the middle of October, between the dolcetto and nebbiolo harvests (though it will mature earlier in prime sites).

Barbera is trained to an average height of 1.5 metres or so with the fruiting cane typically pruned to ten or twelve buds. The foliage (five-lobed leaves) is of medium intensity and the fruit borne in smallish, quite compact, pyramid-shaped bunches of intensely purple grapes. Traditionally barbera requires little green pruning as there is an even, natural balance between fruit and foliage.

The Albese will sometimes acknowledge that barbera generally performs best outside their zone. The obvious rationale behind this point of view is that the best sites in Alba are given over to nebbiolo and the more adaptable grape is used to fill in where nebbiolo would not ripen so well. This often means that barbera will occupy west-facing sites; it is also to be found at the foot of slopes planted to nebbiolo; single vineyard Barbere from famous Barolo and Barbaresco crus are quite commonly found in commerce. Around Asti and Alessandria it occupies prime positions – perhaps the most celebrated example, Bricco dell'Uccellone, is made by the 'King of Barbera', Giacomo Bologna, from a vineyard about 5 kilometres outside Asti. Outside Piemonte it is present in significant quantities throughout most of northwestern and central Italy.

Dolcetto

Although the first mention of dolcetto is to be found in the ordinances of the commune of Dogliani in 1593, references to the 'dozzetto' can be traced back over the previous century. The fact that dolcetto is still referred to as *douset* in dialect tends to confirm that this is one and the same variety. Like barbera and nebbiolo, it has been around for a long time and is a tried and trusted local. The name means 'little sweet one': when fully ripe, the grapes are particularly succulent and because of its fairly low acidity, dolcetto has some history as a table grape.

Like nebbiolo, dolcetto will only perform well in certain locations and is nearly always planted in the miocene soil of the lower (right) bank of the Tanaro and traditionally prefers a calcareous marl ground. In mainly clay or 'cold' (poorly draining) soil, the grapes tend to fall from the vines before they can be harvested. Dolcetto buds around the same time as barbera and is the first of the red grapes to mature (from the middle to the end of September). Because its foliage is not vigorous, dolcetto is normally pruned relatively short with between six and nine buds on the fruiting cane. For the same reason plantings are frequently more dense: the vines are spaced at up to 1 metre apart with a 2–2.25 metre gap between rows. It is usually trained quite low (to a maximum of 1.6 metres) and the shoots are twisted around the last wire – a practice known as *r'caplé* in Piemontese. As it matures early, dolcetto can also be planted at fairly high altitudes: up to 700 metres in parts of central Piemonte.

The plant bears broad, five-lobed leaves and pyramid-shaped bunches of round, vividly coloured, blue-black grapes, the thick skins containing heavy colour pigments. Dolcetto is an easy vine to recognize because of the red veins of its leaves. Owing to its sparse foliage, a number of growers like the Sandrone brothers and Enrico Scavino are experimenting with the removal of the buds on the underside of the shoots in order to achieve a better-balanced arrangement of fruit and foliage. Its presence is almost entirely restricted to central Piemonte where it has no less than seven separate denominations: Dolcetto d'Alba, Dolcetto d'Acqui, Dolcetto d'Asti, Dolcetto delle Langhe Monregalesi, Dolcetto di Diano d'Alba, Dolcetto di Dogliani and Dolcetto di Ovada, a confusing state of affairs justified by often rather subtle differences in style.

Other Red Wine Grapes (Non DOC Wines)

FREISA
Even thirty years ago, freisa was much more widely planted than it is today. However, despite often being relegated to inferior sites, freisa still has a loyal following and demand for the wine – albeit local – remains buoyant. Indeed there are signs that freisa is beginning to make a comeback.

Whilst considered to be of local origin, freisa's presence has only been catalogued since the end of the eighteenth century when Count G. Nuvolone included freisa among the premium black grapes in his work *Sulla coltivazione della vite e sul metodo migliore di fare e di conservare i vini* (1799). Freisa is similar in appearance to nebbiolo; indeed some believe it may belong to the nebbiolo family. Like nebbiolo, freisa's leaves turn yellow in the autumn: with the other red varieties like dolcetto and barbera, the change is from green to red. It is another vigorous vine which produces abundant foliage and requires long pruning. Its leaves are rather small and can have three or five lobes: the grapes, which are a deep, smoky-blue colour, come in long, loose bunches. Freisa is a fairly thick-skinned variety and though production is constant, the grapes do not yield a large quantity of must.

GRIGNOLINO

Although at one time a highly regarded variety, less and less grignolino is planted in the zone today. Indeed some of the better known Albese wineries which include a Grignolino in their line-up (e.g. Bruno Giacosa and the Ceretto brothers) work with grapes from the Asti region. Grignolino originates from the Asti-Casale area and was once probably known as 'barbesino' (the capitular archives of Casale Monferrato mention this variety in the mid-thirteenth century). A few growers in the Barolo and Barbaresco zones (Aldo Conterno and Riccardo Fenocchio in Monforte d'Alba, Fratelli Cavallotto in Castiglione Falletto and Castello di Neive in Neive) still have a few rows of grignolino. Aldo Conterno maintains that the ideal spot for the variety is on the crown of a hill where it might be too windy for nebbiolo, because of the danger of floral abortion. The free circulation of the air helps to protect grignolino's tightly packed bunches from the cryptogamic diseases to which they are otherwise susceptible.

Grignolino is another choosy variety, much preferring a light, sandy soil. Even there its fruiting pattern tends to be irregular: so much so that growers maintain that it is impossible to predict how the vine will fare from one year to the next. The plant does however produce strong vegetative growth of three- or five-lobed, medium-sized leaves and fairly large, compact bunches (often winged) of small, round, pale violet-coloured grapes whose thin skins contain little colour pigment.

Production today is mainly centred on the Alto Monferrato where the subzone of Olivola is considered grignolino's heartland. One interesting curiosity about the variety is that birds will always leave grignolino grapes alone, even when they are fully ripe.

WHITE GRAPE VARIETIES

Moscato

Originally from the eastern European basin, moscato is nowadays widely planted throughout the world. It is an extremely popular variety across the length and breadth of Italy. Almost every part of the peninsula has its own version of a moscato-based dessert wine; they can be found as far apart as the Alto Adige in the country's extreme north and the Italian island of Pantelleria just off the coast of North Africa. Piemonte is no exception: moscato is well-established in the Langa. 'Muscatellum', as the early sixteenth-century statutes of La Morra call the variety, was prized even then for its distinctive aroma and records at the end of that century show the Duke of Mantua placing orders for significant quantities of the Moscato of Santo Stefano Belbo.

The subvariety planted in the Langa is the moscato bianco which is another very demanding vine in terms of where it can be planted to give of its best. Moscato ideally requires a well-drained hillside site of calcium-rich marl or grey-blue loam (often with patches of sand) where it will thrive up to a height of around 400 metres. It does not perform well in a qualitative sense in clay soil or on the valley floor where it produces grapes of diminished aroma and finesse. Following the international success of Asti Spumante, there has been much replanting of moscato to capitalize on a growing demand. This factor has had an ambivalent effect on the wine's image: much of the replanting has been on inferior sites where high production levels have enabled growers to meet the unrealistically low prices demanded by foreign buyers. On the other hand, a number of dedicated moscato specialists have begun to rework some of the region's steeper slopes which had previously been abandoned owing to the difficulty of cultivating them.

The vine bears good foliage of three- to five-lobed leaves and fairly compact, cylindrical bunches of round, golden grapes (they can take on amber tones with a great deal of exposure to the sun), which usually ripen by mid-September. Moscato is normally pruned quite long with nine to eleven buds on the fruiting cane and tends to be planted in greater density than most of the zone's red wine grapes – around 1 metre apart with between 2 and 2.5 metres between rows.

Arneis

Little more than a decade ago this rare and delicate native vine was an obscure local curiosity. By 1989, the first year of Arneis di Roero's official recognition as a DOC wine, arneis grapes were being sold for double the price of those for Barolo. The demand for the wine has now become so great and the availability of arneis grapes so scarce that a new Piemontese word has been coined. *Chardarneis* is a term used to describe an 'Arneis' which tastes as though it might include a healthy dollop of another well-known variety! The rags-to-riches story goes hand in hand with the current trend in Alba towards a reappraisal of winemaking traditions. There is no tradition of still, dry, white wine production in the region, but by the late 1970s, when the area awoke to a new spirit of optimism, many producers identified dry white wine as a vital part of the range which would allow them to compete effectively in a more sophisticated marketplace. A suitable local candidate had to be found (though the more cosmopolitan were prepared to look further afield!). The rediscovery of arneis was under way.

The earliest official records of arneis date back to just over a century ago: G. di Rovasenda mentions that arneis was being grown at Corneliano d'Alba in his *Saggio di una ampelografia universale* (1877). However the real history of arneis goes back much further. In all probability, the variety referred to as 'Renesium' and 'Renexij' in fifteenth- and sixteenth-century documents, had by the eighteenth century become 'arnesio' and finally arrived at its present form by the time Count Traiano Domenico Roero records, in the following century, having several hundred bottles of 'Arneis bianco' from Piobesi in his cellars at Guarene. Much of the uncertainty about the origins of arneis stems from the fact that the Albese were only used to recognizing one white variety, moscato. They tended to lump other white grapes together and refer to them generically as *bianchetto* or *bianchetta* (little white one) – indeed arneis is still known as *bianchetta* although nowadays 'nebbiolo bianco' is a much more common synonym.

Specialized arneis vineyards are only a feature of the last decade or so. Before that it was planted alongside other white varieties (notably favorita) as an *uvaggio* or even in amongst nebbiolo, so that its sweet, early ripening fruit would attract birds away from the more important nebbiolo grapes. Arneis has traditionally been put to a number of uses as a subordinate or substitute. Its most common function, perpetuated today by the production regulations for DOC Roero (p. 117), was to soften or tone down the youthful aggression of nebbiolo. The customary practice was to add arneis as a concentrated, sweet filtrate made by 'freezing' the wine overnight and then discarding the watery liquid which melted first. Its two other main functions make use of the grape's natural sweetness: arneis has a limited history of use as a table grape but, more importantly, it served as an alternative base to moscato for the locally popular semi-sweet, *frizzante* style, white *novello*, the last remaining bottles of which would be consumed during the Easter celebrations following the vintage. Like moscato, arneis can produce an intensely perfumed wine, particularly with some residual sugar remaining. In this form arneis was often served at mass and other religious festivals.

The world 'arneis' has two principal meanings in local dialect: first it can be used to describe someone or something that is stubborn, unpredictable and hard to subdue. The second meaning is 'impudent youngster' (the colloquial alternative is much coarser!) Both reflect the customary problems producers have experienced in working with the grape. Low acid levels often resulted in an unstable wine prone to oxidation. With no tradition of still, dry white wine production, the technical expertise to overcome the wine's inherent fragility did not exist. Subsequent improvements in production techniques are beginning to have a marked effect (cold maceration on the skins is currently in favour) but the most significant work has been done on clonal selection. In conjuction with the University of Turin, Castello di Neive have taken great strides in this area, while the Centro Miglioramento

35

Vite del CNR di Torino (a Turin-based research institute for improving clonal selection) has now isolated a number of superior clones.

The 'nebbiolo bianco' synonym is borne out by the vine's perform-ance in the vineyards. Like nebbiolo, arneis is a very vigorous vine producing a lot of foliage. It is therefore pruned long with ten to twelve buds on the fruiting cane and trained quite high. The leaves which are medium-sized and round in shape can have either three or five lobes. The round grapes come in short, compact bunches of cylindrical form; they are greeny-yellow, taking on smoky amber tones when fully ripe. Arneis is resistant to cold and peronospera but susceptible to oidium; it prefers a light, sandy soil and south-facing sites. The vine typically buds in the third week of April, flowers in the middle of June and is harvested towards the end of September.

Although at one time planted exclusively in the Roero, arneis is beginning to turn up on the right bank of the Tanaro in Barolo and Barbaresco. Aldo Conterno has recently planted 1.5 hectares of sandy south-facing soil in Bussia with the variety. Perhaps the most famous example of this trend is the south-facing slope of Montebertotto in Neive where Castello di Neive planted 2.5 hectares of arneis in the late 1970s. The Albesi's faith in their own vines seems once more to be justified. Arneis has met with instant success, not only on the home market but elsewhere in Europe and in the USA. The 'little bugger' seems to have captured the imagination of the wine-loving public.

The other minor red and white grape varieties will be discussed in the context of their wine styles in chapter 5.

IN AMONGST THE VINES

The most significant current trend in the art of cultivating the vine would be applauded by the environmentalist. The use of organic fertilizers and low-toxicity insecticides has become popular as many growers seek to avoid excessive chemical treatments of the vine and its habitat. Typically the Albesi have not been slow to recognize the tactical benefits of such a policy, though few so far are inclined to wave the 'green' banner. Young Severino Oberto of La Morra and Renato Rabezzana from the hills around Asti are among the first to identify themselves with 'organic' wine production; meanwhile well-established *aziende agricole* like Fratelli Cavallotto of Castiglione Falletto, who have customarily worked along similar lines, continue to pursue a personal crusade. The use of copper- and sulphur-based anti-cryptogamic treatments is generally considered indispensable by all growers.

Many large firms are now beginning to follow the trend, but the small grower is able to adapt his methods more quickly to suit his own particular needs and beliefs. Our study of the vineyard calendar in the Albese is therefore focused on a grower who not only has considerable viticultural experience but who has already evolved a system that represents the general movement towards the production of fine wine from carefully tended vineyards combined with a healthy concern for the environment.

AZIENDA VITIVINICOLA PAOLO SCAVINO: A MODEL VINEYARD

Although he also cultivates apples and peaches, vines are Enrico Scavino's abiding passion. He owns around 5 hectares of vineyards in Codana and Fiasc' close to his home in Garbelletto, a *frazione* of Castiglione Falletto. In addition he has been renting just over half a hectare in Cannubi since 1984: an opportunity, he says, he could not afford to pass over. The Scavino family have been cultivating land around Garbelletto since 1921, but when the founder of the house died in 1949, separate *aziende* were formed by brothers Paolo and Alfonso. Alfonso's family continue to operate a winemaking business today under the Azienda Agricola Azelia label; their winery is no more than a couple of hundred metres away from their cousin Enrico's. This is a common enough feature of the Langa today. The laws of succession have resulted in a proliferation of properties of ever-diminishing size. In many cases the rift this has caused in a family has become permanent through unhealthy fraternal competition, so it is reassuring to find that the Scavino cousins remain on good terms.

Production levels at the Scavino winery are deliberately kept small to reflect Enrico's belief in *un lavoro artigianale* (a small-scale, 'craftsman's' operation). Totals are split up in the following way:

12/13,000 bottles Barolo 'Bric' del Fiasc' from 1.8 hectares (3,700 vines per hectare)

3,800 bottles Barolo 'Cannubi' from just over half a hectare (2,550 vines)

4,000 bottles Barolo from around half a hectare in Garbelletto (about 2,000 vines)

12/13,000 bottles Dolcetto from 1.5 hectares (3,960 vines per hectare)

2/3,000 bottles Barbera from just under half a hectare (2,300 vines)

Over the past few years Scavino has been perfecting a system which will enable him to grow the healthiest possible grapes through a minimal interference with nature. He has gradually abandoned chemical treatments of the soil and nowadays will break up the ground as little as possible. For example he will no longer plough established vineyards: he feels that not only does this disturb the roots of the vines but it also increases the danger of landslips. The plants between the rows help, he argues, to bind the soil together and also perform a number of other useful functions. In addition he maintains that treatments with artificial fertilizers – normally carried out after rain – make ploughed land harder and more impenetrable and therefore more difficult for the vines to take nourishment from.

The Vineyard Calendar

The following account does not allow for the sort of freak weather patterns (hail, drought, etc.) and other natural phenomena (landslips, etc.) that frequently bedevil the lives of the growers. If hail has hit the vineyards particularly hard, growers will resign themselves to losing a part of their crop and may have to adapt their winter pruning at the end of the season to allow for greater foliage so that the vines have a chance to regather their strength; if a landslip has occurred, part or all of the vineyard must be restructured and replanted. These are basic facts of life for the *vignaiolo*. Similarly it is impossible to gauge in advance how great a problem oidium and peronospera will be in any particular year. One answer is to take extensive precautionary measures. Enrico Scavino, however, chooses the more difficult path and will apply anti-cryptogamic treatments only when necessary. All vineyard work depends on the weather and the various tasks can only be carried out when conditions permit.

WINTER AND SPRING
With the ground between the rows cleared of any debris, winter pruning will begin after Epiphany. (Larger firms with available labour, or smaller growers who sell off their grapes and are thus not committed to work in the cellar at the time, may begin pruning in the final months of the year). Scavino uses single Guyot for all three varieties. The trunk is kept very low, leaving one fruiting cane and a reserve spur (*sperone*) with two buds for the following year. He believes in a fairly severe pruning, cutting the vine back as far as he dare to encourage strong growth in the new season. He will prune the fruiting cane of the nebbiolo back to 9 or 11 buds, barbera to 7 or 8 and dolcetto to 6 or 7 (removing some of the buds on the underside of this variety for a longer cane which will produce more foliage). Pruning is a lengthy process and often lasts until the end of March when the vegetative cycle of the vine begins with the rising of the sap. With the cuttings piled up down the middle of the rows, Scavino will pass through with a light mechanical cutter to shred up the grasses and the vine clippings, touching only the surface of the earth. The potassium and nitrogen released through the breakdown of this vegetation will, over the course of the season, help to stimulate the vines' growth. During these early months, the supporting posts and training wires in older vineyards are checked and repaired where necessary. (This task can only be carried out when the ground is not frozen). From March onwards, Scavino begins *legatura*, where the shoots are trained along the bottom wires by bending them into place and tying them up securely. This task is made much easier after the sap has risen and the shoots are more pliable.

The late winter/early spring is also one of two possible times (the other is in the final two months of the year) to carry out any replanting. Scavino normally finds that a healthy vine can continue up to about fifty years old but feels that thirty to thirty-five years is more usual. He rejects the view that older vineyards produce better grapes, insisting that carefully controlled yields are just as effective in ensuring optimum quality fruit. Indeed he has observed that with younger vines, the fruit changes colour perhaps a week earlier and will therefore also ripen more quickly. Scavino will take the decision whether to replant or not on the basis of the health of the individual plant and whether vegetation and fruit production are maintained at satisfactory levels. Every vine, he feels, is different and its state of health depends on the work done in the vineyards during the course of its life. His renewal cycle is a relatively simple one: he is allowed the luxury of 'custom-made' grafts. Cuttings from especially healthy plants are taken down to a nursery in Alba where the grafts are prepared for him. They are then bedded down into large, well-manured holes normally in early March. Other producers prefer a 'hands on' approach and carry out the operation in the vineyards. The American rootstock (a Berlandieri/Riparia crossing, either Kober 5BB or 420(A), is most commonly used) will have been planted out in the vineyard the previous year to establish itself. On the day that grafting is to take place, the workers will have prepared a large reserve of cuttings containing at least one dormant bud from the winter pruning. These will have been soaking in water since the early morning. One end of each cutting is cut to a long, tapering V-shape without damaging the bud. The roots of the American vine are exposed by digging out a surrounding bowl of earth and the top of the trunk is cut off several inches above its roots. The remaining short trunk is then split downwards with a sharp knife. The tapered end of the cutting is inserted into this fissure and the join bound tightly together. The graft is then covered with earth again to protect it from inclement spring weather.

Budding usually starts during the second week in April and the first full leaves will appear on the vine soon after the middle of the month. The shoots grow slowly at first and will only have reached between 5 and 10 centimetres in length by the end of the month. This is the time when oidium is most likely to occur. When they are around 10 centimetres long, Scavino walks between the rows pumping powdered sulphur over the shoots from a container strapped on his back. This task is normally repeated four or five times and is best carried out early in the morning between 5 and 9 o'clock so that the powder will adhere better with the dew.

In May the shoots begin to grow more quickly as temperatures rise. When they are between 60 and 70 centimetres long, green pruning begins. All the infertile or 'feminine' (i.e., non fruit-bearing) shoots are removed, apart from those on the spur canes. The nebbiolo vines, always the earliest to bud since they are planted in the best positions, are done first. This is normally two to three weeks of slow, patient work and must be finished by the end of May. During the second half of the month, a bout of rain may herald the outbreak of peronospera. Using the services of a technical adviser to measure the temperature and humidity in the vineyards, Scavino can anticipate the conditions which favour peronospera and thus carry out preventive treatment with a copper and 'Mancozeb' fungicide preparation. (The use of copper alone is not advisable: it may become toxic in the cold night-time temperatures). In addition, sulphur as powder or in solution may be needed fortnightly against oidium. At one time growers would go ahead with these treatments systematically every eight to ten days for a couple of months but many – like Scavino – have now forsaken the practice. During May he mows the grass between the rows (depending of course on the amount of rain that has fallen).

SUMMER

By the end of May the shoots are growing rapidly and need tying up towards the empty upper wires. As the shoots develop at different times, two or three passages through the vineyards are necessary, removing at the same time any new infertile shoots. Where growth is particularly luxuriant, some shoots may need training along the top wire. This work can take up the whole of June. During this month, flowering, pollination and the formation of the grapes will take place, ideally in warm, dry weather, with a little wind helping good pollination. Depending on heat, humidity and rain levels, anti-oidium and peronospera treatment may again be required. Towards the end of June, when the grapes are between 60 and 70 per cent developed, Scavino will apply Bordeaux mixture (a copper-sulphate solution neutralized with small quantities of lime) for the first time – any earlier, he believes, and the Bordeaux mixture and any previous anti-cryptogamic treatments would cancel each other out.

Around the turn of the month, he will again use the services of a technical adviser to combat the menace of *la tignola*, a moth whose grubs feed off young grapes. Covered traps are suspended near the forming fruit. The bottom half of the trap is smeared with a tenaciously sticky jelly upon which a special capsule is laid. This capsule emits an odour that attracts the male moths, the first to hatch. The numbers of moths caught on the sticky surface is monitored daily. A sudden decline in numbers means that the females, whose scent the males prefer, have also begun to hatch. Eight days after the drop in numbers, the new grubs will start to emerge from the eggs laid on the partially formed bunches. Scavino is thus able to time his treatment to the day and will spray the grapes with a low-toxic, class 3 insecticide. A day too late and the grubs will have started to puncture the grapes in search of nourishment, making later anti-botrytis treatment essential.

When the grapes are fully set in July, Scavino takes steps to control the size of his crop. His ingenious and individual approach to the problem is, like every perfectionist's attention to detail, extremely rigorous and time-consuming. Many years' experience in the vineyards have taught him that the top half of a bunch of grapes takes the sun (and therefore ripens) better. To prove his point, he marched us – just prior to the 1987 vintage – into a neighbouring vineyard. Picking a grape from the top of a bunch, he showed us how the small amount of pulp left clinging to the stalk was already turning red while with a grape taken from the bottom of the same bunch, the pulp was still a clear, pale, watery green. The grape from the top half also had a sweeter, riper flavour. On an average of seven out of the ten shoots off the fruiting cane, there are two bunches of grapes (one between the third and fourth leaves and one between the fourth and fifth). During the first couple of weeks in July, Scavino and his hired help (usually experienced women – they have a more delicate touch, he explains) will cut off the bottom part of each bunch of dolcetto and nebbiolo grapes in his vineyards. Not only is the ripening therefore more homogeneous, he argues, but the remaining grapes will also dry out more quickly after rain, keeping down the risk of rot. As the bunches are typically smaller, the barbera grapes normally escape the prying secateurs. None the less Scavino, vigilant as ever, continues to keep a watchful eye on their dimensions during his daily walk through the vineyards. Other quality-conscious growers will often remove one of the two whole bunches in order to improve quality by reducing quantity. Scavino agrees that this is a valid alternative: the essential thing, he insists, is to reduce yields. He prefers to get this task done as soon as possible (ideally during the first week of July) so that the grapes in the final form will receive maximum nourishment from the vine. In this way Scavino is able to keep down his yields to a maximum of 55–60 quintals of fruit per hectare – the level that the majority of serious producers consider valid for the production of fine wine.

From the middle of July onwards, mowing between the rows becomes more important so that the low-hanging grapes are not shaded out by the grass. The grass is cut once a month, or every two months if the weather is very dry. If it rains, the carpet of grass between the rows helps absorb humidity and the water should not penetrate deep enough for the grapes to swell up. At this stage, as the vegetation is at its lushest, tractors are used. Anti-oidium treatment may again be required; Scavino finds sulphur in powdered form the most effective.

In the first fortnight of August (often the hottest time of the year), Scavino lets his vines work for him. As there is a risk of the grapes scorching in the high temperatures, any shading foliage is not removed. Scavino, normally an almost obsessively neat and orderly man, complains that his vineyards look rather untidy at this point. He gives a characteristic shrug of the shoulders, arms out, palms held up: 'But . . .'. There is indeed little he can do now amongst his vines – his attention turns to the cellar and the bottling of his more important wines (Dolcetto as a rule is bottled earlier). During the second half of the month, if temperatures begin to drop, that unruly shading foliage can finally be cut back.

For the rest of August, Scavino works on his other fruit crops and harvests peaches at the beginning of September. Around the third week of the month he will pick dolcetto, the harvest lasting five or six days. When the apples have been gathered in at the beginning of October, a further two days will see the completion of the small barbera harvest. Nothing is left to chance with the nebbiolo grapes. Regular pre-harvest checks are made on their ripeness with Scavino looking for a pH of between 3.15 and 3.2. Needless to say he is not convinced of the virtues of *surmaturité* and higher sugar levels at the expense of lower acidity. He is aiming for a balanced grape to retain perfume and freshness in his wine. He maintains that the real quality of a vintage is only apparent about eight days prior to the harvest. August and September are clearly crucial months, but truly great vintages are made when the good weather lasts through into the first few weeks of October. It is an extremely anxious time: frequent glances at the sky confirm how vulnerable the grapes are at this stage to a sudden change in the weather. During the picking of the Bric' del Fiasc' vineyard in the second week of October 1987, lunch was interrupted by a phone call from a friend in Milano. A storm was passing over the city and seemed to be heading in the direction of the Langhe. Lunch was abandoned in mid-forkful as Scavino began to shepherd the workers back to the vines to pick what they could before the first drops of rain. In less troublesome vintages the nebbiolo harvest lasts five or six days: the pickers will select the ripest fruit which is then gathered in shallow, plastic trays to avoid damaging the grapes and any loss of their precious juice. Even when the weather has held, this is no time to relax as work in the cellar is now in full swing.

The vineyards are quiet now until at least the middle of November when fertilizer may be used in dry weather. Indeed every three or four years, Scavino will apply fertilizer to his vineyards, but, true to type, it must be of a very particular kind. Scavino's source is high in the mountains where the cattle only eat grass and other natural fodder. He will only use well-seasoned manure which will not ferment any further. A little rain after it has been applied will help the ground absorb the manure.

One glance at his *cantina* confirms that Scavino's approach to the art of wine production is based on deep-seated and serious conviction. It is no exaggeration to say that one could happily eat one's *agnolotti* straight from the cellar floor. The same meticulous care he applies to looking after his vines carries through into the sphere of vinification. Carefully controlled fermentation at fairly low temperatures (below 22°C for Dolcetto and below 28°C for Barbera and Nebbiolo) is followed by frequent racking to ensure complete limpidity. Ageing in *botte* is kept to a minimum for Barolo and rigorously monitored bottling followed by storage at constant temperatures for all his wines helps to retain the fresh and fragrant perfumes all three varietals are potentially so rich in. Enrico Scavino faces the future with justifiable confidence.

4

VINIFICATION

As has been shown in chapters 1 and 3, soil structure and microclimate are of primary importance in defining the individual characteristics of an Albese wine. But the final style of a wine is defined by the individual winemaker. At each stage of vinification the choices he makes will stamp his mark on the finished product.

For some grape varieties there is a more or less standard method of vinification. For example, Dolcetto is usually made as a wine to be consumed in the first two years of its life, Barbera is likely to be a wine of medium longevity given a limited period of wood ageing and so on. In the case of Nebbiolo, however, the exception is the rule. The many permutations of winemaking techniques make a precise definition of *tipicità*, of a benchmark, for Barolo and Barbaresco impossible. The most significant variables are fermentation and maceration technique, as well as the many permutations of wood ageing in various sizes of cask. To the frustration of the marketing men, the confusion of the consumers and the joy of the Barolo fanatic, these wines firmly resist being pigeon-holed. The great wines of this region are produced by individuals who adopt and adapt the principles of vinification according to their own experience, the particular nature of their grapes and their personal goals. It soon becomes apparent that it is self-deluding to speak of 'modernist' or 'traditionalist' schools of vinification in an area where no two winemakers think exactly alike.

RED WINE VINIFICATION

Winemaking in the Langhe revolves around the nebbiolo grape. The following descriptions of vinification practices relate, first and foremost, to nebbiolo as vinified for Barolo and Barbaresco. The variations in technique used for other red varieties and the lighter Nebbiolos will be discussed at the end of this section.

The natural division between the harvesting of different grape varieties means that maximum attention can be given to the vinification of each individual variety. There is great relief when the nebbiolo has been successfully harvested; anxious hours spent watching the sky and listening to the predictions of local soothsayers and meteorologists are at last over. For two weeks the winemaker's life can be focused on a bubbling vat of must beside which he will probably make his bed.

Arrival of Grapes at the Cellar

A great deal of care must be exercised in the vineyard at harvest time if the winemaker is to have the best raw materials at his disposal. As the grapes are picked they are loaded into small crates of 20 kilogram capacity, nowadays normally made of plastic which is much easier to sterilize than wood. Small crates protect the grapes from damage before their arrival at the winery, avoiding any possible precocious fermentation of the must.

Before crushing, the grapes are examined once more, and any bunches showing signs of *muffa* (rot) discarded. Most *cantine* in the Alba area use a small horizontal destemmer/crusher. The grapes are loaded into the top, and the stalks automatically removed to avoid adding extra tannin to the must, and the fruit is lightly milled. The pulp is pumped into a fermentation vat and a small dose of sulphur dioxide is added to inhibit the action of undesirable yeasts and bacteria and to favour the development of ellipsoid yeasts which start the alcoholic fermentation. The dosage of SO_2 at this stage is critical — too much can leave off-flavours in the wine and also prevent the malolactic fermentation. For healthy grapes with a good level of acidity the dose should be as little as 3 to 5 grams per hectolitre but this will probably be doubled if the grapes are unhealthy or deficient in acidity. Few producers admit to using cultured yeasts in the production of red wines in the Langhe. The norm is that the natural yeasts clinging to the grape skins will perform the fermentation. In the case of larger producers, it is becoming more common to inoculate the must with a culture of yeasts taken from the vineyard.

Correction of Musts

The next factor which the winemaker must consider is the ripeness of his grapes. He will already know whether they have an adequate sugar level to meet the DOC(G) minimum. In some cases, where the quality of the grapes fails to match his personal standards he will already have sold the crop to a large negociant. In most vintages the minimum alcohol levels set by DOC(G) should pose no problem for growers with properly sited vineyards where yields are controlled in a sensible fashion. However, in poor vintages, when the grapes lack a degree of sugar, permission is given to adjust the sugar level in the must. A number of producers argue that a better solution would be to lower the DOC(G) requirement for minimum alcohol levels in problematic years.

Since the 1970s some of Italy's top winemakers have been protesting against the Italian law which forbids chaptalization with non-grape sugar. The origins of this legislation are the safeguarding of production of vineyards in Italy's deep south whose excess output is rendered into concentrated must, which is then sold in significant quantities to winemakers in northern Italy. The basic *mosto concentrato* is far too crude to be added to any potentially fine wine. The effect would be to give a cooked or jammy flavour to the finished wine. Nowadays, at least, a better product is available (and legally permitted). This is the rectified concentrated must – *mosto concentrato rectificato* – a relatively neutral form of grape sugar, albeit more costly than saccharose. Some of Piemonte's top names (including Angelo Gaja), however, are still campaigning for Italian winemakers to be put on an equal footing with their French counterparts. Their argument is that, qualitatively, the addition of saccharose to grape must is the least onerous means of increasing the alcoholic degree in a wine. They are sceptical of the must manufacturers' claims for the neutrality of their product: some of the resins used in the concentrate are thought to affect the taste of the wine.

Of course, in Italy, even more than elsewhere, all laws are made to be broken, and many producers have for years flaunted the regulations by adding discreet amounts of sugar solution to deficient musts. Today this is a far more risky practice, since a device has been invented that can detect the presence of alcohol derived from saccharose in a finished wine.

While the battle for the use of saccharose continues, there are a few *cantine* which claim to have found an answer which sweetens the bitter pill of concentrated must. There are the producers, such as Prunotto (p. 176), who concentrate their own must using a slower and more careful technique which avoids ending up with a cooked flavour. The theory is that by using your own concentrate you are at least adding extract to the wines, rather than attenuating them with a higher proportion of alcohol. According to Tino Colla of Prunotto the only disadvantage of doing it yourself, using healthy grapes and your own sophisticated equipment, is the high cost.

The only other corrective occasionally employed in the Langhe in poor vintages (particularly for Barbera) is deacidification of the must. This is done by adding calcium or potassium carbonate prior to fermentation.

The point to be emphasized here is that great wines achieve their harmony through the balance of elements in their raw material – the right proportions of sugars, acidity, extract, tannins and colouring materials in the grapes themselves. To date it has not been possible for the enological scientist to improve on nature; a must with a lack or excess of one component or another can certainly be improved but it will never be transformed into a great wine.

Alcoholic Fermentation

Fermentation is the key to a more precise control over the style of a finished wine. The winemaker who leaves fermentation to chance will rarely produce a wine of exceptional quality. All great winemakers have a profound experience and understanding of fermentation – at least alcoholic fermentation – which to an outsider can resemble the skill of an alchemist.

To understand the variety of styles that make up modern Barolo and Barbaresco it is important to look not only at the variety of vineyard sites, but also at the array of vinification theories proposed by winemakers. It is far too easy to label a producer 'traditionalist' or 'modernist' when in fact he has been influenced by a number of schools of thought. Aldo Conterno, for example, is apparently a traditionalist in the field of Barolo but is simultaneously making up-to-the-minute fruit-dominated, *barrique*-aged wines from the same nebbiolo grapes. Many producers, like Conterno, seek to have the best of both worlds and are open-minded enough to adapt their methods to make better wines.

EARLY FERMENTATION TECHNIQUES

Few producers alive today have first-hand experience of the system of winemaking practised from the nineteenth century until about 1930. Many can remember the wines, however, and have elevated them in their memories to products of a golden age. Today it is impossible to make a judgement on these fabled wines, but one can deduce their essential style. It is important to remember that the wine made by the great grandfathers of today's generation of *Baroliste* is in many ways the archetype for all subsequent interpretations.

The principle of this historical vinification technique, whose last traces were buried in 1980 with the death of Luigi Pira of E. Pira & Figli in Barolo, was based on crushing the grapes by foot.

Extreme care in the selection of the grapes in the vineyard was a major factor in the ultimate quality of these wines. In the rare case that temperatures in the vineyard were high, allowing the grapes to cool overnight reduced the risk of an excessively high temperature in the early stages of fermentation.

Crushing the grapes by foot was a less brutal process than it might sound, indeed less brutal than most of today's mechanical crushers. Another feature of Barolo production in the nineteenth century was *ammostatura*, a process whereby uncrushed grapes are added to the must over a period (Elio Altare has resurrected this technique in the making of his cru Barbera – Vigna Larigi – in an effort to increase fruit flavours in the wine while restricting the amounts of tannin). Little or no SO$_2$ would have been used. Most importantly, the stems and stalks of the grapes were always left in the must for the duration of the fermentation and maceration. In fact this is not a significant factor in increasing the tannin level of the finished wine, as crushing by foot limited the amount of damage to the stalks, which when intact add minimal tannin but do significantly augment the acidity of the must. One benefit of retaining the stalks is that the cap (*cappello*) of solids rising to the top of the fermenting must is more loosely textured and the resulting oxygenation of the must favours a healthy, even fermentation at a time of year when the ambient temperature may well slow fermentation to a snail's pace.

The vessels used for fermentation in this old style were *tini* – usually straight sided, or slightly convex, vertical open-topped wooden vats. The accessibility of these vats made the *follatura* – breaking up the cap of grape pulp, skins and stalks – much easier. The fact that the vats were left open reduced any risk of temperatures rising too high, and the fermentation and maceration were usually all over within fifteen days. On this evidence, it is unlikely that the pre-phylloxera Barolo was any more tannic than its modern-day equivalent, indeed, it may well have been softer and rounder in style than many wines which are today considered to be of the 'old school'.

However, the fact that this system has fallen into disuse suggests that it had major flaws. The main worry is one that would horrify any modern winemaker – the risk of oxidation. The exposure of the cap to air greatly increases the possibility of spoilage by bacteria, in particular acetobacter. Using open-vat fermentation there is in any case a tendency for wines to suffer a higher level of volatile acidity (acetic acid) and to lose both colour and alcoholic degree. In general, a wine made in this way would be likely to mature relatively quickly.

After fermentation the wine would have been racked, the cap pressed, and the results put into large casks to mature for about twelve months. Subsequently the wine would be racked into glass *damigiane* (demijohns) and sold either in these or eventually in bottle.

It is clear that very good wines could have been made using this system but by today's standards the techniques lack precision, and the production of fine wines would have depended even more on the excellence of the raw materials.

CAPPELLO SOMMERSO

The next major development in fermentation technique came in the late 1930s with the widespread adoption of the *cappello sommerso* (submerged cap) system in Piemonte. Today the *cappello sommerso* is considered by winemakers as the 'traditional' approach. This is the system still used at some point in the fermentation of the majority of modern Barolo and Barbaresco. It is not rare to encounter misunderstanding of the relevance of the submerged-cap method of fermentation – even amongst winemakers who practise it themselves.

The system involves a wooden (or nowadays stainless steel) disk or grille that fits into the top of the vessel used for fermentation. The disk is fixed securely several inches below the surface of the must, often jammed down with sticks. The result is that the cap of pulp and skins is pushed up against the disk by the rising carbon dioxide bubbles. Instead of floating on the surface of the fermenting must, the cap is kept submerged.

Technically speaking, this method offers some advantages over the open-vat type of fermentation, principally the lesser risk of acetification because there is no contact between the cap and oxygen. It is also a relatively lazy method, well suited to the farmer who has other crops and beasts to attend to. The labour-intensive work of breaking up the cap to give a more effective and more even maceration of the grape skins is avoided. However, to ferment most efficiently with submerged cap it is important to effect a frequent *rimontaggio* – pumping wine from the bottom of the vat up over the top in order to distribute active yeasts more evenly and to balance the temperature of the must. *Rimontaggio* four times a day is recommended by many experts – but most of the winemakers we have talked to remain content with two pumping sessions – one in the morning and one in the evening.

Nebbiolo-based wines are often very high in tannin, and this is frequently exacerbated by the use of *cappello sommerso*. It is an inefficient method of maceration which takes a long time to extract the best from the grapes. Fifteen to twenty days is the minimum required to draw off sufficient colouring material and extract from the grape skins when using submerged cap. In good vintages some producers, in attempting to make wines of great longevity and extract, will extend the maceration up to about forty days (the longest we have encountered is seventy days at Accomasso). When considering the effects of prolonged maceration it is useful to look at a graph showing the progress of the extraction of tannin (polyphenols) and colour from grapes during fermentation. This example applies to a modern closed-vat style of fermentation, but the principles can equally well be applied to *cappello sommerso*.

The pigments in the grape skins are dissolved in the early period of cuvaison, reaching a peak after only eight days, while the polyphenols (mainly tannins) are released more gradually and continue to increase throughout the maceration period as they are extracted by alcohol.

Source: *Connaissance et travail du vin*, Emile Peynaud 1981, p. 160.

Thus the effect of extended maceration is greatly to increase the proportion of tannins in a wine. It is also true that only musts from top-quality grapes have the potential to stand up to prolonged maceration without the resulting wines suffering serious structural imbalances.

The best practitioners of the submerged-cap technique are flexible in their approach, and, like Castello di Neive for their Barbaresco, only subject wines from good vintages to this slow extraction of tannin. In lesser years they will favour a closed-vat system of fermentation which permits a more efficient and rapid maceration, gaining the maximum colour without overloading the wine with tannin. Many other producers have adopted a compromise, bringing *cappello sommerso* into play only for the latter stages of fermentation to emphasize discreetly the structure of their wines.

TEMPERATURE CONTROL
The effectiveness of maceration is also governed by a factor that has become central to the modern winemaker's philosophy of fermentation: temperature control. The length of the maceration period is a coefficient of the fermentation temperature; at higher temperatures maceration is quicker and more effective.

In late October the nebbiolo grapes will often arrive at the cellar at a very low temperature. Unless there are means of heating either cellar or vats, there is likely to be the problem of a slow start to the fermentation. If the must temperature is below 13°C or 14°C then it will be impossible to initiate any fermentation at all. As a solution, some winemakers will use a starter – for the French a *pied de cuve* – whereby an early picking of ripe grapes is crushed and already vigorously fermenting when the main crop is brought in and added to it a week or so later. This is one of the times of year when the value of a cellar built underground is proven. The modern tendency to build 'cellars' at ground level results in a loss of temperature stability as the walls are exposed to the elements.

A lower fermentation temperature will tend to emphasize the aromatic qualities of the finished wine, while a higher temperature will favour greater extraction of polyphenols including tannins and colouring matter (anthocyanins). The 'normal' fermentation temperature for Barolo and Barbaresco is between 26°C and 30°C. If the temperature rises above 32°C the fermentation will slow and eventually stop as yeasts die. In this case there are dangers of spoilage due to lactic taints and oxidation of the must. As if nursing a new-born child, the devoted winemaker will often sleep in the cellar during the critical initial stages of fermentation to take frequent temperature readings during the night. If he does not have a cooling/heating system built into the tanks – either with water-cooled exterior linings or a spiral in the centre of the tank filled with refrigerant – then he will most likely pump the must out, through a heat exchanger and back into the tank. The crudest method of temperature control is to drop sacks of ice into the vat; in theory, watertight sacks which will avoid dilution of the must. In the hot autumn of 1982, for example, many smaller producers like Enrico Scavino had no alternative but to take emergency measures and procure ice as must temperatures rapidly rose above 30°C. The year 1985 is generally viewed as the first 'modern' Barolo vintage, when virtually all quality producers had access to temperature-control equipment.

Producers favouring a particularly low fermentation temperature include both 'traditional' winemakers such as Giovanni Conterno who ferments his Monfortino at around 26°C and ostensible modernists such as the Cordero family at Monfalletto who claim to ferment nebbiolo as low as 22–3°C. One aim is shared by both winemakers: to give their wines a balance of finesse over power. The divergence comes on the subject of maceration – Conterno will macerate for as long as forty-five days while the Corderos will carry out the *svinatura* (running the wine off the cap) after only ten to fifteen days. To adopt the French concept of *élévage*, the Cordero Barolo will be quite grown up and drinkable at the age of only four years, while after six or seven years Conterno's baby will still be in nappies, lying in cask. The crucial difference in the two wines, apart from difference in the raw materials, is one of tannin level. It is only with a high level of tannin that Giovanni Conterno can make a wine with the structure to withstand such long periods of wood ageing.

CAPPELLO IMMERSO – THE PEYNAUD SCHOOL
In the 1970s one would have said with confidence that obsession with temperature control was limited to a relatively small group of producers who, both in Alba and abroad, were considered the avant-garde. The two most prominent figures amongst them have been the

late Renato Ratti in La Morra and Angelo Gaja in Barbaresco, articulate spokesmen for what might loosely be termed the Peynaud school of vinification. In the field of red wine, Professor Emile Peynaud – described by Jancis Robinson as the 'technical fairy godmother' of Bordeaux winemaking – is one of the most influential and widely read enologists in the world today.

In summary, Peynaud's recommended system for the vinification of high quality red wines destined for lengthy maturation involves fermentation at precisely controlled temperatures in closed stainless steel tanks with frequent pumping over of the must and energetic maceration over a short period. This is the *cappello immerso* system of maceration, which offers a more efficient method of extraction of colour from grape skins with less leaching of tannin, reducing maceration times to as little as one week. This type of fermentation also has technical advantages in protecting against acetification of fermenting must (contact of the must with oxygen is limited and controlled) and favouring an easier malolactic fermentation.

The key to closed-vat fermentation is temperature control. Potentially it allows the winemaker extra precision, especially if he is producing a mould-breaking Barolo which emphasizes fruit over astringency. However, there is a price for such control. The investment in stainless steel equipment is one that might bankrupt the *contadino*. Angelo Gaja (p. 162) is quick to advise caution on the part of the smaller winemaker tempted to follow the trend to new vinification systems. He believes in individual experimentation but in only taking one step at a time. 'There are bad innovations just as there are bad traditions.' Gaja's advice to a young winemaker inheriting the family *cantina* would be to stick to traditional methods of vinification but with cleanliness as the watchword. 'The traditional approach demands a very clean cellar and high quality grapes.' As yet the Langhe lacks its own Peynaud, but there are signs of change. Young, peripatetic consultants such as Donato Lanati (a protégé of Tuscan-based Giacomo Tachis) are now advising several important wineries.

Malolactic Fermentation

The malolactic fermentation is a process that in most red wines naturally follows the alcoholic fermentation. Essentially, it involves the transformation of malic acid into lactic acid and carbon dioxide through the action of lactic bacteria. The effect is a deacidification of the wine by up to 50 per cent: acidity leaves the wine in the form of CO_2. In sensory terms the effect of the *malolattica* is even more significant, because lactic has a far less aggressive character than malic acid. A potentially great Barolo tasted immediately after the alcoholic fermentation is completely unpalatable: a sour and astringent mouthful of aggression.

Today, the significance of the malolactic fermentation is accepted by all major winemakers. Forty or fifty years ago the process was improperly understood and its benefit to the quality of red wine was overlooked. Since then there has been a gradual revolution, and today the enologist will aim to control the course of the malolactic just as he does the alcoholic fermentation. In a conservative region such as Piemonte, of course, these changes in attitude do not happen overnight. There are still many *contadini* whose understanding of the process is minimal – and they may well make good wines despite their ignorance.

Certainly it is possible to argue that, at least in the case of Barolo and Barbaresco, control of the malolactic fermentation is not critical to the quality of the finished wine. Indeed, a traditionalist may well deem the wine which has undergone a haphazard *malolattica* to be the one which shows greater *tipicità*. Because Barolo spends a minimum of two years in cask, the malolactic fermentation will normally have happened naturally before the wine is bottled. An uncontrolled malolactic fermentation is potentially a greater problem for wines sold young with little cask age that may risk fermenting in bottle.

However, as many winemakers in Alba have now realized, there is more significance to the malolactic process than mere stability of the finished product. The modern attitude is that malolactic fermentation should be carried out as soon as possible, usually immediately after the alcoholic fermentation. An early malolactic fermentation results in a wine of greater suppleness, smoother texture and above all with a greater emphasis on secondary fruit flavours. The wines of Gaja and Ceretto spring immediately to mind as influential examples of this style of winemaking.

In order for the malolactic fermentation to take place several factors need to be right. It is worth studying these to see the problems faced by a typical small Barolo producer.

1 Temperature of the wine is vital. Malolactic bacteria act most quickly between 20°C and 25°C. If the cellar is not well insulated or there is no means of heating either cellar or wine, then it is unlikely that any malolactic activity will take place before the spring when the ambient temperature rises.

2 The higher the pH of a wine, the easier the transformation will be. Thus with a Nebbiolo typically high in acidity, the malolactic fermentation may not start by itself every year. In the case of Barbera, deacidification may even be required.

3 The higher the degree of alcohol in the wine the slower the growth of lactic bacteria. This is another natural disadvantage for the great nebbiolo wines.

4 Aeration of the wine favours the growth of lactic bacteria. Racking the wine can help to induce malolactic fermentation, but it is not indispensable, as the bacteria will also develop in the absence of oxygen. In Piemonte traditionalists rack their wine a little as possible.

5 The amounts of certain amino acids and minerals in the wine will affect the speed of growth of the lactic bacteria which feed on these as well as on yeasts in the atmosphere. It is possible to supplement the wine with vitamin B to help the bacterial development.

6 Sulphur dioxide, both in free and combined forms, inhibits the development of lactic bacteria. However, the effect of SO_2 varies greatly according to the level of acidity in the wine. Allied with high levels of total acidity, such as in Barolo and Barbaresco, even an apparently low dose of SO_2 (such as 5 grams per hectolitre) can prevent the malolactic fermentation from taking place.

Some winemakers are experimenting with the technique of inoculating their wines with cultured lactic bacteria to induce the transformation of malic into lactic acid, but this is not a common practice in Piemonte.

An understanding of the *malolattica* is certainly one of the key tools available to Albese winemakers to make their wines more accessible in style to a world audience. The evangelizing work of Ratti and others in the seventies seems to have been heeded in the eighties, and we can look forward to Barolo and Barbaresco of ever greater refinement.

Racking

After the completion of the alcoholic fermentation, and again after the malolactic fermentation, the winemaker will rack his wine. This simply involves pumping the wine from one vat to another to separate it from the deposits of tartrates, yeasts and dead bacteria that have precipitated. To protect the wine from oxidation the level of free SO_2 will usually be checked and adjusted at the time of racking. The traditional approach is to disturb the wine as little as possible, racking normally once or twice in the first year and thereafter annually in the spring. The modern method initially involves more frequent racking: at least three or four times in the first year and then twice in subsequent years. This is a reflection of the modernist's obsession with cleanliness, for a wine left in contact with its lees too long may develop off-flavours from micro-organisms in the lees – the worst example of which is the rotten egg aroma of hydrogen sulphide which one still occasionally meets today in a badly made wine.

Maturation

The process of maturation of a fine red wine is normally divided into two phases: the first a period of time in cask and the second in bottle. The proportional division of these two phases is another critical element in the style of the finished product.

The most common approach among younger winemakers following the Peynaud recipe is to allow shorter periods of cask ageing and to produce a wine designed to reach its maximum potential only after further maturation in bottle. Renato Ratti argued that this was a return to the pre-1930s practice when a Barolo would undergo as little as one year's wood age as few producers could afford more than one barrel. Today's traditionalists aim to make a wine that after lengthy cask age is virtually at its peak by the time it is considered ready for bottling (which is not to say that it will not remain in a stable condition for many years and even develop in bottle). In reality there are many valid points of view which come between the two extremes.

The traditional ageing vessel in Piemonte is the *botte*, a large, horizontal, oval or round cask made of oak (chestnut is no longer used because of its excessive porosity and harsh, tannic flavours) with a capacity of anything from 20 to 150 hectolitres. The most common size in a small winery is about 25 hectolitres or about 2 metres high. Despite the considerable cost of these large casks and the efforts needed to maintain them in a state of both cleanliness and hermeticity, they are still regarded as the optimum medium for slow ageing of fine red wines in the Langhe. In Pio Cesare's cellar there are venerable *botti* from the turn of the century that, although much repaired, are still in use today. More commonly a cellar will now replace one of these casks after twenty or thirty years. The *botte* is a relatively neutral vessel in that it adds only a limited amount of wood flavours to the wine. As a rule, the smaller the cask the more wood flavour it will give the wine. Virtually all *botti* are made of Slovenian oak, which is rather more porous and aggressively tannic than French oak. New *botti* will not normally be used for Nebbiolo for the first two or three years, but instead be broken in with a Barbera to absorb the oaky flavours from the cask (this tradition probably goes some way to explaining the Piemontese predilection for Barbera aged in *barrique*). As Bartolo Mascarello has pointed out, there was a time when a Barolo tasting of oak had to be sold off cheaply. Mascarello recalls his father making the costly error of ageing a Barolo in some newly purchased barrels: because of the oaky flavour they had to sell the Barolo at half price!

It may seem paradoxical to suggest that oxygen is at the same time wine's greatest enemy and yet, in the case of a great red, indispensable to its successful ageing. The key, as with all enological processes, is control. Certainly, it would initially appear that a more traditional approach to winemaking admits a greater role for controlled oxidation. Yet in fact a well-maintained *botte* provides a relatively oxygen-free environment for ageing wine. Evaporation of the wine through the pores of the wood is minimal, the joints of the cask do offer a greater chance of exchange between wine and atmosphere, but most significant of all is the surface area of the wine exposed to the air and thus to potential attack by oxidasic bacteria. The crucial requirement is to keep the casks well filled with wine, with as little ullage as possible. Topping up (*colmatura*) will take place at least every week (in summer even every day) in the dedicated winemaker's *cantina*. The larger the cask, the slower will be the maturation of the wine, as the surface area exposed to air will be smaller in relation to the total volume. Larger casks also allow the wine to retain more CO_2 and thus stay youthful longer. In addition humidity and temperature of the cellar play an important part in determining the speed of maturation of the wine.

There are very few producers left who follow the old practice of transferring their wine from *botte* to *damigiana* for an intermediate period of maturation in an oxygen-free environment. A severe winter in 1929 ushered in a new phase of winemaking as icy temperatures wiped out stocks of these hand-blown glass vessels overnight. Fratelli Barale are the only company with any significant stocks of demijohns; it is an impressive sight to behold the ranks of bulbous glass in their dark cellars. The volume held by the Piemontese demijohn is normally around 50 litres. In explaining the demise of the *damigiana*, producers will point to the time-consuming decanting and filling procedures, and also to great variations in quality between the wine in one vessel and another. Altogether the demijohn system was a haphazard one. Today there is a more hygienic and manageable equivalent in the small stainless steel container into which producers such as Vietti (p.192) and Aldo Conterno (p.153) transfer their wines if they feel that they have had a sufficient period of wood ageing but are not yet ready for bottling.

During the wine's stay in cask, a number of gradual and complex transformations take place. The most significant general development is that of the wine's bouquet from one of rawness and fermentation towards the eventual goal of refinement and fruit. Also obvious is the change in the colour of the wine. As the red pigments (anthocyanins) combine with the tannins (polyphenolic substances), so a purple hue gives way to a characteristic red-brown colour. Some tannins will also combine with oxygen and precipitate, reducing tannin levels, while other tannins condense with proteins. This latter process, known to the chemist as polymerization, is crucial in altering the olfactory characteristics of tannin in the finished wine. The young, unbonded molecules of tannin are much harsher and more astringent on the palate than the chains of tannin molecules formed in a mature wine. These mature tannins are no longer aggressive, but confer an extra richness and solidity on the texture of the wine.

This is a good point at which to consider the role of volatile acidity (VA) in the aroma of a wine. The presence of a high level of VA in a wine is an indication of oxidation, invariably due to attack by acetobacter. The chemical formula expresses it bluntly: alcohol + oxygen $\rightarrow$ acetic acid + water.

The modern school of winemakers argue that even a moderately high level of VA is unacceptable. A wine such as Monfortino, kept in cask for many years, will obviously suffer greater oxidation than one spending two years in wood, hence it is also likely to have a slightly higher level of VA. The effect can be to intensify the aroma of the wine, to 'lift' some of the elements of the bouquet. In fact the reason for this is due to the presence of ethyl acetate, which is always formed at the same time as acetic acid, and which in small quantities can emphasize nuances of the volatile esters and aldehydes that make up the wine's aroma. There are winemakers all over the world who marvel at the extra level of complexity which some alchemists in Barolo achieve with that infinitesimal lift of volatility.

BARRIQUE

Italy's new love affair with the 225 litre capacity *barrique bordelais* is going strong in Piemonte, especially in the field of Barbera. But now the boundaries of this fascination have extended to include Barolo and, in particular, Barbaresco. The use of new *barrique* is expensive: it will add at least L2500 to the ex-cellar cost of a bottle of wine. On the other hand it can make wines enjoyable at an earlier age. The smaller cask certainly helps the wine to become mature more quickly, but most producers in Piemonte are using *barrique* more for the oaky flavour a new barrel confers on the wine. Despite the fact that the DOCG laws for minimum cask age would seem to work against the combination of Barolo and *barrique*, there are a few producers (like Valentino Migliorini of Rocche dei Manzoni) who see this as the path towards greater acceptance of their wines in an international market where the taste of new oak is a symbol of class. Gaja's mould-breaking work in Barbaresco has inspired men such as Pio Boffa of Pio Cesare to admit a percentage of wine aged in new oak into their Barolo.

The crucial question, which will doubtless be debated unto eternity amongst the Albesi, is whether there is any true affinity between the nebbiolo grape and new oak. The most commonly heard argument from the conservative winemaker is that *barrique* is all very well for wines naturally deficient in tannin, such as Barbera, but an absurdity for the high-tannin nebbiolo grape. There is no disputing the fact that Barbera and new oak can be very harmonious partners, but despite the fact that Cabernet wines are often generously endowed with grape tannins you won't hear the Bordelais arguing that Merlot is the only wine suitable for *barrique* ageing. It is important to differentiate between the astringent quality of grape tannins and the sweet, vanillin flavours endowed by new-oak tannins. One must also be aware that a different fermentation technique is required for a wine intended for new-oak ageing: a shorter, more efficient maceration, extracting less grape tannins is more likely to produce better results than the *capello sommerso*.

The only producer in the Langhe with any track record in the *barrique* stakes is Angelo Gaja (p.162). The international consensus is that his results are of the highest quality. Working with Barbaresco he has an advantage in that the minimum wood ageing specified by law is only one year. Gaja is a perfectionist in the field of fermentation, and he limits the contribution of oak to the flavour of his wines by steaming the new casks before they are used and also by transferring the wines to *botte* after a maximum of one year in *barrique*.

While the number of producers jumping on the *barrique* band-wagon will no doubt continue to grow, it seems likely that Barolo and Barbaresco with new-oak flavours will remain an anomaly and a curiosity (and Gaja must be seen as a law unto himself). What is already clear, however, is that there will be an increasing role for fine individualist *vini d'autore*: wines such as Clerico's Arte and Altare's Vigna Arborina. The path to winning over the world's appreciation of noble Barolo may well be made easier by the availability of sister wines with that element of new-oak flavour so highly prized by connoisseurs in both Europe and America.

Bottling

At this point the winemaker must exercise great discretion in choosing the moment when he considers the tannins have lost sufficient aggression, the volatile flavour compounds have developed sufficiently, and the fruit flavours and body of the wine have not begun to deteriorate. This is the moment when the wine is ready to bottle. No two men, however, will choose the same moment, let alone the same month or year.

The main consideration in choosing the time to bottle a Barolo or Barbaresco will be the type and duration of ageing that the wine is subsequently destined for. The moment of bottling will tie in closely with the producer's overall philosophy, and be predetermined not only by the quality of the raw materials, but also by the fermentation technique employed. To consider this in the black and white of the terms 'modernist' and 'traditionalist', we can say that the traditionalist aims to bottle a wine when it is ready for consumption while the modernist will bottle at an earlier stage in order to allow the wine to undergo a significant part of its development in bottle.

The modern theory is that a wine aged reductively (in the absence of oxygen) is capable of greater finesse, especially in terms of bouquet, than one aged in the presence of oxygen. Following this Peynaud-type methodology has led the Albese winemaker to bottle earlier and earlier. At the most extreme point of view there are a handful of producers who ignore the official discipline and keep their Barolo in wood for one year or less (a practice that has much to commend it in lighter vintages where a wine's fruit can easily be lost by overlong wood ageing). There is certainly a value in these pioneering attempts to revitalize Barolo with greater fruit and freshness, but the avoidance of oxidation can all too often seem like a fanatical obsession. Indeed, the control of oxidation in red wines can well be achieved without recourse to enormous investment in modern stainless steel equipment and nitrogen counter-pressure isobaric bottling lines.

Pre-bottling treatments are kept to the minimum by all the quality producers. Filtration of these fine red wines is often considered detrimental to quality and in any case unnecessary, as the sediments of colouring matter and dead bacteria will have already been deposited during the course of wood ageing. Some producers favour a gelatine fining treatment, which clarifies the wine and also reduces the tannin levels, but this may not be used for wines of each and every vintage. Cold stabilization at sub-zero temperatures to precipitate tartrates is now becoming more common in the Albese. Traditionally this is achieved by leaving the wine in casks outdoors in the winter months. Most winemakers will make a slight adjustment of the SO_2 level in the wine before bottling to protect against oxidation and guarantee the future stability of the product.

Ageing

As in most parts of the winemaking world today, the producer in the Langhe is unable to afford to tie up the large amounts of capital necessary to allow him to sell fully mature wines. A very few cellars, like Prunotto, have a laudable policy of holding their bottled stocks of Barolo and Barbaresco for a year before releasing them onto the market. On the whole it is left to the wine merchant, restaurateur and increasingly often the enthusiastic amateur to allow us to follow the progress of great wines as they reach their peak of maturity.

Leaving aside subjective considerations of individual taste, it is difficult to offer sensible guidelines for the potential of Barolo and Barbaresco to improve in bottle. The question of vintage is paramount: a Barolo from a light year such as 1981 would rarely benefit from being given any additional ageing than that already deemed appropriate by the winemaker. On the other hand, the best wines from a fine year such as 1978 have yet to reach their maximum potential (see vintage notes on pp.244–60).

All talk of the quality of a vintage must always be put in perspective by looking at the individual producer and his raw materials. In a potentially good year such as 1987 we visited top adjacent cru vineyards in Barolo. In one row hung sparse, small neat bunches of perfectly healthy nebbiolo grapes, while in the other an almost obscene abundance of gigantic bunches flaunted themselves. The yields from the vines with large bunches would have been at least double that of the vines with small bunches.

Apart from the question of vintage, a Barolo subjected to long cask maturation will on the whole derive less benefit from significant bottle age, whereas some of the more modern interpretations of Barolo, while appealing in their youth because of their prominent primary and secondary fruit flavours, look likely to go on improving for decades.

OTHER RED WINES

Nebbiolo d'Alba DOC

Although it used to be vinified as a sweet wine, today's Nebbiolo d'Alba is often looked upon as the baby brother of Barolo and Barbaresco. This view is generally reflected in a vinification technique which mirrors that of the two DOCG wines.

The nebbiolo grown on the sandy soil of the Roero rarely offers the option of making a wine that needs long ageing. The most appropriate style here is that of a warm, fruity wine – softer and less tannic than either Barbaresco or Barolo. The wine is fermented at similar or slightly lower temperatures than Barolo, sometimes with *cappello sommerso*, but with a much shorter maceration on the grape skins (typically around ten days).

DOC law specifies a minimum one-year ageing period, and normally this takes place in *botte*; softening the wine and giving it some characteristics of maturity. The wine will customarily be bottled in the summer some eighteen months after the vintage.

Nebbiolo delle Langhe

This *vino da tavola* could well have started life being groomed for DOCG status as a Barolo or Barbaresco and declassified by either producer or DOCG selection panel at a later stage in the wine's development. Alternatively the winemaker, deeming the grapes not up to scratch for a nobler appellation, may have vinified the wine in a lighter style for early consumption.

Roero DOC

As Alba's most modern DOC it is no surprise that Roero should in many ways be the Langarolo wine vinified in the most up-to-date fashion.

The mandatory 2–5 per cent of white arneis grapes may be crushed or fermented together with the nebbiolo; but more commonly they will be blended in in the form of wine at a later stage.

Most Roero producers are aiming at a style that is racy, fruity and fresh. This means that cool fermentation temperatures are the norm (20°C) and maceration periods very short (often only six or seven days).

Wood ageing is usually kept to a minimum for Roero, many producers storing the wine only in stainless steel. Bottling will take place in the summer after the vintage.

Barbera d'Alba DOC

In the Langhe barbera is vinifed in a similar fashion to nebbiolo. Indeed, the best examples of mature Barbera often show an uncanny resemblance to mature Nebbiolo.

On the whole, however, Barbera is rarely destined for long ageing because of its relatively low tannin content. As a result, fermentation temperatures are invariably a degree or two lower than those used for Nebbiolo – Pio Cesare for instance work at 24–5°C instead of the 25–6°C used for Nebbiolo – and maceration times are shorter: ten days is typical. Use of *cappello sommerso* is becoming less common for Barbera these days, except where a wine of exceptional power is the aim. Barbera's aggressive acidity means that a complete malolactic fermentation is indispensable if a balanced wine is to be produced.

The Barbera of immense concentration, as produced in good vintages by Vietti, G. Conterno and Vajra, is principally a result of using superb-quality fruit, but also due to longer maceration and higher fermentation temperatures. At the other end of the scale, Barbera's high acidity can make it well suited for a light, fruity and even slightly *frizzante* role, but most Barbera d'Alba occupies the middle ground.

The DOC requirement of two year's ageing (including one in wood) has recently been dropped altogether. While this appears to go against the traditional style of the wine, it does open the door to a wider range of interpretations.

The modernist, *barrique*-aged version was, by chance, already accommodated by DOC. Today, almost every cellar has its obligatory *barrique* or two tucked away in a corner, and usually the contents will be Barbera. Even traditional cellars such as Castello di Neive have tried new oak with Barbera. One of the earliest and most successful examples is produced by Aldo Conterno, who uses a combination of new and used French *barriques* for a limited maturation period of up to nine months.

Dolcetto

The first thing you notice about Dolcetto is its colour: vivid, deep, purple-rimmed and at times virtually opaque. The grapes give freely of their colour without contributing great quantities of tannin. This means that dolcetto receives the briefest maceration of all the Albese red grapes. Sometimes only three or four days will suffice to extract a healthy colour, but in an effort to give a more tannic balance, the more old-fashioned winemaker will normally wait for ten to twelve days before the *svinatura* when the juice is run off the skins before the end of the alcoholic fermentation. In exceptional cases, such as with Mauro Mascarello's Gagliassi (produced from old vines), a maceration of up to eighteen days will produce a Dolcetto of considerable tannic structure.

The average producer's aim in making Dolcetto, however, is more likely to be a wine which, whether light or full-bodied, retains the taste of the grape: very fresh and bursting with fruit. Dolcetto's low acidity mitigates against making a wine with the capacity to improve for more than one or two years in bottle. The route to freshness is via a cool fermentation temperature of 20°C to 23°C. For the ill-equipped producer in a hot September, it may well be a problem to exercise this type of control. Certainly it is not difficult to find examples of Dolcetto with a baked, cooked or jammy flavour resulting from a very high fermentation temperature.

67

No minimum ageing period is stipulated for Dolcetto d'Alba, and most winemakers will either keep the wine out of wood altogether or bottle when the malolactic transformation is complete in the spring or summer after the vintage. Some producers even deliberately partially inhibit the *malolattica* to give the wine greater acidity. We have come across a few examples of Dolcetti where the malolactic fermentation has been blithely continuing in the bottle: a bad advertisement for a wine that surely has great potential on the export market.

Freisa

Today a relatively unknown variety outside Piemonte, at the beginning of the century freisa was much more widely planted. The reason for its demise is that, if grown indiscriminately, freisa tends to an overproduction of feeble grapes. Like nebbiolo, good sites and hard pruning are needed to bring out the best in freisa.

A 1967 Freisa from Prunotto tasted on its twentieth anniversary with the Colla brothers showed what could be done with Freisa in the Langhe. It still had a deep colour and plenty of sweet fruit. Beppe Colla explained how the new (and in his opinion inappropriate) fashion for a *frizzante* style of wine in the sixties and seventies led him to stop producing Freisa.

The characteristics of this grape have something in common with nebbiolo; Freisa is also high in acidity but somewhat less abundantly blessed with tannin. In the Alba zone there is a history of producing a full-bodied dry Freisa capable of some cask and bottle age, but the *frizzante* mode dominates production today. The best example of Freisa fermented at low temperature (20°C) in a sealed vat or autoclave and bottled with a slight fizz is perhaps Domenico Clerico's fragrant and fruity wine from Ginestra. Also in Monforte, Aldo Conterno produces a weightier style which finishes its fermentation in bottle and needs decanting due to a sediment.

A lone flag for a more weighty, demanding wood-aged style Freisa is being flown by young Aldo Vajra. He has achieved notable results from the 1985 vintage with a wine of very limited yields fermented at 30°C. His wine combines structure, texture and a unique perfume in a way that leads us to hope for a revival of interest in this type of Freisa amongst the best winemakers in the area.

WHITE WINE VINIFICATION

Moscato d'Asti DOC and Asti Spumante DOC

There is a certain irony in the fact that the spontaneous charms of Moscato – surely the wine whose flavour stays nearer to that of the original grape than any other – are the results of much toil and effort in the cellar, not to mention investment in technology!

In his monograph *Asti*, Renato Ratti traced the origins of today's production technique for Moscato back to the end of the sixteenth century, when Giovan Battista Croce developed the methods of decanting and filtration which are still used today to keep the fermentation process in check and maintain the wine's natural sweetness.

The first stage in this sequence of controlling measures is the clarification of the must. Immediately after what is today a very soft pressing, the must is clarified to remove yeasts together with the pectins and nitrogenous substances which are important elements in feeding the yeasts during fermentation. As a result the risk of unwanted fermentation is reduced.

Traditionally this clarification was carried out by a laborious technique involving multiple decanting of the must while skimming solids off the surface, and then a coarse filtration through cloth-lined hessian filters. These long *salame*-like tubes are known as 'Dutch sacks' – *filtri olandesi*.

Technology has made life easier for the Moscato producer. Nowadays he can obtain excellent results by initially centrifuging the must to remove any particles and then using a bentonite fining for a thorough clarification. The single biggest advance in production techniques over the last forty years is the availability of sophisticated refrigeration equipment to inhibit the must's tendency to ferment.

After the Moscato must has been stabilized it may then be stored at 0°C until the wine is to be produced. This enables the producer to ensure the freshest possible product. Asti Spumante may legally have its must enriched by the addition of saccharose up to the equivalent of 2 per cent in terms of alcohol, whereas a Moscato *naturale* which comes under still, as opposed to sparkling, wine legislation is not permitted such latitude. As a result the finest grapes tend to be used for the Moscato d'Asti, while the larger, industrialized Asti Spumante producers are understandably more concerned about keeping their costs under control.

The final fermentation, *preso di spuma*, is carried out in the auto-clave – a costly pressure- and temperature-controlled tank (usually stainless steel) which gives the winemaker full command over his subject. Using the autoclave, the producer can achieve the second, continuous, phase of fermentation, often aided by cultured yeasts (and for Asti Spumante by the legal addition of saccharose), over a period of a few weeks at a temperature below 20°C. The fermentation is stopped by refrigeration when the alcohol level reaches 5.5 or 6.5 per cent with about 5.5 per cent of the potential alcohol remaining as sugar. Asti Spumante is allowed to ferment one or two degrees of alcohol further towards dryness, and will be bottled at 5 atmospheres pressure rather than Moscato d'Asti's 3 atmospheres.

The traditional fermentation process was lengthy and interrupted by repeated filtrations to keep matters under control. After some five, six, or seven small fermentations, the result was a wine of great richness: fatter, softer but less freshly perfumed than today's typical Moscato. The old method also involved finishing fermentation in bottle with the attendant risk of things going out of control. Ratti spoke of the days when cellar workers would protect their faces by wearing fencing masks!

The culmination of modern Moscato production is a final refriger-ation to eliminate tartrates, a sterile filtration and bottling in a stout bottle with a jumbo cork. As at all stages of production, impeccable hygiene is essential to avoid any risks of bacterial contamination.

Dry White Wines

Dry white wine is a small but growing star in the firmament of winemaking in the Langhe. Producers with years of experience of red wine vinification are virtually going back to school to learn the new science of white wine production. Anyone who has become familiar with the Arneis and Favorita produced on the right bank of the Tanaro over the last ten years will be aware of the considerable technical progress that has been made.

Given the right weather conditions, it is possible for the smallest *contadino* to produce a great Barolo. White wine is a relatively delicate substance, and it is notoriously difficult to make a good example without recourse to sophisticated technology. In the 1980s we have seen the small producer invest in the equipment to produce reliable, fresh whites every year.

With the exception of Chardonnay, the white wines of the Langhe are all characterized by their delicacy and lack of structure. In order to make the most of their limited personalities, the winemaker needs to take great care at all stages of production. Arneis in particular is low in acid and the wine often subject to premature oxidation.

After gentle crushing of the grapes and removal of the skins and stalks, the pulp is pressed as softly as possible to avoid extracting excessive polyphenolic substances which may encourage oxidation. The more forward-looking producers are incorporating a percentage of wine made using criomaceration, a technique of cold macerating the grape skins in the must at 0°C to extract more aromatic perfumes. The resulting must will then ideally be refrigerated, given a low dose of SO_2, and clarified to remove further polyphenols and bacteria.

Precise temperature control during fermentation is far more critical for white wines than red. The fashion for the uniform 'bubble-gum' flavours that typically result from very low temperature fermentation (below 16°C) is on the wane. Today the consensus is that the end product will have more personality if fermented at around 18–20°C. Many producers aim to leave a few grams of residual sugar in their arneis to give the wine a more aromatic quality.

After fermentation, a neutral container, ideally stainless steel, provides the best medium to preserve these slight and fragile wines. Storage under a blanket of carbon dioxide, or nitrogen offers an additional guarantee against oxidation. Malolactic fermentation is a contentious subject. Many producers preserve the maximum total acidity in the wine, avoiding the malolactic by storing the wine in a cool and oxygen-free environment. Others, including influential names such as Bruno Giacosa, allow a complete *malo* to happen. In the case of Arneis this makes for a richly textured, but often spinelessly soft and flat white wine. Bottling takes place in the spring after the vintage following further clarification through fining and sterile filtration.

In the case of the new phenomenon of the wood-matured Chardonnay as made by Gaja, Pio Cesare and increasing numbers of others, the wine is matured in the 225 litre *barrique*. In Gaja's case the wine is fermented in stainless steel and then transferred to a combination of previously steamed new and one-year-old oak for a period of two or three months. Pio Cesare on the other hand follows the more common Burgundian technique of fermenting the must directly in *barrique*. Because the cask becomes lined with tartrates, the wine can rest there for a year without taking on excessive amounts of oak. The oak-matured Chardonnay will normally undergo a full malolactic transformation in cask which contributes to its round, velvety texture.

The Arneis boom in Italy has inspired more and more new plantings of different white grape varieties. At the moment production levels are rarely enough to stimulate much more than academic curiosity. But the potential for quality – if not quantity – has been proven, and the Langhe can be expected to produce some fascinating new white wines over the next few years.

5

VINEYARDS AND DENOMINATIONS

Just as the topography of the zone determines the nature and distribution of the many and varying microclimates, so in combination with appropriate exposure and altitude it has a fundamental bearing on pinpointing the prime sites for the relevant grape varieties. As we have seen, the vines planted have an affinity with the differing soil types that make up the viticultural Langhe/Roero. The icing on the cake is that the land's geophysical structure is diverse enough to permit variations in wine styles from one hillside to the next. These styles are examined within the context of both the wine denominations and their principal vineyards.

BAROLO

PRODUCTION REGULATIONS
Minimum alcohol content: 13 per cent.
Minimum ageing requirements: 3 years, at least two of which must be in oak or chestnut barrels: 5 years for *riserva*.
Maximum production levels: 80 quintals of grapes per hectare (1 quintal = 100 kilograms) with a 70 per cent *resa in vino* (the crushed grapes may yield a maximum of 70 per cent of their weight in wine). The *resa in vino* drops to 65 per cent after the compulsory ageing period (i.e., to 65 per cent of the original weight after the minimum 3

years' maturation). The final maximum output from a hectare of nebbiolo vines is therefore 52 hectolitres of Barolo.

DOC granted: 23 April 1966; DOCG as of 1 July 1980.

A maximum of 15 per cent of older Barolo can be used to 'improve' the quality of a younger vintage and vice versa.

The Barolo zone, covering the region's southwestern section, was officially defined in 1909 by the Comizio Agrario d'Alba, though the Ministry of Agriculture had begun a similar project in 1896 and a decade earlier, Fantini – a land surveyor from Monforte d'Alba – had virtually mapped out the finished 1909 version. Ironically he did not include Monforte itself, which at that time, like neighbouring Novello, was regarded principally for its Barbera and Dolcetto production. Even after Monforte's inclusion in 1933, it was difficult to persuade many growers to replant with nebbiolo. Those who did still liked to improve their wine with liberal additions of barbera to boost both colour and acidity! The final delimited area covers eleven different communes, though only five form the classic heartland. Altogether the eleven communes produce around 6.5 million bottles a year from just over 1,200 hectares tended by some 1,200 growers. Production levels have remained constant over recent years (in 1973 just under 7 million bottles of Barolo were produced, whereas in the all-time peak vintage of 1985 the figure was just over 7 million). This clearly demonstrates that we are dealing with an area operating somewhere near its full capacity. The following breakdown, based on production figures for 1988, illustrates the point:

Table 3

Commune	Growers	Registered Barolo vineyards	% of total Barolo production
La Morra	372	380.93 ha	32.32
Serralunga d'Alba	149	197.36 ha	16.74
Monforte d'Alba	185	193.70 ha	16.43
Barolo	139	149.97 ha	12.72
Castiglione Falletto	93	102.74 ha	8.72
Verduno	81	50.06 ha	4.25
Novello	62	45.82 ha	3.89
Grinzane Cavour	51	29.23 ha	2.48
Diano d'Alba	8	17.09 ha	1.45
Roddi	22	10.47 ha	0.89
Cherasco	1	1.26 ha	0.11
TOTALS	1163	1178.69 ha	100.00

Source: Camera di Commercio Industria e Agricultura di Cuneo.

The number of growers and amount of land under vine in each commune varies slightly from year to year. In the great vintages everyone with a nebbiolo vineyard falling within the delimited area will probably want to produce a Barolo from it; in lesser vintages this will not be the case. The figures for 1988 are thus taken from the actual production declarations made. The 1,200 growers and their 1,200 hectares represent a notional average over some fifteen vintages.

The first five communes form the core of production and the minor communes account for much smaller percentages. It can also be seen that the average holding there is generally much smaller (well under 1 ha in most cases) indicating fewer specialized nebbiolo vineyards. Though Serralunga has fewer growers than Monforte, the total land under vine and percentage of the production is greater owing to the presence of the area's largest privately owned winery, Fontanafredda. The fact that their estate overlaps into Diano d'Alba goes some way towards explaining the apparently high average holding there too.

The figures for the major communes are worth contrasting with those for 1975:

Table 4

Commune	Registered Barolo vineyards	% of total Barolo production
La Morra	382.42 ha	33.5
Serralunga d'Alba	178.28 ha	16.6
Barolo	145.66 ha	13.5
Monforte d'Alba	140.10 ha	13.0
Castiglione Falletto	96.64 ha	9.0
TOTALS	943.08 ha	87.6

Source: Camera di Commercio Industria e Agricultura di Cuneo.

The contribution of the minor communes has remained fairly static (12.4 per cent in 1975 and 13.07 per cent in 1988). These percentages are based on totals of 1,076 hectares in 1975 and 1,178 hectares in 1988. Most interestingly, the data reveal the fall and rise of Barolo and Monforte respectively. The hectares under vine in Barolo have increased marginally (145.6 in 1975 and 149.9 in 1988) whereas the extra land planted to nebbiolo in Monforte has increased dramatically from 140.10 hectares in 1975 to 193.7 hectares in 1988. The more recent tradition of growing nebbiolo in Monforte means that it is here, if anywhere, that the vineyards of Barolo can be expanded, while in Barolo itself, the nebbiolo appears to be fully established.

The Geographical Perspective

The Barolo zone is a narrow-mouthed, horseshoe-shaped basin bounded to west by the high crest which reaches along the western edge of the communes of Barolo and La Morra. This merges, towards Monforte, into a cluster of hills where the crest that skirts the eastern edge of Serralunga begins. The horseshoe is bisected by a spine-like ridge beginning just north of Castiglione Falletto and extending south to the village of Monforte. The basin is thus split into two distinct sections. The western part consists of the valley stretching from Gallo d'Alba to Barolo and taking in the commune of La Morra. Its eastern border is marked by the Talloria dell'Annunziata stream which separates La Morra from most of Castiglione Falletto and from there on the Valle dei Fischi (the course of the Bussia stream) divides Barolo from the lower part of Castiglione Falletto and from Monforte. Apart from the low-lying hills of Cannubi and to the east Costa di Rosé and Castellero (overlooking the Valle dei Fischi to the east again), most of the major vineyards are all within the gently undulating slopes which start northeast of the village of Annunziata and continue in a broad sweep along the zone's western flank to curve back behind the village of Barolo towards Monforte.

At the eastern edge of these boundaries the Serralunga valley begins, comprising the communes of Castiglione Falletto, Monforte and Serralunga itself. This valley falls between two steep ridges, one connecting Castiglione Falletto and Monforte, the other defining the eastern edge of Serralunga (there are roads along the top of both). The physical make-up of the eastern section is markedly different: a series of south and southwest facing lateral spurs off the western edge of the ridges (marked by a series of *conche* between them) create a much more varied topographical structure with fewer unbroken tracts of vines. On the southerly stretch of the Castiglione Falletto–Monforte ridge vines are also planted on the eastern side of the hills below the village of Castelletto and facing Serralunga across the valley of the

Talloria di Castiglione (the famous Rocche vineyard of Castiglione Falletto occupies this side of the ridge too).

As we have seen, the formation of the two valleys occurred during the third phase of the Tertiary epoch. This Miocene period can be further broken down into four geological subdivisions: Langhian, Helvetian, Tortonian and Messinian, categories which are used to characterize differing types of soil structure. The terrain of the western (or Barolo) Valley is Tortonian and is typically a calcareous bluish-grey marl while the eastern (Serralunga) valley has a Helvetian soil type (mainly sand and limestone conglomerates). Thus in terms of basic soil composition the Barolo valley has rather more clay and the Serralunga valley more sand and further to the east more chalk. In addition there is a differing balance of mineral and trace elements (usually more iron, phosphorus and potassium in Serralunga and more manganese and magnesium oxide in Barolo). The structure of the Tortonian soil is also less compact and therefore more prone to erosion from its water courses.

As a consequence of these marked differences in terrain (it must be remembered that the nebbiolo mutates very easily in response to its soil conditions) and topography (characteristically more south to southeast facing sites to the west and more south to southwest exposures in the centre and east), there is a discernible contrast in styles between the wines of the two valleys. The wines from the western section are generally a little less alcoholic, somewhat lighter in body and faster maturing; they are prized for their perfume, elegance and velvety texture. Those from the east tend to have greater structure, body, extract and alcohol and are usually harder and longer-lived.

Many of the vineyard slopes are steep without being precipitous. As the basin is relatively low-lying – the highest points are the Bricco del Dente at 553 metres on the ridge behind La Morra and Bricco Tappa at 549 metres just northeast of Monforte – most vineyards lie between 150 and 400 metres where the nebbiolo fares best.

Although the boundaries are first and foremost parochial ones, each commune has its own distinctive style. These characteristics become a little more blurred towards the extremities of the communes and even more so where the vineyards overlap from one to another. As any winemaker will tell you, you cannot make a wine from La Morra taste like one from Serralunga; but the ultimate determining factor in the

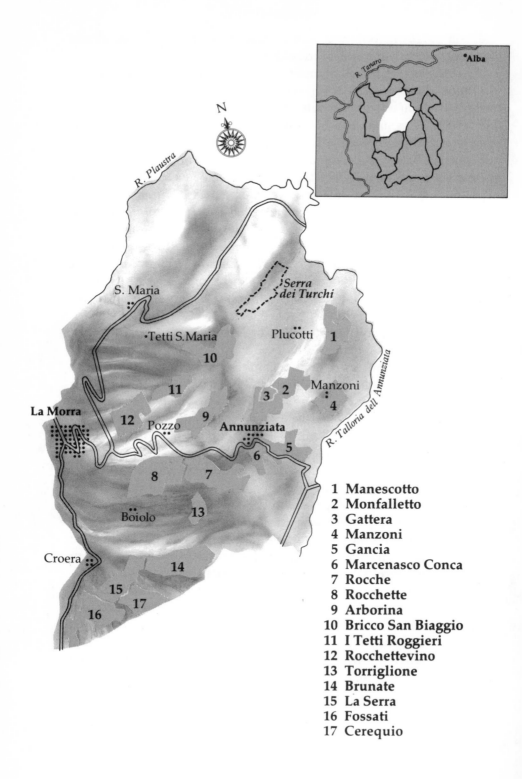

N

R. Plaustra

Serra
dei Turchi

S. Maria

•Tetti S.Maria

Plucotti   1

10

Manzoni

11   3 2

La Morra   4

12   Pozzo   9

Annunziata

8   7   5

6

Boiolo   13

Croera

14

15

17

16

R. Talloria dell'Annunziata

R. Tanaro   •Alba

1 Manescotto
2 Monfalletto
3 Gattera
4 Manzoni
5 Gancia
6 Marcenasco Conca
7 Rocche
8 Rocchette
9 Arborina
10 Bricco San Biaggio
11 I Tetti Roggieri
12 Rocchettevino
13 Torriglione
14 Brunate
15 La Serra
16 Fossati
17 Cerequio

style of an individual wine is often the method of vinification and differences in origin can be obscured by the techniques favoured by the particular winemaker. Clearly the most fruitful method of isolating the special characteristics of the various zones is to taste different crus from the same producer: Ceretto, Bruno Giacosa, Prunotto and Vietti all have appropriate ranges.

La Morra

La Morra lies in the northwest of the 'classic' zone. It is an old town dating back to Roman times, perched on top of a series of sprawling hills and reached from the Alba–Barolo road by a switchback lane up through a cascade of vineyards. La Morra is the biggest commune in terms of inhabitants and also of production levels both historically (at the turn of the century the largest negociant outside Alba and Bra was the La Morra house of Tarditi) and today, when it continues to produce nearly twice as much Barolo as its nearest rival Serralunga.

La Morra takes in the satellite village of Santa Maria to the northeast where a number of wineries are based. Although this area has a few vineyards of some renown (Ciocchini, La Serra dei Turchi and Plaustra-Convento in particular), they are just outside the central part of the zone where it is unanimously agreed the great crus of Barolo are all gathered.

The most important vineyard areas lie much closer to La Morra itself, to the east and south of the town. Due east and covering a complex of hills that face the Castiglione slopes across the valley, the major nebbiolo sites lie close to the villages of Annunziata, Pozzo and i Tetti-Roggieri. The village of Annunziata, once known as Marcenascum, is built around the fifteenth-century abbey which nowadays houses an excellent museum dedicated to the history of Albese wines and to Barolo in particular. The vineyards of Annunziata, and above it Pozzo, form a southwest through to southeast facing crescent which begins at Rocchette just below La Morra and ends east of the Cordero di Montezemolo's Monfalletto estate at the Manescotto hill. Arborina, Rocche, Marcenasco Conca, Gattera and the lesser-known sites of Gancia and Manzoni also fall within this district. In the next group of hills to the north around the tiny village of Roggieri, the

79

vineyards of Tettimorra, Rocchettevino and San Biaggio lie midway between La Morra and Santa Maria.

Some of these sites, though well situated, are relatively minor: Gancia, Manzoni, Manescotto, Rocchettevino and San Biaggio may become more important in the future as the crus of Barolo become better known and more closely defined (and, of course, their market more secure). For the moment they are normally reserved for the production of generic Barolo or other varietals (Rocchettevino is a renowned Dolcetto vineyard). In general the eastern La Morra slopes have the classic Barolo valley soil-mix of lowish sand, average limestone and a relatively high clay content (an average of around 38 per cent) and most are south to southeast facing. Important growers are Abbazia dell'Annunziata, Accommasso, Altare, Bovio, Cordero di Montezemolo, Grasso, Oberto, Oddero, Rocche Costamagna, Scarpa and Settimo.

A deep valley divides the 'eastern' from the 'southern' crus of La Morra. Towards the head of the valley lies the *frazione* of Boiolo and below it, the *frazione* of Torriglione sits on top of a small conical hill. Much of the valley's land is planted to Dolcetto but on the hill below Torriglione, a few well-known growers like Bartolo Mascarello work nebbiolo vines on the southeast-facing slopes.

The vineyards to the southeast of La Morra occupy the flanks of a large bowl which faces south towards the village of Barolo. They begin at Brunate. This famous south-facing hillside, where almost every plot of vines has perfect exposure on the smooth slopes, is one of the great crus of Barolo (a small part of its eastern tip extends into the commune of Barolo). Brunate's 25 per cent sand content is one of the lowest of the entire zone and clay at 39 per cent among the highest. Iron levels are relatively high for its westerly position while the presence of above-average manganese is more typical. The northern limit of Brunate is formed by a small track which connects the two tiny hamlets (really just groups of three or four houses) of Fontanazza Soprana (the source of Cogno-Marcarini's cru Brunate) and Fontanazza Sottana where Ceretto are based. Other parcels of vines within Brunate are owned by Fratelli Dogliani, Marchesi di Barolo, Fratelli Oddero and Ponte Rocca. Separated from Brunate by a dry ditch along a narrow dip in the land is the famous Cerequio cru. Lying just south of its neighbour, Cerequio has a similarly ideal exposure. By far the largest landowner here is Vinicola Piemontese (formerly Tenuta Cerequio) who farm some 6.5 hectares of nebbiolo vines.

Straddling Brunate and Cerequio above the head of the dry ditch is the La Serra cru. Cogno-Marcarini is the major landowner here with smaller sections owned by Gianni and Roberto Voerzio. The La Serra vineyards merge into the adjoining cru of Fossati to the south which extends over the communal border into Barolo.

WINE STYLES AND PRINCIPAL PRODUCERS
The typical style of La Morra is an 'ambassadorial' one: these are the zone's most approachable wines, representing the softer and more seductive side of Barolo. Though great Barolo is never without a healthy measure of structure and concentration, in La Morra these qualities are generally maintained in close harmony with the wines' more accessible characteristics. Their velvety, perfumed and forward style provides an ideal starting point for the would-be student.
The eastern vineyards: elegant, medium-bodied wines with a pronounced aromatic character (often with a hint of aniseed, licorice and tobacco) and a fairly intense structure.
Aborina: Elio Altare, Gianfranco Bovio
Gattera: Gianfranco Bovio
Marcenasco Conca: Abbazia dell'Annunziata
Monfalletto: Cordero di Montezemolo
Rocche: Lorenzo Accommasso, Abbazia dell'Annunziata, Renato Corino, Fratelli Oberto, Severino Oberto, Rocche Castamagna, Aurelio Settimo
Rocchette: Accommasso, Rocche Castamagna, Aurelio Settimo
Tettimorra: Scarpa
The western vineyards: archetypal La Morra – rich, ripe, velvety wines of great finesse which can also age quite well.
Brunate: Ceretto, Cogno-Marcarini, Marchesi di Barolo, Terre del Barolo, Vietti, Roberto Voerzio
Cerequio: Vinicola Piemontese, Roberto Voerzio
La Serra: Cogno-Marcarini, Gianni Voerzio, Roberto Voerzio
Fossati: Giuseppe Dosio
The differing attitudes of these vineyards account for discernible differences in style between the southern crus. Thus the lower-lying Cerequio has a little more solidity than Brunate, while La Serra and Fossati (higher vineyards) tend to be lighter in body and a little less

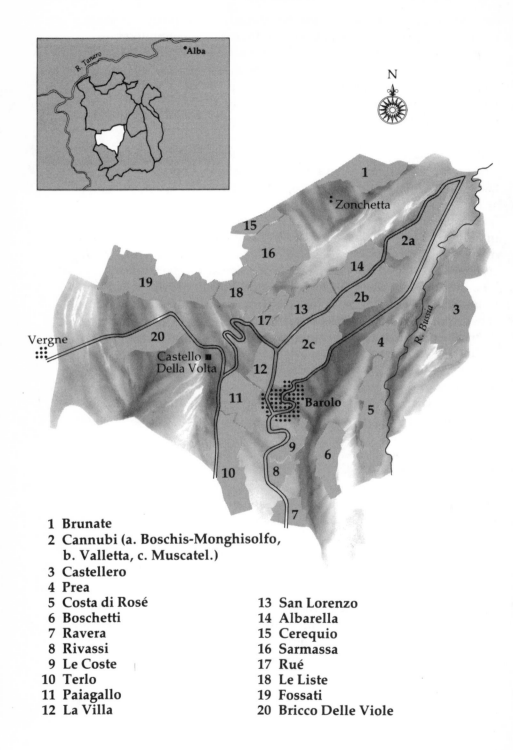

N

1 **Brunate**
2 **Cannubi (a. Boschis-Monghisolfo,**
   b. Valletta, c. Muscatel.)
3 **Castellero**
4 **Prea**
5 **Costa di Rosé**
6 **Boschetti**
7 **Ravera**
8 **Rivassi**
9 **Le Coste**
10 **Terlo**
11 **Paiagallo**
12 **La Villa**

13 **San Lorenzo**
14 **Albarella**
15 **Cerequio**
16 **Sarmassa**
17 **Rué**
18 **Le Liste**
19 **Fossati**
20 **Bricco Delle Viole**

fleshy. Though generally showing an intense and heady fragrance, wines from these last two crus are usually a little shorter lived.

Barolo

The commune of Barolo is the historical centre of the zone (though west of centre in geographical terms). It was once the feudal seat of the Marchesi di Falletto, the family credited with laying the foundations for Barolo as we know it today. Their castle, owned by the commune, houses a small museum and doubles up as the headquarters of the Enoteca Regionale del Vino Barolo (the regional wine library of Barolo). High on the hills to the west near the *frazione* of Vergne, stands the impressive Castello della Volta; otherwise Barolo is given over to its many *cantine* and most of its 700 or so inhabitants are involved in wine.

The commune's most famous vineyard has a fabled reputation. Cannubi is a low-lying hill shaped like an extended tongue; it begins at the northern edge of the town and extends in a northeasterly direction almost to where the three communes of Barolo, Castiglione Falletto and La Morra converge. Cannubi lies at the point where the Helvetian and Tortonian soil types of the two valleys meet – a fact the locals are quick to seize upon to justify the vineyard's reputation for combining the best of both worlds: the perfume and velvet of the western valley with some of the structure and concentration of the eastern section. Cannubi is also known as Cannubio, some growers prefer one name, some the other. The latter bears a close resemblance to the Italian word for union or marriage, *connubio*, and the vineyard's soil structure certainly bears out the connection: it has a high sand content for the western valley (over 35 per cent where 31 per cent is the overall average), highish limestone (just under 35 per cent) and low clay (30 per cent as opposed to the 37 per cent norm). Much of Cannubi is southeast, south southeast and south facing but as the hill is undulating, it also contains parcels of land which face north and northeast. Cannubi is bounded by the two roads leading into the small town from the direction of Alba.

The vineyard is divided between many different owners, many of whom tend no more than a few rows of vines. Two contrasting theories have grown up around the proliferation of the many 'subplots' that characterize the vineyard today. One maintains that over the course of the years individual names have been used to identify the different parcels. Among the most common are Muscatel (the most southern reaches), Valletta (close to the middle), San Lorenzo (which skirts the central section on its western side and continues over the top road overlooking Brunate/Cerequio) and Boschis, also know as Monghisolfo (the vineyard's northern tip). The other theory, favoured by Bartolo Mascarello in particular, is that at one time Cannubi was the name of a relatively small vineyard at the central section of the hill surrounding Cascina Ferrero (nowadays the site of the Borgogno brothers' winery) and that Muscatel, Valletta, San Lorenzo and Boschis were the traditional names for those parts of the hill. These days they are usually combined with Cannubi as growers seek to identify their wines with the zone's best-known name. While Cannubi and the various subsections apparently have a more homogeneous identity now, Mascarello describes the 'oral tradition' of naming vineyards in the area: growers have always been content to use the names handed down by their fathers and the sites have never been clearly mapped out.

There is no doubt that many parts of the vineyard have a splendid position, but to cash in on Cannubi's reputation, nebbiolo vines have frequently been planted on the inferior sections of the hill (for similar reasons, many growers in the commune like to insist that their vines lie within or just adjoining the famous site). Wines from Cannubi do not always match up to the elevated status Barolo's supposedly number one cru enjoys.

Despite its standing, we had to wait for our first taste of the great Cannubi. Probably the closest for a long time was the 1971 Cannubi from Ceretto, made on a one-off basis. Prunotto's Cannubi can show delicious fruit but does not have the intensity or staying power of their Bussia for example, and is sold by the Colla brothers as their faster-maturing cru Barolo. Most of the other examples we came across were a distinct let-down. Recently however we've been luckier: the three Cannubi-based crus (Cannubi, Cannubi Muscatel and Valletta) from Marchesi di Barolo showed definite promise as this famous house begins to revive its reputation. The finest examples we have tasted so far have been from two small producers, both only recently involved with the vineyard: Luciano Sandrone and Enrico Scavino. Local growers hold Cannubi in great esteem because of the unique perfume and fragrance of its wines: from Sandrone's Cannubi Boschis (first labelled as such from the 1985 vintage) and Scavino's Cannubi (first produced in 1985), that glory finally shone through in a wealth of ripe, heady and alluring soft fruit perfumes recalling raspberries and black cherries. Cannubi's reputation began at last to look as if it might be justified.

Owning vines in Cannubi is a mark of real prestige and land in the vineyard rarely becomes available: when it does, even a small plot can cost a great deal of money. Not surprisingly as Barolo's star rises, big business is keeping a close eye on developments. In spring 1989, the massive sparkling wine house Gancia, based in Canelli, invested some L800 million (around £370,000) in their purchase of 2.59 hectares of the vineyard. The wine will be made by Mauro Sebaste (p. 220) and the combination of his winemaking skills and their marketing and distribution experience may mark another milestone in the history of Barolo.

Owing to its central position within a relatively small commune, the other vineyards tend to radiate around Cannubi. To the east and adjoining the communes of Castiglione Falletto and Monforte are the low-lying vineyards of Castellero and Preda (mainly west-facing) and Costa di Rosé (a particularly sandy site facing east towards Bussia in Monforte). Below Barolo to the south, Le Coste and Terlo also have quite good reputations but are not seen as cru bottlings while the Ravera, Rivassi and Boschetti vineyards in this district are mainly planted to dolcetto. Adjoining the Muscatel section of Cannubi, Fontanafredda's mainly east-facing La Villa is a part of the old Mirafiore estate. Paiagallo, sitting between La Villa and Terlo, is highly regarded for barbera.

To the west of Barolo on the hills above the Castello della Volta, is the small *frazione* of Vergne situated close to the communal boundary with Narzole and thus right on the confines of the DOCG area. At up to 400 metres above sea-level, the vineyards – planted on quite chalky soil rich in magnesium oxide – are among the highest in the zone. The grapes ripen late at this altitude and harvest time can extend into November. Fossati (an extension of the vineyards in neighbouring La Morra) and Bricco delle Viole are the most renowned vineyards here.

Below Castello della Volta, Le Liste, Rué, Albarella and San Lorenzo are the vineyards covering the southern and eastern slopes of the valley which separates Cannubi from Brunate/Cerequio. Some of these are relatively minor sites owing to their primarily easterly or westerly aspect and are usually the source of generic Barolo. On the eastern flank of the valley however are the two remaining great crus of the commune. Below Barolo's small section of Cerequio lie the south and southeast facing Sarmassa (or Sarmazza) vineyards. Merenda and Le Mandorle are two small subsections of Sarmassa; Le Mandorle in particular has a distinctive character with a notable almond-like flavour and perfume though the name has rarely been cited on labels. To the northeast of Sarmassa is the small section of Brunate that falls into the commune of Barolo and the last of its prime sites. Marchesi di Barolo, Giuseppe Rinaldi, Luciano Rinaldi and Cogno-Marcarini own plots of land here (the Cogno-Marcarini vineyard is known as 'Canun'). Lying between the feet of the Cerequio and Brunate hillsides is the small *conca* of Zonchera (or Zonchetta) which partly overlaps into La Morra. Zonchera takes its name from *giunchera*: at one time the now-drained lake below the property was the source of the reeds (*i giunchi*) which growers used to tie up their vine shoots in late spring.

WINE STYLES AND PRINCIPAL PRODUCERS
The wines of the commune present a fairly classic and balanced character. While showing many of the accessible and perfumed qualities that characterize the wines of La Morra, they are often seen as having a little more backbone and intensity of flavour. The differences though can rest on the slightest nuance. If La Morra is the Margaux of Barolo, then Barolo itself is St Julien.

Cannubi: at best a sublime fusion of striking perfumes and ripe, silky soft fruit flavours, at worst a grave disappointment. Producers: Serio and Battista Borgogno; Tenuta Carreta; Tenute Colué; Giacomo Fenocchio; Marchesi di Barolo (Cannubi, Cannubi Muscatel, La Valletta); Prunotto; Luciano Rinaldi (Cannubio); Luciano Sandrone (Cannubi Boschis); Enrico Scavino.

Castellero: easy, approachable and quite perfumed wines. Producers: Fratelli Barale; Brezza.

Costa di Rosé: the only cru bottling widely available is from Marchesi di Barolo and has a lean and distinctively aromatic character; it promises the ability to age quite well.

La Villa: rich, structured Barolo from Fontanafredda.

Sarmassa: ripe, perfumed wines that mature fairly quickly. Producers: Brezza; Marchesi di Barolo.

Brunate: (see La Morra). Producers: Cogno-Marcarini (Canun); Giuseppe Rinaldi (Brunata); Luciano Rinaldi.
Bricco delle Viole: firm, medium-bodied and aromatic wine from Aldo Vajra.

Castiglione Falletto

Whereas Barolo is the zone's historical heartland, Castiglione Falletto lies at its geographical centre, only contributing to the outline of the DOCG limits as a small strip of land at the commune's most northerly point. Castiglione Falletto covers the northern end of the spine of hills between, to the west, the Talloria dell' Annunziata and, to the east, the Talloria di Castiglione. You reach the village by turning left, up towards Monforte, off the Alba–Barolo road: it clusters around the brow of a hill with vineyards dropping away to all sides. A small place of around 500 inhabitants, Castiglione Falletto is dominated by another intriguing but inaccessible castle. Apart from a small bar/restaurant, a newsagent/tobacconist and a grocer's shop, there are a few narrow streets of tiny houses. The road through to Monforte skirts the centre but clinging to the top of the slope on its western side are several small but important wineries like the Bricco Boschis estate of Fratelli Cavallotto and the home of one of Barolo's great characters, sadly no longer involved in winemaking, Violante Sobrero. Towards the floor of the valley separating Castiglione Falletto from La Morra is the small *frazione* of Garbelletto. The Scavino cousins and Fratelli Brovia are the main growers based here.

At the highest point of the commune, just south of the village towards Monforte, is the Ceretto brothers' awesome Bricco Rocche estate. It offers a marvellous panorama of much of the Barolo zone.

The commune is wholly given over to vines and despite its size (half that of Serralunga or a quarter of La Morra in terms of both hectares under vine and production levels), it is the base not only of small, high quality wineries like those of Cavallotto, Ceretto, Paolo Scavino and Vietti (whose *cantina* lies almost under the castle walls), but also of the largest single source of Barolo, the Terre del Barolo cooperative. Their cellars are housed in an industrial building on the Alba–Barolo road

87

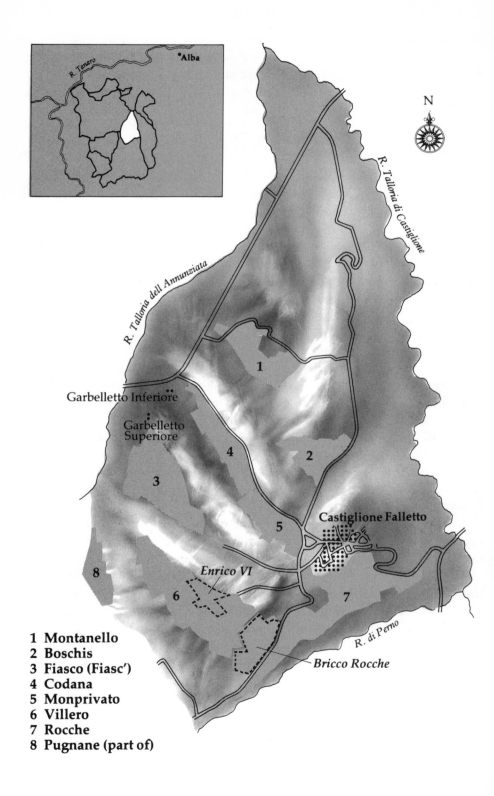

N

R. Tanaro
•Alba

R. Talloria di Castiglione

R. Talloria dell'Annunziata

1

Garbelletto Inferiore

Garbelletto
Superiore

4

2

3

5

Castiglione Falletto

8

Enrico VI

6

7

R. di Perno

Bricco Rocche

1 **Montanello**
2 **Boschis**
3 **Fiasco (Fiasc')**
4 **Codana**
5 **Monprivato**
6 **Villero**
7 **Rocche**
8 **Pugnane (part of)**

near the beginning of the Talloria dell'Annunziata valley.

Castiglione Falletto boasts some outstanding vineyards. Rocche is the most famous. The only major vineyard on the eastern side of the ridge, Rocche is mainly southeast facing and follows the curve of the hill on top of which the castle sits, through into Villero to the west. Rocche's soil is the classic mid-zone mix of high sand with a medium limestone content and low clay; it also shows an above-average level of phosphorus. Rocche is divided between many growers few of whom actually bottle their own wine – the rich and sturdy Rocche dei Brovia from Fratelli Brovia is a notable exception and Vietti own around one hectare of the vineyard. Bruno Giacosa produces a cru Rocche from bought-in grapes and Terre del Barolo also bring out a single vineyard bottling from their member's holdings. Some growers argue that Rocche's boundary to the west and at its highest point is the Alba–Monforte road. This would therefore exclude Ceretto's Bricco Rocche whose vines are planted above the road. As this part of the hill has an identical exposure to the lower-lying section of the vineyard, this would seem to smack of 'sour grapes' (although old maps show that the farm on top of the hill was traditionally known as Cascina Serra).

The other important vineyards also lie fairly close to the village. The most northerly of these is Montanello. Although now under the ownership of the Monchiero brothers, the Montanello hill was, until the early part of the century, the site of the Castiglione Falletto cooperative. The 18 hectares of excellent south to southwest facing vineyards have a markedly high sand content of around 40 per cent. Lying between Montanello and the next spur off the ridge (Monprivato) is Bricco Boschis. Although the highest part of the Cavallotto brothers' estate, Punta Marcello, has again a very sandy soil, their other two Barolo vineyards, San Giuseppe and Colle Sud Ovest, have a more evenly balanced soil structure.

This great variation in soil is once more apparent in the southwest facing Monprivato hillside. Nowadays it is almost entirely owned by Mauro Mascarello (p. 168). Seen from across the valley at La Morra, Monprivato is a patchwork of differently coloured plots. The lower part of the same hill where it extends down behind Garbelletto is known as Codana. The next lateral spur is the large southwest facing Villero hillside which, according to Mauro Mascarello who owns part of it, has a far more homogeneous soil structure. Cordero di

Montezemolo are also important owners here with the 'subcru' Enrico VI. Both Bruno Giacosa and Vietti also produce cru Villero. Nestling in the valley between these last two crus is the small Fiasc' or Fiasco hill (so called because it is shaped like the famous Chianti-type flask). The Scavino cousins Enrico and Lorenzo are the major owners of this south to southwest facing vineyard. While the actual *cascine* of Fontanile and Pugnane lie just inside the most westerly point of Castiglione Falletto's boundary, their vineyards creep into the commune of Monforte.

WINE STYLES AND PRINCIPAL PRODUCERS

To return briefly to our earlier comparison with the communes of Bordeaux, Castiglione vies with Monforte, its immediate neighbour to the south, for the mantle of Pauillac. The character of the Castiglione wines is quintessential Barolo: they are rich and perfumed yet structured too, becoming more velvety and graceful as they age. The small commune embraces the whole spectrum of winemaking styles, from the dogged traditionalism championed until the early eighties by Violante Sobrero and continued in a modified form by Cavallotto and Mascarello, to the dynamically modern as typified by Ceretto.

Rocche: richly-flavoured, well-balanced and aromatic wines, often with notably spicy and herbal tones, that age well. Producers: Fratelli Brovia (Rocche dei Brovia); Ceretto (Bricco Rocche); Bruno Giacosa; Terre del Barolo; Vietti.

Montanello: the Monchiero brothers produce a heavier, densely structured style of wine.

Bricco Boschis: Cavallotto's three crus, Punta Marcello, Colle Sud Ovest and San Giuseppe, are rich, ripe and scented wines bearing the violets and tar stamp of old school Barolo.

Monprivato: intense, structured and complex wine that ages superbly; benchmark Castiglione Falletto from Mauro Mascarello.

Villero: the wines show similarities with Monprivato but tend to have a more open and fruity style. Producers: Cordero di Montezemolo (Enrico VI); Bruno Giacosa; Mauro Mascarello; Vietti.

Fiasc'/Fiasco: elegant and supple wines of fine structure and excellent concentration of fruit; classic Barolo in a more modern style from Paolo Scavino (Bric' del Fiasc') and Lorenzo Scavino, under the Azelia label (Bricco Fiasco and, from the crown of the hillside, Bricco Punta).

Monforte

Continuing south along the road from Castiglione Falletto, you are soon in the commune of Monforte: it begins just beyond the southernmost part of Villero. Monforte forms the southern central section of the Barolo zone. Its natural boundaries are the Valle dei Fischi to the west and the Talloria di Castiglione to the east, which divides it from Serralunga. A few kilometres down the road is Monforte itself. The old town covers the western side of a steep hill at one of the highest points in the zone. Tiny crumbling houses crowd the narrow twisting streets up to the summit. It's worth the struggle to the top though, for the view from the perimeter walls of the old church is another spectacular one. At the bottom of the hill the newer part of the town centres on a quiet square: just off here is one of the region's top restaurants, Il Giardino da Felicin. Not only is owner, Giorgio Rocca, an inspired chef, but his young son Nino takes his responsibility of looking after the wines very seriously. He is a real enthusiast with, not surprisingly, a marked preference for the wines of Monforte.

Monforte is generally home to the smaller producer. It continues to grow (witness its development between 1975 and 1988) and has the potential to produce more Barolo than Serralunga eventually. In terms of hectares under vine, Monforte is second only to La Morra, yet only half the commune comes within the delimited Barolo area; indeed, the town itself just scrapes in at the very southern limits. Moreover the Monforte hills are planted to a greater variety of grapes than is found in the other communes: freisa is quite strong – even grignolino – as well as barbera, dolcetto and nebbiolo. Monforte is still seen by many as the optimum area for barbera and dolcetto. The simple fact is that there is more room here and tradition has less of a stranglehold; a growing number of producers are busy experimenting with white grapes, for example.

Most of Monforte's top sites are situated on the two sides of the same elongated complex of hills. They are closer to the *frazioni* of Perno on the western flank, and Castelletto, overlooking the eastern slopes, than to Monforte itself.

Right on the communal boundary with Castiglione Falletto are the vineyards of Fontanile and Pugnane. The southwest facing vineyards of Bussia Sottana (lower Bussia) lie in a *conca* below the village itself.

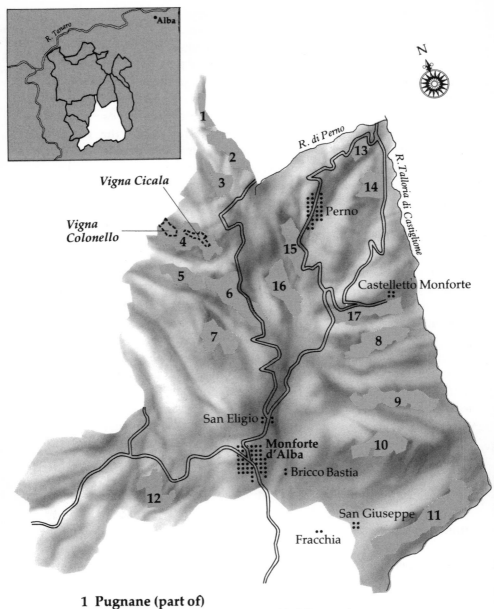

R. di Perno

R. Talloria di Castiglione

Vigna Cicala

Vigna Colonello

Perno

Castelletto Monforte

San Eligio

Monforte d'Alba

Bricco Bastia

San Giuseppe

Fracchia

1 Pugnane (part of)
2 Fontanile
3 Bussia Sottana
4 Bussia Soprana
5 Dardi
6 Pianpolvere
7 Arnulfo
8 Grassi/Gavarini
9 Ginestra

10 Mosconi
11 Le Coste
12 Manzoni Soprana
13 Colombera
14 Disa
15 Santo Stefano
16 Gremolere
17 La Villa

They overlook the start of the long winding Bussia hill which faces the village of Barolo across the valley to the west. Nestling beneath the rounded peak (Bricco Bussia at just under 400 metres) are the Bussia Soprana (upper Bussia) vineyards, Monforte's most highly reputed cru. This steep, sheltered site has an ideal *mezzogiorno* exposure and shares a similar soil structure with its sister site to the north: highish sand, medium clay and lowish limestone with the typical Serralunga valley high iron content. Various plots of vines in Bussia Soprana are identified by individual names: Bricotto, Ciabot, Cicala, Colonello, Mondoca and Romirasco, some of which are produced as a 'cru within a cru' Barolo by producers such as Domenico Clerico and Aldo Conterno.

After Bussia Soprana, the hill curves westwards again and on the southern slopes of this spur is the lower-lying Dardi cru. Adjoining it to the southeast are the fine southwest facing Pian della Polvere vineyards at the head of the valley. The last 'subcru' of Bussia, Arnulfo, lies on the south side of the next outward curve of the hills; part of Arnulfo's fame lies in the fact that an earlier owner of the estate is supposed to have been among the first to bottle his own Barolo towards the end of the nineteenth century.

To the east, above the road connecting Castiglione Falletto to Monforte, is the small *frazione* of Perno. There are a number of excellent though little-known sites on these high slopes including, to the northeast of the village, Colombera and Disa, but the most reputed cru is the famous Santo Stefano vineyard, a sandy southwest facing hillside rich in potassium, phosphorus and iron. Few if any of these wines are available commercially: they are either sold off in bulk to negociant houses or in demijohns to private customers. Given the limited amount of land available in the zone, this may well change in the near future; indeed Valentino Migliorini of Rocche dei Manzoni has recently acquired a large parcel of land in Santo Stefano. Perno looks to be an area of much greater future interest.

Separated from Perno by the conical hill of il Bric' (just over 400 metres), the nearby *frazione* of Castelletto sits on the eastern edge of the ridge. In Gremolera and La Villa, Castelletto has a couple of good if underdeveloped sites, though to the south of the village overlooking the southern reaches of Serralunga are a number of established crus: Grassi, Ginestra, Mosconi and Le Coste, which have mainly southeast to south facing exposures. This area has the sandiest soil with the lowest clay content of the entire zone. The road below the lowest-lying cru, Le Coste, takes us back into Monforte again. The only other vineyard area of importance lies just inside the DOCG limits to the west of the village: the south facing hillside at Manzoni Soprana below Valentino Migliorini's winery.

The big name in Monforte is Conterno. Brothers Aldo and Giovanni are among the most prestigious names in Barolo today: the fact that their ideas are no longer compatible seems to preclude any meaningful exchange between the two. Many of the smaller Monforte-based producers are quite new, a measure of the commune's developing fortunes as more, specialized nebbiolo vineyards become established along with the determination to make great wines from them. Nowadays the small *azienda agricola* is very much the thing for the craggy individualists of Monforte: Baroliste like Clerico, Conterno-Fantino (Diego and Claudio Conterno are apparently not related to Aldo and Giovanni), Grasso, Giacomo Fenocchio and Riccardo Fenocchio produce smallish quantities of, in some instances, outstanding wine.

WINE STYLES AND PRINCIPAL PRODUCERS
In general, the Baroli of Monforte are among the zone's longest lived. The classic examples are characterized by their striking concentration of rich fruit flavours and firm structure, factors consistent with their overall proportions: the Monforte wines are among the biggest and most powerful Barolo produced.
Bussia: rich, deeply flavoured and classically structured wines that count among the finest Barolo (especially the various Bussia Soprana wines). Producers: Giacomo Fenocchio (Sottana); Domenico Clerico (Soprana: Bricotto); Aldo Conterno (Soprana: Cicala, Colonello, Granbussia); Bruno Giacosa, Prunotto, Mauro Sebaste, Vietti, Maura Mascarello (Dardi); Riccardo Fenocchio (Pian della Polvere); Accademia Torregiorgi (Arnulfo).
Grassi: medium-bodied, full-flavoured wines in a slightly coarser style from Elio Grasso (Gavarini-Runcot, Gavarini-Chiniera, Gavarini dei Grassi).
Ginestra: ripe, balanced wines of notable elegance. Producers: Clerico (Ciabot, Mentin, Ginestra); Conterno-Fantino (Vigna del Gris, Sori' Ginestra); Feyles, Grasso (Casa Matè); Prunotto.

Le Coste: a softer style of Barolo, elegant and complex, from Scarpa.
Mosconi: Giovanni Scarzello produces a powerful, old-fashioned
Barolo.

Serralunga d'Alba

Serralunga is a long, narrow strip of land which, with small sections of
Grinzane Cavour and Diano d'Alba, forms the eastern border of the
Barolo zone. The commune consists of the slopes off both sides of a
long ridge which rises close to the Fontanafredda estate and finally
curls to the west at Serralunga's southern limits back towards the town
of Monforte.

Despite the presence of the region's largest privately owned winery,
Fontanafredda, whose annual production of Barolo accounts for over
70 per cent of the commune's total, Serralunga remains something of
an enigma. The commune is otherwise an area of small growers,
whose grapes or wine are often swallowed up by larger houses, rather
than the grower/bottler as is the emerging pattern in Monforte. A
number of up and coming growers like Franco Boasso, Giovanni
Porro and Renato Massoci may reverse the trend before long.
Similarly, top flight sites like Baudana, Briccolina and Gabutti-
Parafada do not as yet roll off the tongue as readily as Brunate, Bussia
or Cannubi. For the moment there are few examples of cru wines being
vinified by a number of different producers – the stuff that reputations
are made of. Bussia, Brunate and Cannubi etc., are clearly identifiable
as 'grands crus' firstly because they have a longstanding tradition of
producing great wines and secondly because, as examples are made by
several winemakers, the unique characteristics of the vineyard can
shine through their various interpretations of the winemaking process.

Like the other towns of the Barolo zone, Serralunga dates back to
before the Middle Ages and at one time was also the feudal domain of
the Falletti. Nowadays to talk of Serralunga is to talk principally of
Fontanafredda: their estate is situated at the centre of a bowl of hills at
the northern tip of the valley. Indeed the first vineyard you see heading
towards the zone from Alba is their San Pietro. According to Livio
Testa, Fontanafredda's enologist, it is a unique site, being the only
patch of Tortonian soil in the whole of the eastern valley. Sharing a

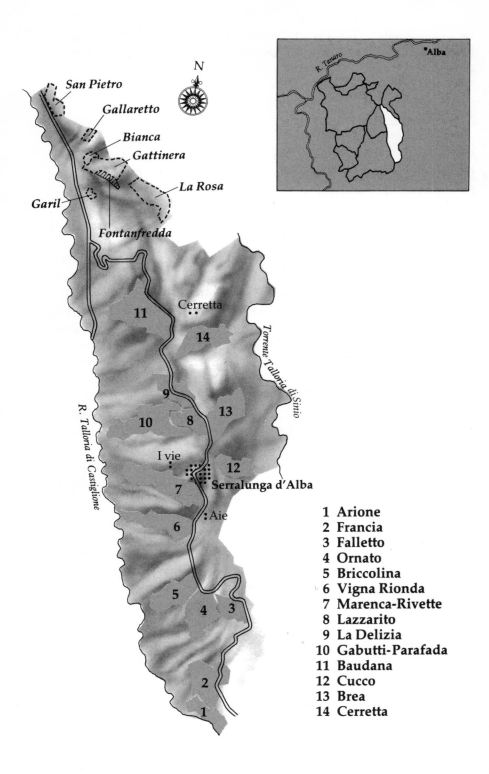

N

San Pietro
Gallaretto
Bianca
Gattinera
La Rosa
Garil
Fontanfredda

*Alba
R. Tanaro

Cerretta
11
14
Torrente Talloria di Sinio
9
13
10   8
R. Talloria di Castiglione
I vie
12
7
Serralunga d'Alba
6
Aie
5
4   3
2
1

1 Arione
2 Francia
3 Falletto
4 Ornato
5 Briccolina
6 Vigna Rionda
7 Marenca-Rivette
8 Lazzarito
9 La Delizia
10 Gabutti-Parafada
11 Baudana
12 Cucco
13 Brea
14 Cerretta

similar, mineral rich, clay-based soil, five more of Fontanafredda's nine cru vineyards surround the elegant winery, its buildings striped in colours of terracotta and sand. Gallaretto, Bianco, Gattinera and La Rosa occupy the south and southwest facing slopes of this bowl with Garil just over the lip to the south. The estate overlooks the hamlet (*borgata*) of Sorano whose vineyards, including Bruni and Carpegna, also have a good reputation.

But Serralunga's other major sites start south of here again at the *frazione* of Baudana. The southwest facing hillside just below the village has a distinctively white, chalky soil and is a prime example of the commune's many excellent but sadly rather unknown sites. Further down the road on its eastern side, Cerretta is a large south-southeast facing slope. A group of fine south and southwest facing vineyards lie on the opposite side of the road immediately to the south along the next spur off the ridge: Gabutti-Parafada (two tiny *borgate* normally considered as one) occupies the furthest extension of the hill with Lazzarito at the opposite end back below the road again. Sandwiched between the two and lying both above and below the road is La Delizia. This stretch of fine sites again shows that sparkling, chalk-white soil: in fact the average limestone content in the commune is around 36 per cent (32 per cent is the norm for the Barolo zone).

The next curve of the hill brings you into Serralunga itself. Just beyond the quiet narrow streets to the northeast are two well-reputed sites, Brea and Cucco. On the western edge the steep white slopes of Marenca-Rivette with their perfect *mezzogiorno* exposure begin. The sight of that same limestone soil must have made quite an impression on Angelo Gaja: he bought the 28-hectare site in July 1988 from Pietro Lanzavecchia (otherwise associated with the infamous merchant house of Villadoria). The Barolo-loving world waits with bated breath to see what the great man comes up with.

Serralunga's most famous vineyard, Vigna Rionda, is just south of the village. Rionda is a small site on the south facing slope of a low-lying tongue of land; although typically high in limestone (36 per cent), the soil also has a high clay content (39 per cent) but surprisingly little sand. Vigna Rionda generally enjoys wider recognition as a source of exceptional wine than most of the commune's other crus, largely because of Bruno Giacosa's association with the vineyard.

As the road winds along towards the southern reaches of the

commune, several vineyards with less of a reputation none the less show similar potential. A fine strip of south and southwest facing sites hugs the tapering hill that marks the last great curve in the road towards the east. At the western tip, Briccolina is one of Fratelli Dogliani's 'seven farms' (*sette cascine*). Adjoining it to the east is Pio Cesare's Ornato estate while Falletto, the only vineyard owned by Bruno Giacosa, completes the stretch as the road swings back to the southwest. Where it temporarily straightens out just before Serralunga's southern border lie the commune's final two important estates: Giovanni Conterno's Cascina Francia (which the owner maintains dates back to the times of Julius Caesar) and Gigi Rosso's Cascina Arione. Both are steep, rather exposed, southwest facing sites dropping down towards the floor of the valley.

Serralunga clearly has vineyards of splendid potential but as traditionally the poorest of the major five communes, it is still something of a forgotten land and lacks the air of purpose and quiet prosperity the others share. Like Monforte just over a decade ago, Serralunga remains a happy hunting ground for negociant houses who buy in much of the commune's grapes and wine. The arrival of Angelo Gaja will no doubt bring about a shift in the balance. The spotlight that inevitably trains on him should serve to revitalize the efforts and ambitions not only of his neighbours but also possible investors from outside the zone. Serralunga, the quiet one, the poor one, has intriguing times ahead.

WINE STYLES AND PRINCIPAL PRODUCERS
The wines of Serralunga have a fearsome reputation, reflecting the rather 'backward' nature of the commune. The winemaking techniques of the smaller producers seem often to lag a little behind the times, resulting in some rather uncommercially coarse and stiffly structured Barolo. On the one hand the structure, richness and durability that some view as working against the wines' image, is seen by others as the foundation stone of great Barolo: for them at least Serralunga represents the pinnacle.
Fontanafredda: The six crus produced from vineyards around the winery show a marked house style epitomizing the robust, rather tough and tannic but long-lasting wines for which Serralunga is renowned (San Pietro, Gallaretto, Bianca, Gattinera, La Rosa, Garil).

Baudana: this seems to show a little less of the commune's customary leanness and a rather more rounded and accessible style; Zunino (Sorì' Baudana), Eredi Virginia Ferrero (San Rocco).

Cerretta: the source of Ceretto's cru Prapò: a more austere wine than their Brunate or Bricco Rocche but its firm frame carries good, rich fruit.

La Delizia: one of the more forward of the Fontanafredda crus, it is also produced in an archtraditional dense and rich style by Luigi Artusio of Diano-based Cantina della Porta Rossa.

Lazzarito: a robust rather hard wine in its youth, Lazzarito is potentially the longest-lived of the Fontanafredda crus.

Vigna Rionda: may well be Bruno Giacosa's finest Barolo: this monolithic wine with its remarkable depth of rich, ripe fruit and awesome structure shows just how good the wines of Serralunga can be. Massolino's cru Rionda (they are also known as Azienda Agricola Vigna Rionda) shows promising raw material too.

Falletto: good wine that seems to lack a little of the depth and intensity of Bruno Giacosa's other crus.

Cascina Francia: in great vintages, the wines from Giovanni Conterno's 17-hectare estate (Vigneto Francia and Monfortino) have few peers: rich, powerful, structured and complex Barolo that can age magnificently.

Cascina Arione: Gigi Rosso produces big, old-fashioned, aromatic wines.

The Minor Communes

The peripheral communes that make up the outskirts of the zone are of lesser importance in terms of the quantity of Barolo they produce. Verduno and Novello have around 4 per cent each of the total production, but only Verduno has any real reputation and crus of note. A number of firms including Ascheri and Commendatore G.B. Burlotto produce Barolo Monvigliero from the commune's most important site (the soft, round and accessible wine from Fratelli Allessandria is a good example). Bel Colle also produce a promising *vino da tavola* nebbiolo Monvijé (the traditional Piemontese name for the vineyard). Barolo Massara from the Burlotto sisters at the Castello di Verduno can also be worth watching out for. Although Novello produces almost as much Barolo as Verduno, like the remaining four communes its vineyards are mainly given over to barbera and dolcetto. Barolo by now has become almost an afterthought.

BARBARESCO

PRODUCTION REGULATIONS
Minimum alcohol content: 12.5 per cent.
Minimum ageing requirements: 2 years, at least one of which must be in oak or chestnut barrels; 4 years for *riserva*.
Maximum production levels: 80 quintals per hectare with a 70 per cent *resa in vino* dropping to 65 per cent following the statutory ageing period.
DOC granted: 23 April 1966; DOCG as of 3 October 1980.
A maximum 15 per cent of older Barbaresco can be used to improve the quality of a younger vintage and vice versa.

Just under 500 firms (482 in 1988) produce a maximum of 28,000 hectolitres of wine from about 500 hectares of vines grown in four communes to the northeast of Alba: Barbaresco, Neive, Treiso and a small section of Alba (San Rocco Seno d'Elvio) between the western edge of Treiso and the Seno d'Elvio stream. Annual production averages out at just over 2.5 million bottles representing approximately 70 per cent of the theoretical permitted maximum amount. From around 1.25 million bottles in the mid-seventies, production peaked to roughly 3.25 million in the late seventies. This is now levelling out to somewhere much closer to the average figure (2,361,466 in 1988). The percentage of land under vines in the different communes has remained fairly constant since the boom planting period of the late sixties/early seventies.

The area was first defined through the efforts of a Barbaresco-based syndicate in 1926 and in 1933 was enlarged to include Neive, thanks largely to the determination of Count Riccardo Candiani of Neive (then proprietor of Castello di Neive). The vineyards are generally planted at altitudes of between 150 and 300 metres, often at a gentler

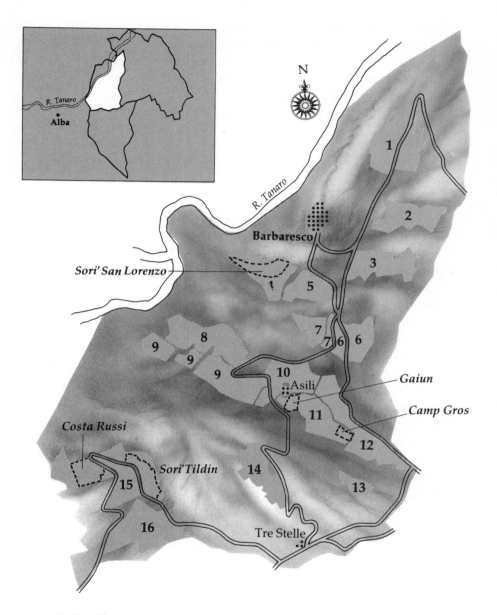

N

R. Tanaro
Alba

R. Tanaro

Barbaresco

Sori' San Lorenzo

1 Ovello
2 Montefico
3 Montestefano
4 Secondine
5 Ghiga
6 Moccagatta
7 Paglieri/Pajé
8 Faset

Gaiun

Camp Gros

Asili

Costa Russi

Sori'Tildin

Tre Stelle

9 Porra
10 Asili
11 Martinenga
12 Rabaja'
13 Trifolera
14 Rio Sordo
15 Roncagliette
16 Roncaglia

incline than in Barolo. The prime sites are southeast through to southwest facing and the terrain is the classic 'white earth' of the Langhe: compact, greyish-white clay and limestone marl with an even balance of macro- and micro-elements. Typically there is a higher clay content in Barbaresco than Barolo (close to 40 per cent), yet while the soil structure is in general more uniform throughout the zone, the communes are renowned for differing styles of wine.

Barbaresco

Barbaresco lies a few kilometres to the northeast of Alba just off the secondary road heading east towards Acqui Terme. An alternative route beginning in the backstreets of Alba takes you up through the most southerly vineyards of the commune via the village of Tre Stelle. As you approach Barbaresco along the valley below, the famous tower stands proud of the vines that otherwise dominate the scene: an impressive landmark, from a distance. Turning right, you wind up through the vineyards into a still, silent world.

In 1988 the commune accounted for 44.45 per cent of the total production of Barbaresco from 217 hectares tended by 132 growers. The average holding of around 1.7 hectares is high for the region partly owing to the large amount of land – over 30 hectares – owned by Barbaresco's most famous son, Angelo Gaja. The village gives its name to the denomination; barbaresco is in fact the Italian word for barbarian. The tower, which when you reach the centre of the village looks in a pretty sorry state, is said to have been built originally by the Romans. The present tower was constructed on top of the original foundations to serve as a lookout point on top of which fires could be lit to warn of invaders. There is nothing else remotely remarkable about the place, unless of course it's wine you're looking for.

Most of the major vineyards apart from the important crus of Montefico, Montestefano and Ovello, lie due south of the village towards Tre Stelle on Barbaresco's southern communal boundary with Treiso.

The vineyards to the north and west of Barbaresco and those to the south and east belong to two different chains of hills both beginning at the banks of the Tanaro to the northwest of the village. The first chain starts at the southern reaches of the village and contains much the greater proportion of the commune's great crus. The hill winds back on itself several times before its slow ascent to the small *borgata* of Bongiovanni just west of the village of Treiso. The first stretch of the hill includes two major south facing sites which lie at the foot of Barbaresco itself. The more westerly of them is Secondine which incorporates Gaja's famous 3.23 hectare San Lorenzo vineyard. Adjoining Secondine to the east is the Ghiga estate. After a brief twist in the hill, the steep southwest facing *conca* of Paglieri (Pajé in Piemontese – it means piles of straw) lies just below the more westerly oriented Moccagatta.

The hill sweeps back to the west at this point and on its undulating southern face lie Barbaresco's finest sites. They begin at Faset, a south facing *conca* below a small double peak at around 275 metres. Directly below Faset is the winding Porra cru. To the east the broad *conca* which forms the largest and most prestigious vineyard area of the commune begins at the steep, mainly southeast facing vineyards of Asili. They make up the western edge of the *conca* and merge into La Martinenga right at its centre. The superb southeast through to southwest facing site is wholly owned by Tenuta Cisa Asinari dei Marchesi di Gresy. In addition to Barbaresco Martinenga, di Gresy produces two 'subcrus' in favourable vintages from Gaiun (adjoining Asili) and Camp Gros – arguably their finest wine – the vineyard immediately below Rabajà (in lighter vintages di Gresy vinifies all the grapes together and the wine is sold as Barbaresco Martinenga). The southwest facing Rabajà occupies the softer, broader, eastern flank of the hill. The soil composition of the area is typical of the southern Barbaresco vineyards, made up of around 25 per cent sand, 35 per cent limestone and 40 per cent clay, rich in iron and manganese.

Immediately after the lesser known Trifolera vineyard, close to Rabajà to the south, the hill snakes back to the west again. There is one southwest facing spur directly south of Asili: the site of the Rivosordo, or Rio Sordo cru. At the point where the hill swings back eastwards, the Roncagliette estate overlooks the Tanaro. The back road up to Barbaresco goes through almost a 360° turn here: above and below it and both facing plumb southwest are Sori' Tildin (3.78 hectares) and Costa Russi (4.06 hectares), Gaja's other two cru Barbareschi. Almost adjoining Roncagliette to the south and right on the border with Treiso is the more westerly facing Roncaglia.

The northern and easterly vineyards of Barbaresco are encapsulated within the second chain of hills which begins almost on the communal boundary with Neive to the north of the village. Ovello, the commune's most northerly site, occupies the western slopes of the hillside. Over the brow of the hill two steep and sheltered south to southeast facing *conche* lie in its fold, Montefico and a little further south, Montestefano. The vineyards of this eastern area are planted on harder ground where the reddish earth has a higher clay content. The wines have a distinctive style: Prunotto's Montestefano is a case in point, showing more firmness and structure than their Rabajà and needing more time in bottle to soften the higher tannin content. Gianni Testa, winemaker for the Produttori del Barbaresco (p. 171), identifies the difference in style between the two vineyard areas in terms of macro-and micro-structure. Ovello, Montefico and Montestefano have bigger 'macro-structures' (a greater concentration of tannins and other poly-phenols) while the crus to the west (where the ground is richer in limestone and other active micro-elements) tend to have greater elegance and finesse with, therefore, 'micro-structure' to the fore.

WINE STYLES AND PRINCIPAL PRODUCERS

Secondine: The definitive example of Secondine (indeed perhaps the definitive example of Barbaresco) is Gaja's Sori' San Lorenzo, much the largest section of the vineyard. Of the three Gaja crus, it is the firmest and most closed in its youth yet with an almost unique richness of flavour and concentration of fruit underpinning its slightly austere frame: an amazingly impressive wine with the ability to age for many years.

Ghiga: Pietro Berutti of La Spinona owns the largest section of this vineyard and bottles a La Ghiga cru: old-fashioned winemaking techniques result in a firm, full-bodied and heavier style of Barbaresco.

Pajé: elegant and balanced wines with rich fruit in a tight structure: Alfredo Roagna (Crichet Pajé), Produttori di Barbaresco.

Moccagatta: the lightest of the Produttori crus: a soft, forward wine with lowish acidity which matures early; also produced by Mauro Minuto of Azienda Agricola Moccagatta.

Faset: forward, medium-weight wines of impressive aroma. Producers: Ceretto (Bricco Faset); Cantina della Porta Rossa, Luigi Bianco (Faset).

Asili: one of Barbaresco's great vineyards giving balanced, perfumed and complex wines of great breed. Producers: Ceretto (Bricco Asili); Donato Giacosa, Produttori di Barbaresco.

La Martinenga: includes the two single vineyard crus 'Gaiun' and 'Camp Gros'. La Martinenga is a forward, medium-weight, aromatic wine, Gaiun particularly perfumed and approachable, even at an early stage and Camp Gros the firmest, fullest and most complex of the three (Marchesi di Gresy).

Rabajà: archetypal Barbaresco, presenting the softer face of nebbiolo to the world. Rabajà is characterized by its rich ripe, almost chocolate-like fruit and expansive, velvety texture: a silky and supple wine. Producers: Fratelli Barale; Luigi Bianco: Giuseppe Cortese; Azienda Agricola de Forville; Produttori di Barbaresco; Prunotto; Vietti.

Riosordo: produces rather more structured and concentrated (though ultimately less complex) wines than the Asili-Martinenga-Rabajà 'Golden Triangle'. The wines have a distinctive aroma of 'underbrush' (*sottobosco*), herbs and licorice. Producers: Fratelli Brovia; Bruno Giacosa (from 1985); Mussa; Produttori di Barbaresco.

Roncagliette: just under half this 13 hectare estate is divided up between the Costa Russi and Sori' Tildin crus. The slightly lower-lying Costa Russi is Gaja's most forward cru Barbaresco: a rich, ripe wine with scented and cedary overlays. Sori' Tildin (made from later-harvested grapes) can equal and even surpass Sori' San Lorenzo in some vintages. It shows an opulent, mouth-filling richness of sweet fruit backed up with an underlying firmness of tone. Gaja's most sumptuous Barbaresco.

Roncaglia: not surprisingly the Roncaglia wines have always seemed rather lighter and less impressive than those from Roncagliette. Roncaglia can produce good if rather tannic Barbaresco none the less. Producer: Fratelli Giacosa.

Ovello: the biggest and firmest of the Produttori crus, with a rather earthy, even coarse style. It ages very well in better vintages when its warm, rich, earthy flavours can make a very satisfying glass of wine.

Montefico: a big, meaty style of wine with rich, gamey flavours in a firm structure (Produttori di Barbaresco).

Montestefano: the Produttori di Barbaresco Montestefano lies between their Montefico and Ovello in style – a big, gamey Barbaresco, harder and more austere than Montefico though less structured than Ovello. Prunotto's Montestefano is also impressive in its rather firm and tannic way.

Given their range of nine different crus from some of the commune's finest vineyards, a comparative study of the wines of the Produttori di Barbaresco is an excellent way of identifying the nuances that characterize the various sites.

Barbaresco's wealth is solely in its vines. The village has staked everything, including its name, on glorifying noble nebbiolo. Although Angelo Gaja, regarded by the more traditional fraternity as both mad and sinful for his decision, has planted foreign pretenders like cabernet and chardonnay in the precious soil, there is little threat to nebbiolo's monopoly of the better sites. Gaja's example has been taken up by producers like Marchesi di Gresy and Alfredo Roagna (and even some of the old guard like La Spinona). Others may well join in the game of follow my leader, but it is the less prestigious vineyards that will be targeted, and mainly for chardonnay. For the moment the combined total of land planted to other varieties is around one-third of that given over to nebbiolo.

Neive

Lying due east of Barbaresco a few kilometres along the same secondary road is Neive. There are two parts to the town: along both sides of the road which, for a few kilometres, follows the valley of the river Tinella is the 'new' town (Borgonuovo) and on top of a steepish hill to the northwest, the medieval town lies at around 300 metres above sea level. Although the new town is home to several important wineries, including Bruno Giacosa, it is inevitable that the visitor will head up the hill to the more picturesque historical centre. The tiny, narrow streets contain several interesting buildings: as well as the elegant, gently fading castle, the church of Saints Peter and Paul has an impressive front and there is the irresistible lure of one of the Langhe's top restaurants, La Contea. Even up here there is no getting away from the real focus of interest: the cellars of both the castle and the church are given over to wineries (Castello di Neive and Parocco di Neive) and La Contea has one of the best selections of Barbaresco to be found.

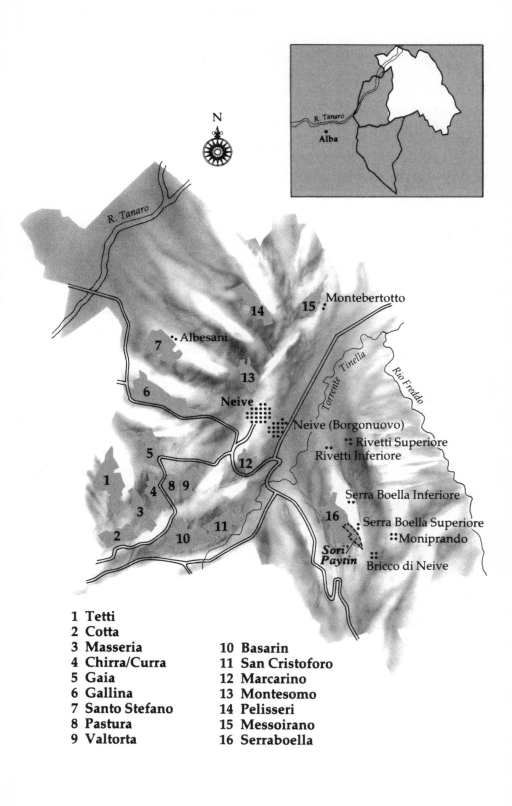

N

R. Tanaro

Alba

R. Tanaro

Montebertotto

14   15

7   Albesani

13

6

Neive

Torrente Tinella

Rio Freddo

Neive (Borgonuovo)

Rivetti Superiore
Rivetti Inferiore

5

12

1

4   8   9

3

Serra Boella Inferiore

16   Serra Boella Superiore

2

10

11

Moniprando

*Sori/
Paytin*

Bricco di Neive

1 Tetti
2 Cotta
3 Masseria
4 Chirra/Curra   10 Basarin
5 Gaia   11 San Cristoforo
6 Gallina   12 Marcarino
7 Santo Stefano   13 Montesomo
8 Pastura   14 Pelisseri
9 Valtorta   15 Messoirano
                               16 Serraboella

Neive is by far the biggest in area of the Barbaresco producing communes. It has almost twice as many registered growers as Barbaresco yet they produce less than one-third of the total: in 1988 230 growers accounted for 30.68 per cent of all Barbaresco. The average holding is much smaller in Neive (approximately two-thirds of a hectare) and there are only around 150 hectares planted to nebbiolo (220 hectares in Barbaresco). This is the realm of the small grower whose wine is often destined to the melting pot of anonymous blends. It is significant that far more dolcetto is grown in Neive than in Barbaresco – well over half as much again – and indeed some of the well-known vineyards like Basarin are as renowned for this varietal as they are for nebbiolo. The situation becomes even clearer when we consider barbera: Neive has almost ten times as much barbera planted as Barbaresco. Furthermore Neive is one of the designated Moscato d'Asti communes (unlike Barbaresco) and makes a significant contribution to its total production. It is clearly easier for the small growers and winemakers of Neive to work with these 'lesser' grapes. Given the minimum ageing requirements for the wines, there is less capital to be tied up in young varietals and at present the market for them (particularly Dolcetto and Moscato) remains very secure.

The Barbareschi of Neive have the reputation of being the fullest, most tannic and longest-lived of the denomination – they certainly tend to be less immediate and opulent than those from their neighbour to the west but are capable of redressing the balance with their impressive structure and power. How much these differences can be attributed to the provenance of the wines and how much to the corresponding levels of winemaking expertise in the two communes is a sensitive question. Neive has a typically sandier soil than Barbaresco (at the expense of limestone though the clay content is normally lower too). At the same time there is no denying that a more sophisticated approach to the question of vinification is generally apparent in Barbaresco.

Neive's great nebbiolo vineyards are located on the western side of the town towards Barbaresco. There are two principal areas – the vineyards to the north of the main road into Neive (following the course of the Rio di Vassellera), and those to the south. Neive's two most esteemed crus lie in the northern section both overlooking Barbaresco's Montefico. The more northerly (indeed the furthest

north of the denomination's great sites) is Santo Stefano. Santo
Stefano occupies around 8 hectares of the steep southwest facing
slope below the *borgata* of Albesani: it is wholly owned by Castello di
Neive (they also sell grapes to Bruno Giacosa for his version) and is
widely regarded as Neive's number one cru. The next south facing
slope of the same winding hill forms the Gallina cru: this shallow low-
lying *conca* sits between two small peaks in the hill (at around 250
metres) and stretches down as far as the road at its lowest point. A
third peak just to the east marks the tiny Crocetta estate. A little
further to the east, Montesomo sits directly above the old town facing
southwest and below it, along the southwest to southeast slopes of a
small rounded bricco, lies Marcarino. Apart from two smallish sites
further above the old town to the north and northwest (Pelissero and
Messoirano), most of the rest of this part of Neive is planted to other
grape varieties.

Below the road and east-southeast of Neive, a horseshoe-shaped bowl
open to the northwest, really a continuation of the more northerly
hillchain of Barbaresco, contains nearly all the major remaining nebbiolo
vineyards of the commune. The quite steeply sloped peaks along the ridge
lie at an altitude of about 300 metres and offer a wide range of exposures
from mainly west through to southeast facing. The principal sites lie
along the western and southern slopes and inside the eastern edge. Right
on the border with Barbaresco and directly overlooking the tower in the
distance, is the primarily west facing *borgata* of i Tetti and on the
southwestern lip of the bowl, the more southerly orientated Masseria.
Three adjacent crus are situated on the southwest facing 'inside' curve of
the hillside: Pastura at the highest point with Chirrà (Currà) just below it
merging into the *borgata* of Gaia to the north. On the southeast facing
slopes below Pastura on the other side of the ridge, Valtorta is mainly
noted for Dolcetto.

To the southeast and southwest of the horseshoe are two conical
hills: the southern slope of the more westerly hill forms the Cottà cru
while the Bric San Cristoforo is the highest point to the east of Neive at
370 metres. The San Cristoforo vineyards lie on the southeastern flank
of the hill adjoining Basarin to the west.

To the southeast of the town a number of long, tapering spurs reach
down into the valley of the Tinella. There is really only one area of note
for nebbiolo on this side of the river: the southwest facing slopes

below the village of Bricco di Neive at the tiny *frazione* of Serra Boella Superiore (Upper Serra Boella). So far only two small producers actually bottle their own wine but Renato Cigliutti and the Pasquero family are setting high standards. Further to the east and overlooking the *frazione* of Rivetti, the tiny Cascina Chiabotto estate belonging to winemaker Giuseppe Traversa marks a lonely outpost for the production of quality Barbaresco.

The terrain of Neive has a complex topographical structure of folding hills surrounded by a number of isolated outlying peaks. This gives rise to many scattered smallholdings with fewer unbroken stretches of vine. The nebbiolo therefore tends to have less dominance in the commune and only the Stupino family at the Castello di Neive have managed to piece together a sizeable estate (around 25 hectares) from parcels of land in some of the better regarded sites. As well as Santo Stefano, they own parts of Gallina, Messoirano, Basarin, Valtorta and Marcarino and the lesser known vineyards of Montebertotto (for arneis) and Mattarello (for barbera). The next largest landowners are the church with their 13-hectare Parocco di Neive estate, including land in Gallina, Basarin and San Cristoforo.

Neive has its fair share of good, if smallish, nebbiolo vineyards though as yet, as with Serralunga in Barolo, few of the smallholders are bottling Barbaresco from them. The forward-looking Cantina del Glicine, while owning land in Gallina and Marcarino, supplements its range of the Neive crus by buying in grapes from some of these lesser-known sites. They are currently the exception to the rule. Another alternative, the pooling of resources, is being tried out by the Confratelli di San Michele. While the members own separate, often adjacent vineyards, winemaking facilities and sales are a joint responsibility for this group of small producers. Although the results may sometimes be uneven, the principle must be applauded.

The Barbareschi of Neive are often said to be the closest in style to Barolo with their distinctively firm, full-bodied character. Despite the few small Bricco di Neive producers and the lighter but intensely fruity and approachable wines of Cantine del Glicine (whose Adriana Marzi is one of the zone's few female winemakers), the Barbareschi from the commune's two best-known wineries, Castello di Neive and Bruno Giacosa, remain the paragons of the essential Neive character.

WINE STYLES AND PRINCIPAL PRODUCERS

Santo Stefano: structured yet balanced wines needing plenty of bottle age in the great vintages to show their full richness and complexity of flavour. Producers: Castello di Neive; Bruno Giacosa.

Gallina: fruitier, softer and more approachable than the Santo Stefano wines though ultimately without their intensity and staying power. Producers: Cantina del Glicine; Confratelli di San Michele; Bruno Giacosa; Parocco di Neive.

Crocetta: rich, chunky and aromatic wines from Accademia Torregiorgi (San Giuliano).

Marcarino: stylish, fruity and quickly maturing wine from Cantina del Glicine.

Messoirano: a firmer, leaner and more tannic style of Barbaresco. Producers: Castello di Neive; Accademia Torregiorgi.

Tettineive: the more forward of Scarpa's two Barbareschi with a spicy, aromatic style.

Cottà: fairly soft and forward wine in the rustic mould from Confratelli di San Michele; Dario Rocca's La Ca' Nova vineyard is also part of Cottà, he makes a rich, characterful, traditionally styled Barbaresco.

Masseria: the firmer and more structured of the two Barbareschi from Vietti.

Currà/Chirrà: elegant and perfumed wine from Cantina del Glicine.

Gaia: rich, old-fashioned Barbaresco from Maria Feyles.

Basarin: soft, floral-toned wines from Azienda Agricola Moccagatta and Parocco di Neive.

San Cristoforo: Confratelli di San Michele make a full, soft and earthy style of wine from here.

Serra Boella: elegant and balanced wines of unobtrusive structure with fruit to the fore. Producers: Renato Cigliutti; Pasquero (Sori' Paytin).

Treiso and San Rocco Seno d'Elvio

In 1988, Treiso and San Rocco Seno d'Elvio accounted for 19.58 per cent and 5.29 per cent respectively of the total Barbaresco production. Treiso, where around 100 growers cultivate approximately 95

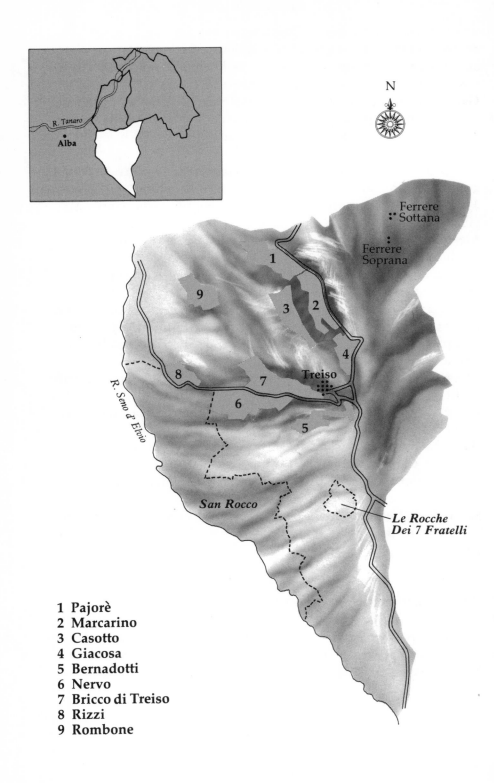

N

R. Tanaro

Alba

Ferrere
Sottana

Ferrere
Soprana

1

9

3   2

4

Treiso

7

8

6

5

R. Seno d' Elvio

San Rocco

Le Rocche
Dei 7 Fratelli

1 Pajorè
2 Marcarino
3 Casotto
4 Giacosa
5 Bernadotti
6 Nervo
7 Bricco di Treiso
8 Rizzi
9 Rombone

hectares of nebbiolo vines, is by far the more important of the two in terms of quality as well as quantity; indeed San Rocco Seno d'Elvio has no specialized nebbiolo vineyards of any renown, and is normally considered as an adjunct to Treiso. As in Neive, barbera and dolcetto are widely planted and even cabernet (from Pio Cesare, for example) is on the increase. Even so, Treiso has a number of Barbaresco vineyards of real merit. These are mainly situated close to the communal boundary with Barbaresco and occupy the southwest facing flank of the same hillchain that continues down from Roncagliette and Roncaglia.

The most prestigious sites lie just to the south and west of Monte Aribaldo where the elegant Villa Gresy is located (di Gresy's cru Dolcetto is Monte Aribaldo). The most northerly cru is Pajoré, a steep, sunny site with a considerable reputation, based at least in part on the Podere del Pajoré Barbaresco once produced by Enrico Giovannini Moresco. His last vintage was made in 1979 and his vineyards are now owned by Angelo Gaja. The slope winds gently southwards taking in the *borgate* of Marcarini and a little further south Giacosa. Beneath the two, the vineyards of Casotto occupy the lower slopes. The hill doubles back on itself at the *frazione* of Bongiovanni to form a steep-sided tongue of land jutting out from the western edge of Treiso. On the southern side of the spur, some of the steepest vineyards in the Barbaresco zone overlook a deep valley. The major sites here are Bricco di Treiso and, almost hanging from the edge of the precipice, San Bernadotti. To the west, the Nervo vineyards merge into Rizzi on the lower of two further tongues of land. To the north Cascina Rombone is almost an extension of the Bricco di Treiso vineyards.

Few other areas of Treiso seem particularly well adapted for nebbiolo. Large tracts of wooded land to the northwest of the commune cover the mainly north facing slopes of a long, high hill centring on the *borgata* of Ferrero and facing Bric' San Cristoforo and Cottà across the valley. The southern reaches of Treiso remain for the most part, undiscovered territory.

The few top-quality examples of Barbaresco from Treiso show considerable style and seem capable of real finesse and longevity. The area looks to be ripe for development, though so far, of the major houses, only Pio Cesare, Angelo Gaja, Mauro Mascarello and Scarpa seem to have recognized the potential.

113

WINE STYLES AND PRINCIPAL PRODUCERS

Pajoré: the only widely available cru bottling is Scarpa's Podere Barberis, a perfumed and complex wine of excellent concentration and sleek structure, longer lasting than their Tettineive.

Marcarini: tight, scented and stylish wine of considerable elegance from Mauro Mascarello; the Treiso based cooperative Cantina Vignaioli Elvio Pertinace also produces a meaty and aromatic Barbaresco from here.

Bricco di Treiso: the source of Pio Cesare's uncommonly full-bodied Barbaresco (it is not, however, a cru bottling).

Other cru wines in Treiso are produced by Ernesto Dellapiana (Rizzi), Giuseppe Nada (Podere Casot), Luigi Pelissero (Vanotu), and Bruno Nada of Azienda Agricola Fiorenzo Nada (Rombone). The Vignaioli Elvio Pertinace bring out other Treiso crus (Castellizano and Nervo) which are usually soundly made in a rather rustic style. These wines tend to be produced in very limited quantities and are not generally available outside the area.

Barbaresco v. Barolo

Barbaresco has always been the underdog to Barolo even during the last decade or so when Angelo Gaja has, by association, given greater lustre and credibility to the name. Much less is available (almost three times as much Barolo is made) but in the hands of the right producers – Castello di Neive, Ceretto, Gaja, Giacosa, Marchesi di Gresy, Produttori di Barbaresco and Scarpa spring most readily to mind – it can be a definite equal. A number of up and coming small producers like Alfredo Roagna, Giuseppe Cortese, Renato Cigliutti, Cantina del Glicine and Pasquero seem determined to continue the trend.

Barbaresco is often less austere, less structured and less long lived than Barolo, but, taken together, these factors can be a definite advantage for the unconverted. Though no lightweight (often reaching 13.5 per cent with ease), Barbaresco has a reputation for elegance and consistency. While the *riserva* category still exists, it is becoming increasingly unfashionable these days as modernizing views gain wider acceptance. Thanks to a significant presence of forward-thinking winemakers and the minimum one year's cask ageing, wood-attenuated Barbaresco is starting to disappear.

Given its less demanding nature, there is an obvious danger of seeing Barbaresco as first and foremost a stepping stone into the world of fine Albese wines – and therefore as introduction to Barolo. This does Barbaresco a great disservice as anyone who has tasted one of the top crus from the top producers will testify. Good Barbaresco is above all easier to drink: there is no shortage of *conoscenti* who respect and admire Barolo but who drink Barbaresco. The attendant marketing problem must however be faced and Barbaresco assert its individuality by focusing on its unique attributes. Balance, elegance and style are the key points. Angelo Gaja has taken the bit firmly between his teeth, concentrated his methods of vinification to those ends and gone beyond the confines of the Langhe (where many Albese still fear to tread) to promote and sell his wines. Given the fierce intermural rivalry between so many of the producers, we can only hope that more individualists do likewise.

OTHER DOC REDS

Nebbiolo d'Alba

PRODUCTION REGULATIONS
Minimum alcohol content: 12 per cent.
Minimum ageing requirement: 1 year (part of which may be in barrel).
Maximum production levels: 90 quintals per hectare with a 70 per cent *resa in vino* (i.e. 63 hl/ha).
DOC granted: 27 May 1970.

According to local legend, the most famous champion of Nebbiolo d'Alba was Frederick Barbarossa, the twelfth-century Holy Roman Emperor. While often a very traditionally styled product, the much-travelled Frederick's favourite wine would have borne little resemblance to today's. Nebbiolo d'Alba was in fact the last of the Albese Nebbioli to be vinified dry, indeed DOC regulations still allow for the historically popular sweet and sparkling styles. The shift to complete fermentation took place as recently as the beginning of the sixties. Nowadays the sweet version is strictly of historical interest though is apparently still made by a few tiny producers in the northern and western Roero (around Canale, Priocca and Santo Stefano Belbo) for themselves and their friends: it is doubtful that these wines are ever bottled and they are not available commercially.

Where Barolo and Barbaresco are often cited as the king and queen of Piemontese reds, the prince's crown is usually handed to Nebbiolo d' Alba. The 'pimply youth' is destined for a lifetime in short trousers: Nebbiolo d'Alba never achieves the stature of its grander relatives though occasionally can serve as a worthy introduction to them. These days there is an average production of around 1.5 million bottles from some 1,300 growers cultivating approximately 600 hectares. The DOC zone is restricted to twenty-seven communes of Alba. Though the traditional area of production is the sandy hills of the Roero between Bra and Canale, three main subzones are evident.

The first is the 'central strip' of the Roero (the traditional growing zone) bordered to the west by the rocche. The most important communes for volume are Vezza, Corneliano, Montaldo Roero, Monteu Roero, Canale and Santo Stefano Roero. The wines of this section account for over 70 per cent of the production totals and are therefore much the most typical. Traditionally two of the finest crus are the steep sheltered vineyards of Valmaggiore, a frazione of Vezza (bottled by Fratelli Brovia and Bruno Giacosa) and Ochetti of Monteu Roero (Abbazia dell'Annunziata and Prunotto are noted producers).

The northeastern communes of the Roero, principally Guarene, Castagnito, Magliano Alfiero, Castellinaldo and Priocca, produce just under 20 per cent of the total. These wines tend to be the lightest in style, but the best examples such as Scarpa's San Carlo di Castelli-naldo, have an intense, soft fruit character and can be very enjoyable.

The third subzone lies on the right bank of the Tanaro, comprising Alba itself and parts of the Barolo-producing communes of Verduno, Roddi, Grinzane Cavour and Diano d'Alba (as far as the confines of the DOCG zone). The wines tend to be the closest in style to 'mainstream' nebbiolo and are usually vinified more like Barolo and Barbaresco, but without seeing so much wood. Production levels for this subzone are relatively low, accounting for perhaps 10 per cent of all Nebbiolo d'Alba produced. However the area has now been extended through the crescent shape formed by the communes of Montelupo Albese, Sinio, Monforte d'Alba, Monchiero and Novello,

Autumn view of Castiglione Falletto with the vineyards of
Annunziata in the background above the fog.

Cannubi seen from the east, with the Borgogno winery halfway along the hill.

The Rocche vineyard lies below the castle at Castiglione Falletto.

The nebbiolo harvest in the Bric' del Fiasc' vineyard.

Winter view of the southern edge of the Monforte commune.

Serralunga, seen from the east.

The great crus of Barbaresco viewed from Tre Stelle. From left to right: Faset, with Porra below; Asili; La Martinenga and Rabajà.

The tower of Barbaresco with vineyards below.

though as with the other Barolo-producing communes, the vineyards lie outside the DOCG limits. For the moment the classic example from this subzone is Pio Cesare's.

Unlike Barolo and Barbaresco, the DOC discipline does not specify particular clones of nebbiolo. However, as the production zones of the wines do not overlap, Nebbiolo d'Alba is not a convenience package for the excess production of its two seniors: Barolo and Barbaresco can only be declassified to Nebbiolo delle Langhe *vino da tavola* (p. 133).

Roero

PRODUCTION REGULATIONS
Minimum alcohol content: 11.5 per cent.
Minimum ageing period: until 1 June following the vintage.
Maximum production levels: 80 quintals per hectare with a 70 per cent *resa in vino* (i.e. 56 hl/ha).
DOC granted: 18 March 1985.

Roero is a new DOC in a unique position. Even more than Nebbiolo d'Alba it is charged with the daunting task of presenting the more open and accessible face of nebbiolo to the world; at the same time, the potential rewards are boundless. Nebbiolo d'Alba is a wine with a past rooted in a distinct winemaking tradition, Roero is a wine of the future with a tradition still to build.

Roero's chosen form sets it apart immediately: every other DOC(G) Albese wine must be vinified as a pure varietal but the grape mix for Roero (*uvaggio* is a useful term, similar to the French *cépage*) calls for between 95 and 98 per cent nebbiolo with other local varieties (barbera, bonarda, etc.) making up the balance. A minimum of 2 per cent of arneis must also be included. Some growers take advantage of using the full 5 per cent arneis for maximum freshness and fragrance. We have already seen an instance of barbera being used as an 'improver' grape for nebbiolo in Monforte d'Alba: there is in fact a widely accepted but scantly publicized tradition in the Alba zone of lesser-known varietals, arneis and pelaverga for example, being used in this way. With Roero, arneis is in fact fulfilling one of its traditional roles of helping to 'pacify' the nebbiolo.

Roero has yet to realize its full potential but examples from

Deltetto, Malvirà, Negro and the Pasquero family (cousins to the Barbaresco producers) promise well for the future. There is a small *consorzio*, whose president, Giuseppe Rabino, makes one of the best Roeri we have come across so far, and several major Albese firms like Marchesi di Barolo and Prunotto have now included a Roero in their line-up.

In 1988, the fourth year of production, 195 growers produced over 750,000 bottles of Roero from around 150 hectares of land. The figures have increased dramatically from the first vintage (1985) when under 400,000 bottles were made from vineyards tended by 80 growers. The DOC Roero zone covers a similar area to the first two subzones for Nebbiolo d'Alba, excluding much of the western parts of the communes of Govone, Priocca and Guarene (where there are only a total of three growers – one in each commune – for Roero and eighty-four for Nebbiolo d'Alba). These are early days but Roero is a wine to watch: there must be many Nebbiolo d'Alba producers casting anxious glances over their shoulders.

Barbera d'Alba

Because of its easy adaptability to local conditions, its vigour and its ability to bear good quantities of fruit consistently, barbera has been the most widely planted red grape in the Langhe during the post-phylloxera period. These days, however, the chameleon-like personality arising from its versatility has created a troublesome 'image' problem. Barbera serves to accommodate the many individual whims of the region's winemakers: from the brooding *vin de garde* that Giovanni Conterno, for example, will create in vintages like 1985, through wines of tremendous fruit, intensity and structure from producers like Mauro Mascarello, Aldo Vajra and Vietti and the *barrique*-aged modern masterpieces of Elio Altare, Aldo Conterno and Angelo Gaja, via a profusion of supple, medium-bodied quaffers to the light, fruity and instantly forgettable, the answer is Barbera. It is often found fizzy, as a rosé, as a dry, medium or occasionally sweet white (the recently launched Verbesco is a dry white based on barbera vinified off the skins); we have even come across a dry white *metodo classico* sparkling version! It is hardly surprising that the methyl alcohol scandal of the mid-eighties should revolve around Barbera: so much is available and in such a diversity of styles, it is an easy assumption that producers will go to almost any lengths to get rid of it.

Its consequent downmarket image is a travesty – in the hands of the right winemaker, barbera is a budding superstar. Its reputation took a telling body blow during the 1986 crisis when part of the generally weak 1984 vintage was found to contain lethal doses of methyl alcohol. Fortunately this was confined to Barbera at the very lowest end of the scale. Some of the lost ground was made up quickly with the following vintage – the best for Barbera since 1947 for many producers. It is now rightly undergoing something of a revival, indeed in recent years the prices for top quality barbera grapes have been close to those for nebbiolo.

PRODUCTION REGULATIONS

Minimum alcohol content: 12 per cent; 13 per cent for the *superiore*.
Minimum ageing requirements: none specified; 1 year for *superiore*.
Maximum production levels: 100 quintals per hectare with a 70 per cent *resa in vino* (i.e. 70 hl/ha).
DOC granted: 27 May 1970.

The Barbera d'Alba zone is restricted to all or part of fifty-two communes centred around Alba. Almost 3,800 growers produce on average more than 5 million bottles per annum of the DOC version from about 2,500 hectares of vineyards (a relatively small proportion of the total barbera output). Like Barolo, Barbera's production peaked in 1979 with more than 11 million bottles of DOC wine (though from a very modest base of 2–3 million bottles in the early seventies). Though present to a greater or lesser extent throughout the zone, there are two areas of most intense planting.

In the northernmost part of the region, the communes of Monteu Roero, Canale, Vezza, Castellinaldo, Castagnito, Corneliano, Guarene, Priocca, Monticello, Magliano Alfiero and Govone account for just over 40 per cent of the production total. Govone, in particular, is widely planted to the variety. The wines from this area tend to be made in a lighter, early drinking style.

The 'wedge' from Barbaresco and Neive into Alba and Treiso and encompassing the Barolo zone is usually seen as the classic area. Paiagallo in Barolo and Pianromualdo in Monforte are two of the great sites.

Until the 1987 vintage, DOC allowed Barbera d'Alba a 'correction' of up to 15 per cent nebbiolo must or wine produced within the province of Cuneo. This officially sanctioned *uvaggio* set an interesting precedent by rubber stamping the tradition we have already referred to, but barbera is increasingly vinified as a pure varietal in keeping with the general tendency throughout the zone towards single grape wines. The old tradition in Monforte has now been revived through 'designer' *vini da tavola* like Migliorini's Bricco Manzoni. The recent change in law that has done away with a minimum ageing period for the wine has also decreed that Barbera d'Alba must now be made from 100 per cent barbera grapes.

Barbera is typically a high-acid, low-tannin grape, hence its suitability, some producers argue, for *barrique* ageing. It gives deep, dark, purple-coloured wine full of extract and bramble/cherry fruit often characterized by spicy and aromatic tones reminiscent of seasoned leather. This 'platonic' form of Barbera is capable of taking plenty of bottle age in its stride – up to ten years or so – when, as if by magic, its mature flavours can develop a marked affinity to those of the nebbiolo: there is even a word to describe the process, *baroleggiare* means 'to become like a Barolo'. To achieve this level of quality, yields are as ever the key; the lower the yield, the less piercing the acidity seems to be. Moreover certain producers swear by the superiority of the restricted bunches of smaller grapes that, they insist, only old vines are capable of bearing – the sort, Carlo Brovia, winemaker for Fratelli Brovia in Castiglione Falletto maintains, that many *contadini* would grub up for not being productive enough. Angelo Gaja who once talked of phasing out his Barbera production because of the grape's unfashionable image, argues that the timing of the harvest is crucial: he prefers to pick for an optimum balance of flavours rather than an elevated sugar content. He is now also considering planting barbera on his new Marenca-Rivette estate in Serralunga.

Despite the bewildering variation in styles, Barbera can, from winemakers like those above, be a truly fine wine; indeed amongst the best the zone has to offer. Production levels were once much higher but over the past decade there has been much replanting with dolcetto and moscato which have proved, at least temporarily, much easier to sell. In recognition of these marketing problems, a promotional campaign, La Rosa di Barbera, has been launched to remind people of what they're missing. A little more understanding on behalf of the consumer and a rather more concerted effort by the winemakers to emphasize the quality aspect of their products, could indeed ensure a rosy future for Barbera.

Dolcetto

Known as the lifeblood of the Langaroli (the story goes that if you analysed an Albese's blood sample, it would contain at least 50 per cent Dolcetto), this is the classic *vino da tutto pasto*: a wine for all day, every day and an automatic choice at the beginning of almost every meal. Indeed in some traditional *trattorie* there is no choice at all: a bottle of the local Dolcetto appears, unsolicited, at the same time as the cutlery!

While Dolcetto retains a distinctively Piemontese character, it has the great advantage of a remarkably 'easy' nature. Always an accessible and appetizing, intensely purple-coloured wine, Dolcetto's unrestrained fruit and youthful exuberance often come as a breath of fresh air in a land dominated by its serious red wines. Quality standards are moreover pretty reliable and there is a more uniform image to the product than with Barbera, for example. Dolcetto represents a rather more light-hearted side of the Piemontese character, though comparisons to a 'Beaujolais with guts' hardly do it justice. Like the Albesi themselves, its charm may be rustic, even earthy, yet is rarely without style.

PRODUCTION REGULATIONS: DOLCETTO D'ALBA
Minimum alcohol content: 11.5 per cent; 12.5 per cent for *superiore* (a category rarely seen and not, as the term would seem to imply, a 'superior' product: it merely indicates a higher alcohol content).
Minimum ageing requirements: none specified; 1 year for *superiore*.
Maximum production levels: 90 quintals per hectare with a 70 per cent *resa in vino* (i.e. 63 hl/ha).
DOC granted: 6 July 1974.
The Dolcetto d'Alba zone extends over thirty-four communes on the right bank of the river Tanaro; the only exception is a fractional slice of Alba itself as far as its northern border with the Roero

communes of Monticello, Piobesi and Guarene. The zone's eastern limits are very nearly defined by those communes through which the river Belbo passes – Santo Stefano Belbo, Cossano Belbo, Rocchetta Belbo, Castino and Bosia. An average of 7 million bottles is produced annually, although only just over 100,000 bottles were made in its first year as a DOC wine. Production levels, because of Dolcetto's immense and growing popularity on the domestic market, are still creeping up: 1988 was the biggest vintage to date with just under 8 million bottles. Over 2,500 growers farm nearly 2,600 hectares of vines.

The biggest concentration of dolcetto vines is around Barolo and Barbaresco, especially the communes of Alba, La Morra, Neive and Treiso. Monforte accounts for 18 per cent of the production total, making it the single most important commune. Everyone seems to grow a little, even the otherwise strictly monogamous *Barolista* Bartolo Mascarello! The most famous sites for dolcetto fall within this classic area: Ravera in Barolo, Gagliassi in Monforte, Rocchettevino in La Morra and Basarin in Neive all have excellent reputations. Mango, to the east of Treiso, is also seen as a prime area where dolcetto will not have to compete with nebbiolo for the better positions (Abbazia dell'Annunziata produce a couple of superb Dolcetti from this commune).

Dolcetto comes in two principal styles which, by and large, tie in with the winemaker's tendency towards a more 'traditional' or 'modern' approach to vinification. The classic, traditional Dolcetto as made by Giovanni Conterno and Mauro Mascarello is a big wine with masses of ripe, chocolate-like fruit. The emphasis is on richness and concentration and this style can often sustain several years of bottle age. In particularly ripe vintages such as 1985, wines of almost monstrous dimensions can occasionally be made: Fratelli Brovia's Solatio from that vintage achieved 15 per cent alcohol, not exactly the ideal quaffing wine but remarkable none the less for its power and size. A unique Dolcetto in the more traditional style is made by Elvio Cogno at La Morra, whose Boschi dei Berri comes from a quarter hectare plot to the southwest of the town. Cogno-Marcarini rent the vineyard from Giovanni Burdese: the vines have never been grafted on to American rootstocks and, although their exact age is unknown, Elvio estimates that some of them could be as much 115 years old. Boschi dei Berri, made in lots of around 2,000 bottles a year, has no rivals for sheer intensity of flavour.

The more elegant, lighter and supple 'modern' versions have the accent on freshness, clarity and fragrance of fruit. Excellent examples are available from Domenico Clerico, Aldo Conterno and Marchesi di Gresy. The exception to the rule is Elio Altare: although a passionate believer in radical winemaking techniques, Elio works with such low yields (the key to success with all his wines), that his wine is as full, rich and concentrated as any of the 'old style' Dolcetti.

Roberto Voerzio of La Morra believes that the vinification process for dolcetto will bear further experimentation – at least for Priavino, his 'cru' Dolcetto. He has gradually been reducing yields in recent years – an advocate of severe pruning, he prefers to work with a maximum six bunches per vine and around forty quintals of fruit per hectare – and at the same time is increasing the period of maceration in better vintages, while adding less sulphur to the must. This may in fact be leading him back towards the more traditional methods as championed by Giovanni Conterno, for example, though Roberto favours a more classically 'modern' approach for his Pria San Francesco Croera wine. Angelo Gaja, naturally enough, does his own thing and gives his Dolcetto Vignabaila three to four months in *barrique*. With a wine where freshness, primary fruit flavours and lowish acidity are normally its most prized features, this shouldn't really work. Of course it does, Vignabaila is a very attractive wine with a far sleeker structure and higher acidity than most Dolcetti.

A handful of young producers – Paolo and Enrico Cordero di Montezemolo, Alfredo Roagna and Mauro Sebaste – have in recent years brought out a *novello* version which is on sale by the Christmas following the vintage. Mauro Sebaste makes his Dolcetto San Pietro delle Viole using the *maceration carbonique* method, thus giving greater emphasis to the freshness and primary fruit characters for which dolcetto is renowned. He argues that this osmotic form of fermentation is particularly well suited to dolcetto. His customers seem to agree; Mauro has usually sold out of the wine within two weeks of its release.

PRODUCTION REGULATIONS: DOLCETTO DI DIANO D'ALBA
Minimum alcohol content: 12 per cent; 12.5 per cent for *superiore*.
Minimum ageing period: none specified; 1 year for *superiore*.

Maximum production levels: 80 quintals per hectare with a 70 per cent *resa in vino* (i.e. 56 hl/ha).

DOC granted: 3 May 1974.

If Dolcetto has not yet established its true position in the hierarchy of Albese wines, the separate DOC of Dolcetto di Diano d'Alba confirms that its potential is at least acknowledged. Around 240 growers, though numbers are increasing, cultivate about 280 hectares of land in the Barolo producing commune of Diano d'Alba. Though still a relatively small denomination, DOC was granted before Dolcetto d'Alba and operates a stricter set of controls: yields are lower and mandatory bottling inside the production zone was a first for Diano. Production levels average out at 750,000 bottles per annum. The figure peaked quickly in 1979 (over 800,000) following the tiny 1978 vintage of just under 300,000. This came from a low base of only 16,666 in the first year of production. A new record of 850,000 was set again in 1986 demonstrating that 'Diano' is still on the up.

Although both Fontanafredda and Gigi Rosso produce cru Dolcetti di Diano, the area is at present dominated by smaller houses like Mario Savigliano and the Accomo family of Bricco Maiolica. These two small firms make ripe, fleshy wines with an underlying stalky tone that gives the rich, plummy fruit a clearer perspective. The largest producer and leading figure in the commune, Luigi Artusio of Cantina della Porta Rossa, defiantly sells his wine as Diano d'Alba (qualified by the name of the cru). 'Diano is Dolcetto,' he insists. The former enologist of Fontanafredda is not a man to argue with!

Dolcetto di Diano d'Alba may be seen as an attempt to create a super-Dolcetto; indeed it was the first area in the Langhe to organize and map out its seventy-seven crus (practicable because of its small size). However the marketing concept is arguably as interesting as the product itself – the finest Dolcetti are mostly made by Barolo and Barbaresco producers. This is not entirely surprising: both tradition and technology are more readily at their disposal. The area must be applauded for its forward thinking though: we clearly have not seen the best of Diano yet.

DOC WHITES

Moscato d'Asti

PRODUCTION REGULATIONS
Minimum alcohol content: 10.5 per cent (potential) with a minimum
of one-third 'undeveloped', i.e., present as residual sugar.
Minimum ageing period: none specified.
Maximum production levels: 110 quintals per hectare with a 75 per
cent *resa in vino*, (i.e. 82.5 hl/ha).
DOC granted: 9 July 1967.

In a region where small-scale wineries and extraordinary winemakers
are the norm, a typically low-priced and widely available product like
Moscato d'Asti may seem out of place. At least Moscato d'Asti is often
seen in those terms and with some justification, but it is by no means the
whole story. Production costs are certainly not cheap: as well as the
sophisticated equipment involved, moscato grapes are among the most
expensive to buy in the zone. Corners must therefore be cut when
Moscato d'Asti is bought to the constraints of a low budget.

The cause of quality production was not helped when in 1982
permitted yields were increased to 110 quintals per hectare from their
previous limit of 100. Similarly the *resa in vino* is the highest for any
DOC wine in the zone.

The redeeming factor that shines through is the nature of the
product itself. At its best, Moscato d'Asti is sublime stuff – an
explosion of freshness and piercingly fragrant fruit, the natural
sweetness tempered by a lift of light sparkle and slightly 'green'
acidity. It remains one of the world's finest and most frequently
misconstrued dessert wines – there is nothing better with fresh fruit for
example. At the end of a rich and lengthy Piemontese dinner, its
unique freshness and delicacy have a magically restorative effect.

Over 30 million bottles of Moscato d'Asti are produced annually in
the Albese, where about 2,300 growers farm around 4,000 hectares of
land. Although the Asti and Alessandria zones account for more than
50 per cent of the entire Moscato d'Asti production total, the fourteen
full communes and part of Alba itself delimited in the province of
Cuneo form the most favoured subzone. The eastern part of the
region where it borders on Asti is seen as the optimum area, especially

the communes of Como, Mango, Cossano Belbo, Castiglione Tinella and Santo Stefano Belbo (the last three in particular are reputed to produce the finest wines characterized by their delicacy of aroma and lightness of style). The Barbaresco communes of Neive and Treiso have good reputations too. Given Fontanafredda's involvement with all types of sparkling wine it is hardly surprising that Serralunga d'Alba is also part of the zone. The inclusion of Santa Vittoria d'Alba, stranded on the left bank of the Tanaro, is similarly linked to Cinzano's presence there.

The wine may be still or sparkling (there is no minimum atmospheric pressure specified) but must contain a potential alcohol content of at least 10.5 per cent with no less than 33 per cent remaining undeveloped – the unique fragrance of the grape would be lost if the wines were fully fermented. The individual winemaker is thus able to determine his preferred style: not only the degree of sparkle but also whether the wine be slightly drier and more delicate as with Roberto Voerzio's La Serra di Valdivilla or the full-blown, perfumed style of a Moscato specialist like Rivetti (La Spinetta). Although many large concerns are heavily involved in production, individually styled wines from small producers in the east of the zone like Dogliotti (Cascina Caudrina) and Saracco are still widely available. Thankfully, buoyant sales of more specialized products on the home market prevent them from becoming an endangered species.

Arneis

PRODUCTION REGULATIONS
Minimum alcohol content: 10 per cent.
Minimum ageing requirement: none specified.
Maximum production levels: 100 quintals per hectare with a 70 per cent *resa in vino* (i.e. 70 hl/ha).
DOC granted: 3 January 1989.

The fact that a still, dry, white Albese wine has achieved DOC recognition in such a short space of time is a measure of the zone's growing confidence in matters commercial. As with the rise of the cru concept however, a long line of producers stands ready to take a share of the credit for Arneis' upturn in fortunes and the bandwagon is once more dangerously overloaded. While there is a lengthy tradition of growing the variety in the Roero, its potential long went unrecognized. Three names emerge as being instrumental in popularizing the revival. Bruno Giacosa and Vietti were certainly among the first to produce Arneis commercially, while in the Roero itself La Cornarea have acted as an example to many smaller producers by growing, vinifying and bottling Arneis for themselves.

The DOC Roero Arneis zone has now been defined and covers the same sixteen communes as Roero (*rosso*), though Monteu Roero, Vezza and Canale seem likely to form the centre of prᵒduction. There is a close parallel to be drawn with Barolo in the secoᵔd half of the 1970s in the way that many small firms have suddenly appeared with carefully packaged products from supposedly traditional Arneis crus (usually bizarre-sounding Piemontese names). For the moment DOC regulations allow for the production of sparkling Arneis, though as with the several *passito* versions, the variety's lack of acidity would seem to work against this option. Once the dust settles, production levels and the subzones of true vocation should begin to be established in some sort of pattern.

Given its inherent fragility, almost all Arneis is best drunk young. It can be very stylish: the nose fresh, expansive yet elusive, often fruit salad-like with notes of apples, peaches and cardamom (it is sometimes compared with the *viognier* of the northern Rhône). Though the palate rarely shows much weight, it has some complexity with subtle underlying spiciness. Castello di Neive have given new impetus to the emergent tradition with their Arneis Montebertotto from a vineyard planted in 1979. In a good vintage, Montebertotto can even take a little bottle age when it begins to smell almost like old Champagne. That hint of decadence carries through onto the palate giving the wine a suggestion of real richness which could well appeal to lovers of white Burgundy. Ironically, though, the DOC zone excludes Neive and one of the most interesting examples so far of Arneis can therefore only be sold as a *vino da tavola*! Also showing definite promise are Deltetto (San Michele), Malvirà (Renesio), Negro (Perdaudin) and La Cornarea in the Roero, and amongst the Barolo and Barbaresco houses, Vietti and both Gianni and Roberto Voerzio.

So is Arneis the great white hope of the Albese? These are early days though potential is evident. At least one producer, in typically hard-headed fashion, put Arneis firmly in its place as 'an interesting curiosity from a red wine region'.

VINI DA TAVOLA

Red Wines

While freisa and grignolino are still reasonably common in the Albese, the other minor red grapes are present in much smaller quantities. Some are planted on an experimental basis, others seem to be under almost constant threat of extinction while one isolated case seems to be hovering in the uncertain area between obscurity and cult status.

FREISA
Freisa is still a great favourite locally and is loved by all from the most traditional producers like Giovanni Conterno through to radical modernists like Domenico Clerico and Roberto Voerzio. Assuming that your real interest is Barolo, few producers will actually offer you Freisa to taste but seem genuinely pleased if you express an interest. As it performs well at higher altitudes, Freisa gives producers another string to their bow and the modern version with its fresh, fragrant fruit and light fizz is readily consumed with *antipasti* as an alternative to Dolcetto. A few examples of still Freisa are available: though the weighty style as produced by Aldo Vajra is a one-off, similarly vibrant perfumes are evident in the lighter wines of Giovanni Conterno and Conterno-Fantino. Freisa is mainly grown in and around the Barolo zone, especially the communes of Barolo, Monforte and La Morra.

GRIGNOLINO
Grignolino used to occupy a special place in the hearts of many Piemontesi probably because in a region with more than its fair share of *impegnativi* (demanding) wines, a pale, light red with a marked tendency towards astringency came as a welcome and digestible rarity. Grignolino is also said to have medicinal properties. Planting of the

variety is nowadays mainly restricted to a few isolated vineyards in the Barolo and Barbaresco zones.

The best examples of Grignolino have a delicate, floral-toned bouquet often reminiscent of rose petals and a fresh, lively palate with keen acidity and an uncompromising dryness. The wine always comes first in pouring order at a Piemontese table and, with so few dry whites available until recently, Grignolino often assumed that role. When we asked one famous Barolista what he drank with fish, the reply was immediate: 'Grignolino.'

PELAVERGA AND OTHERS

Brachetto ('braghat' in Piemontese) is only made by a handful of producers in the Albese today. Its traditional style – an aromatic and often sparkling dessert wine – has long since fallen out of fashion. The few examples still available are made as light, rather lean, dry reds of striking and expansive aroma. Bricco Maiolica and Angelo Negro make authentic versions.

Even rarer is the bonarda Piemontese. Small quantities are grown in the Roero though usually end up as part of the red DOC *uvaggio*. The only 'varietal' Bonarda we have tasted comes from Angelo Negro; his Bric' Millon would seem to suggest a brighter future for the grape, a point of view corroborated by Professor Morando at Alba's Enological School who maintains that bonarda has 'everything, including a future'.

Amongst the more unusual indigenous varieties, pelaverga is enjoying a healthy revival at the moment and is becoming very much *alla moda* in certain parts. Its reputation as an 'erotic' wine (the literal translation is 'bared rod') may have something to do with this! Though pelaverga is thought to originate from the Bronda valley in the Saluzzo area, it is now grown almost exclusively in the Barolo commune of Verduno where Massara is a noted cru. Pelaverga has some history as an 'improver' grape but the current emphasis is on what the variety can achieve in its own right. With the backing of the commune, a small *consorzio* of growers has been formed to develop a production discipline and carry out research into clonal selection (apparently one vineyard is planted to thirty different pelaverga clones). Early signs show a dark, full-bodied wine with rich, dried fruit tones.

Little has so far been seen of the so-called 'international' red varieties. Pinot nero (pinot noir) has been around for a century and more, and is used mainly as a component in sparkling wines. Fontanafredda market a 100 per cent Pinot Nero *metodo classico* from their Gattinera vineyard at Serralunga d'Alba. Rather like grignolino, pinot nero is susceptible to rot because of its highly compact fruit. A rare example of still Pinot Nero is made by Luciano de Giacomi at his Bricco del Drago estate near San Rocco: a pale, light, herbal-toned red that would come as a shock to those used to Côte d'Or or New World examples.

While Angelo Gaja's cabernet sauvignon vineyard below his house in Barbaresco has attracted a great deal of interest and comment, Angelo quite openly admits that nebbiolo remains his abiding passion. With a wary eye on the competition, Pio Cesare have planted both cabernets in their vineyards at Treiso (like Gaja, Pio Boffa has spent time with winemakers in California). While others may well have the occasional row of cabernet discreetly tucked in amongst their native vines, few, as yet, are prepared to admit it! When it comes to red grapes, the Albesi have an unshakeable belief in their own varieties: with nebbiolo around, who needs cabernet?

White Wines

FAVORITA

It is thought that favorita — so-called as it is a 'favourite' locally, a reference to its popular use as a table grape — may be a clone of the vermentino variety from just across the Maritime Alps in Liguria. There is certainly a long history of trade between the Piemontesi and Liguri, and the adoption of one of their neighbours' white grapes would seem, in a world dominated by red varieties, an obvious step. Favorita has a poorly documented history and is not as well established in the Roero as arneis, though traditionally it has been put to the same uses. However, as the dry white becomes all the rage in the Langhe, demand for favorita grapes often outstrips supply these days.

On the whole, favorita shows less distinction and character than arneis. A non-aromatic variety according to almost all the people who grow it, Favorita displays a broad, vinous nose with clear, fresh fruit on the palate, but too often seems disappointingly neutral. The best examples from left-bank producers like Deltetto, Malvira and Negro can be very pleasant though rarely more than that. Favorita has not so far fired too many imaginations outside the Roero and few right-bank houses are as yet working with the variety (Bel Colle and Franco Fiorina are two exceptions). Though its basic neutrality would seem to indicate a minor future role, favorita's revival continues unabated.

CHARDONNAY

Amongst the less insular winemaking community chardonnay is the 'in' thing. It has had such a spectacular worldwide success story that almost anything with chardonnay on the label is easy to sell; a rather alarming reflection of the prestige in which it is held by winemaker and consumer alike. The chardonnay phenomenon began in the Barbaresco zone initially thanks to Angelo Gaja, but many others now boast chardonnay vineyards. It can now be found all over the Albese as producers seek to cash in on an apparently insatiable demand. Aldo Conterno, Conterno-Fantino and Valentino Migliorini have all planted chardonnay in Monforte d'Alba and Fratelli Barale in Barolo itself. Fontanafredda have been growing chardonnay for almost fifty years on north and west facing slopes of their Serralunga estate: so far it has been used principally for sparkling wine production. Like the other white grapes, chardonnay frequently occupies north facing slopes in order to prolong its ripening season and is thus no threat to nebbiolo.

PINOT BIANCO AND PINOT GRIGIO

Many Italians have the confusing habit of referring to the 'pinot' grape, leaving you to guess which subvariety they mean. It could be the pinot bianco (white), pinot grigio (grey), pinot nero (black) or even pinot giallo (yellow) as the chardonnay is still known in some areas. The Albesi are no exception. The various pinots were introduced to the area in the middle of the nineteenth century and have been going in and out of fashion ever since. Their most significant presence these days is at Fontanafredda where they have been planted for over forty years. Fontanafredda are founder members of the Istituto Spumante Metodo Classico Italiano, a marketing consortium of sixteen members who have banded together to promote the use of the champagne method, and vinify their pinot grapes into an impressive range of sparkling wines. Castello di Neive produce a Castelborgo Brut from pinot bianco and pinot grigio grapes grown in Neive's Gallina vineyard, but otherwise only a few producers are working with 'pinot' (there is rather more bianco planted than grigio). A rare still version is made by Fratelli Giacosa of Neive.

Minor White Grapes

There are only isolated examples of other white varieties in the region (usually present on an experimental basis) and amounts grown are impossible to quantify. For the sake of completeness we must mention cortese (extremely common further to the east in the Monferrato hills and around the town of Gavi, it is also planted in negligible quantities along the Belbo valley communes of Rocchetta, Cossano, Castiglione Tinella and Santo Stefano) and furmentin. Although some claim the latter may be derived from the Hungarian furmint, a rather more plausible explanation is that like favorita, it could be related to the Ligurian vermentino variety. The nature of the Piemontese dialect supports the latter alternative: the omission of the final vowel is a characteristic trait and the similarity between 'fur' and 'ver' obvious. A tiny amount is grown in Cossano and Rochetta Belbo and the Cantina Sociale di Dolcetto e Moscato produce both still and sparkling versions. Neither grape though, in our limited experience, produces a wine of any distinction.

Vino da Tavola con Indicazione Geografica

With the exception of furmentin, all the above red and white grapes for DOC and non-DOC wines have since late 1987 qualified for the Vino da Tavola con Indicazione Geografica category (table wine from a specific area). The description *delle Langhe* can therefore be appended to the relevant grape variety as in, for example, Favorita delle Langhe. This can also apply to riesling italico, riesling renano (Rhein riesling) and Sauvignon blanc, none of which is planted in any significant quantities in the Langhe yet. In addition to recognizing the production of wines from varieties grown outside the various DOCG limits, the *delle Langhe* denomination can encompass declassified wine from within them. Barolo and Barbaresco producers may for a variety of reasons register their products as Nebbiolo delle Langhe. Thus with wine that does not match up to their own or the tasting commission's standards, or if production methods have not conformed to the DOCG discipline, the *delle Langhe* category exists as an optional safety net. Nebbiolo di Barolo aged for say twelve months in *barrique,* and thereafter only in stainless steel or bottle, could in theory be sold in this form although in this instance most producers would prefer an individual 'designer' package. More commonly seen under this guise are the *novello*-style Nebbioli like the Produttori di Barbaresco's Langhe or Conterno-Fantino's Ginestrino: fresh, fruity varietals made with little or no wood ageing.

'Vini d'Autore'

Although Angelo Gaja for one maintains that Alba has both a tradition of and vocation for thoroughbred varietal wines, a quiet undercurrent – hitherto mainly at the *contadino* level – of discreet blending has been going on for many years. Some of the grapes described above, such as arneis and pelaverga or, latterly, cabernet, have traditionally been used as 'improvers' (*cépage améliorateurs* in French) to soften or even 'beef up' some of the more illustrious names. The prototype *uvaggio* was Barbera d'Alba which until the 1987 vintage allowed for the addition of up to 15 per cent nebbiolo. In Monforte d'Alba custom favours a blend of reverse proportions and today's most famous *uvaggio* is a direct descendant of this tradition. Valentino Migliorini has been producing Bricco Manzoni (an 80–20 per cent nebbiolo/barbera blend) since the seventies. Since the early eighties Migliorini has given the wine between twelve and eighteen months in new *barriques.* The presence of barbera 'plumps out' the nebbiolo and, in combination with the cedary new oak tones, gives Bricco Manzoni the sort of elegant international appeal that could make the area many new friends. Domenico Clerico's Arte (90 per cent nebbiolo, 10 per cent barbera), Conterno-Fantino's Mon Pra' (50–50) and Mauro Sebaste's Bricco Viole (around 50–50 again) are all aged in *barrique* and fuel the argument that tradition must adapt in order to remain strong.

Although Barolo and Barbaresco producers are to be applauded for their decision to keep faith with the traditional denominations, some exceptional wines coming out of the Langhe today are made in defiance of the DOCG rules. These individual expressions of the winemaker's art have become known as *vini d'autore* (literally 'authors' wines').

While nebbiolo, barbera and *barrique* are an increasingly popular combination, other *vini d'autore* are made to different specifications. Ageing Nebbiolo di Barolo in *barrique* seems to outrage many winemakers and commentators alike. While a spell in *barrique* can certainly never turn a poor wine into a good one or enhance one that has not been vinified in the appropriate fashion, the evidence of Elio Altare's Vigna Arborina or Aldo Conterno's Il Favot is hard to refute. Nebbiolo in *barrique* can and does work if the base product is right and – personal tastes aside – must therefore be seen as a valid variation on the nebbiolo theme. How far the idea of *barrique* ageing will be taken is as yet uncertain. One of the more esoteric experiments is being carried out by Alfredo Roagna in Barbaresco. His first release of 'Opera Prima' (Opus One in Italian) was a blend of different vintages of *barrique*-aged nebbiolo. It is ultimately the consumer who will decide whether the use of new oak has added enough to a wine to justify its necessarily higher price and also whether he is willing to pay a premium for a product which in some cases is first and foremost an experiment.

Fewer winemakers are working with a nebbiolo-dolcetto blend though Luciano de Giacomi's Bricco del Drago (85 per cent dolcetto, 15 per cent nebbiolo) is one of the most persuasive arguments yet in favour of the *uvaggio*. Ironically Bricco del Drago was a chance discovery. The Dolcetti from the San Rocco area had always, according to de Giacomi, shown an uncommon capacity for ageing. When he unearthed some bottles made by his father twenty years earlier, he tasted them out of curiosity. He saw enough to feel convinced that, with the addition of a little nebbiolo for backbone, he had stumbled on something rather exciting. That was in the sixties and de Giacomi has not looked back since. In particularly good years, the President of the Cavaliere del Tartufo also produces a Vigna del Mace version from the highest vineyard on his estate. The Cordero di Montezemolo family are trying out the combination with an 80 per cent nebbiolo, 20 per cent dolcetto blend. The year 1984 was the first vintage for their 'Elioro', but the wine has yet to match the standards set by their Barolo.

At least two famous producers are looking at broader-based, *barrique*-aged *uvaggi*. Vietti blend nebbiolo and barbera with dolcetto and neyrano (an obscure local variety also used as a table grape) from their Fioretto vineyard close to the village of Castiglione Falletto. The wine is made in tiny quantities and only in good vintages. Abbazia dell'Annunziata combine barbera (80 per cent) and freisa (15 per cent) with the rare uvalino grape from the Villa Pattòno vineyard at Costigliole d'Asti. Renato Ratti smiled wryly the time he recalled his first shopping expedition in France to buy *barriques*. He was wholly unprepared for the different kinds of wood on offer, while as for which 'toast' he required . . .

There are numerous other minor proprietary blends, not only permutations of the nebbiolo, barbera, dolcetto trio. De Giacomi combines pinot nero with freisa to make Campo Romano (so called because Roman artefacts have been found in the vineyard), while Moscato specialist Romano Dogliotti blends the latter variety with barbera for a bizarre but tasty, fizzy red called Campo del Ghein which is vinified in autoclave. From here on, though the stories behind them are sometimes fascinating, the wines head off into the realms of obscurity.

With the exception of Villa Pattòno (born outside the Albese in Costigliole d'Asti) there is a clear common denominator amongst the major *uvaggi*: the presence of nebbiolo. As Angelo Gaja's Cabernet Sauvignon 'Darmagi' has served to generate new interest and credibility in the region as a whole, so the *uvaggio* wines can perform a similar function with the additional advantage that the focus is firmly on the versatility of the nebbiolo grape. Supported by wines such as the fruit-dominated Nebbioli delle Langhe, they may be about to open a new chapter in the history of Albese wines.

6

PRODUCER PROFILES

To understand a wine beyond the sensations it offers to the palate, you must study the land, the grapes, the winemaking traditions of the area, as well as the cultural environment in which it is born. All of this however, can remain sterile data if not put into human perspective by the individuals behind the wines.

Before considering some of the Langhe's most influential and typical characters, an examination of the background issues shaping the way in which today's Albese wines are made and marketed is called for.

BROADER HORIZONS

Barolo and Barbaresco have yet to conquer the rest of Italy, let alone the world. Most other Italians seem content to take their reputation on trust: mention of the Langaroli and their wines elsewhere in Italy is likely to be greeted with a knowing smile and a sympathetic nod of the head. Their compatriots seem to feel more at home with a glass of Moscato d'Asti than with a glass of Barolo. Indeed Barolo is considered the sort of wine to be broached two or three times a year, and then only when game is plentiful. The Langaroli are viewed as a race apart – a proud, silent and stubborn people who are about as impenetrable as young Nebbiolo. There is much circumstantial evidence to bear the view out: two young brothers, on inheriting the family winery, find their ideas about how to make wine to be wholly irreconcilable; they therefore build a dividing wall down the middle of the cellar and now run totally separate businesses. If their fellow countrymen have difficulty in understanding the Langaroli, what chance has the poor foreigner?

While most Italian regions have a substantial history of turning up excellent winemakers, none can boast a long and unbroken tradition of fine wine production. Where Bordeaux and Burgundy have – if only in the eyes of the wine-loving public – centuries of expertise behind them, comparable zones like Chianti and Alba have pasts that are, at best, murky. Unlike the Californians and to a lesser extent the Australians, the Italians were unable to launch their new assault on wider markets with a clean sheet. Scandal and inconsistency were already writ large at the top of the page. If the odds were thus heavily stacked against the average Italian producer in pursuit of international recognition, they were even more punishing for the Langaroli.

The Langaroli were confronted with a major paradox: what was at once the greatest attraction of their wines, their very singularity, was at the same time their most forbidding feature. For wine drinkers brought up on Cabernet Sauvignon, Pinot Noir and Chardonnay, Barbera, Nebbiolo and Arneis are not easy to understand and appreciate. A wealth of new flavours, often as difficult as they are exciting, are as likely to put prospective customers off as they are to attract them. In many parts of Italy there was a mad rush in the seventies to supplement existing indigenous varieties with 'international' grapes like cabernet and chardonnay. With a few notable exceptions, the Albesi have stuck to their guns and continued to work with the likes of nebbiolo, sublimely confident that the world would one day wake up to what it was missing. While robust and assertive reds may indeed have been the ideal foil for hearty Piemontese cooking, were wines from another era really what the rest of the world wanted?

A CHANGING WORLD

Until the 1960s, production in the Alba zone was limited and demand relatively high. What was not drunk within the immediate area was readily bought up by a hardy band of *conoscenti* in the wealthier towns of northern Italy. There was little need therefore for wine-makers to modify the tried and trusted techniques handed down from their fathers and grandfathers. However, as more and more new vineyards were planted by both small farmers and large companies to supply a buoyant market, production increased dramatically. In Barolo the spur for this was the official blessing of DOC; in the twenty years that followed its introduction in 1967 the area under vine all but doubled. Ironically, the 1970s brought a slump in consumption – a drop of as much as 25 per cent over the course of a decade. Full-bodied red wines were the first to suffer as tastes veered towards lighter, fruitier styles. Instead of the customer beating a path to his door, the producer was forced to go out and sell his wares. In an increasingly competitive market, few wineries could be certain of turning over their annual production.

Before the mid-seventies, few producers had made serious assaults on the export market, but with falling sales at home they could no longer afford to ignore the possibility. There was no guarantee, however, that their traditional winemaking methods would be accepted in more critical international markets.

Though tradition remained strong, the radical views on wine-making first voiced in the mid-sixties by men like Renato Ratti were steadily gaining credence. The modern school's concern for clean-liness highlighted the more obvious flaws of the old style wines. In doing so they proclaimed the greater suitability of their products for a wider market. The period of great enological change which began in the sixties extended through the following decade and into the mid-eighties. By 1985 the majority of cellars in the Albese had invested in sophisticated new equipment.

During the 1970s the rise of the *azienda agricola* (the term has come to signify the 'estate-bottling' specialist who works only with his own grapes) was to have an equally profound effect on the structure of the wine trade. Hitherto production had been dominated by negociant houses who based their product on bought-in grapes or wine. Falling domestic consumption resulted in a downward price spiral for grapes as stocks built up. The brunt was borne principally by growers who were being asked to sell their crop for an unrealistically low price. In the ensuing buyer's market, significant numbers of these small growers took the logical step of vinifying and bottling their own wine in order to claim their share of the dwindling profits. The trickle of small producers who had set a precedent during the previous two decades had become a bubbling stream by the end of the seventies. There was no shortage of canny *contadini* who managed to dig out sufficient funds from under the mattress to invest in the necessary cellar equipment.

THE EMERGENCE OF THE CRU

The fairly rudimentary understanding of the winemaking process shown by some of the new producers was matched by the arrival of a number of exceptional 'hand crafted' products made in tiny quantities and usually sold as single vineyard or 'cru' wines. Although restricted by law to various French Appellation Contrôlée wines, the term 'cru' has arrived to stay in Alba. Despite local and more widespread terms – *bricco, sori'*, and *vigna* or *vigneto* – the word 'cru' conveys a precise idea, especially to an international audience.

Vinifying grapes from separate plots is a long standing practice in the Albese; the oldest known bottles of 'Barolo' are labelled simply 'Cannubi 1752'. At the beginning of the sixties the influential wine and food writer Luigi Veronelli was an early champion of the cru concept and was already pressing for official recognition of Italy's top sites. The call was taken up in the Langhe by Renato Ratti amongst others, and nowadays the idea has widespread acceptance in the area. Fierce individual competition, ever an Albese trait, rears its head when you try to pinpoint the start of the cru bottling trend. Quite simply, they all did it first.

There exists as yet no official definition of what constitutes a cru, and therefore no control of its use on the label. The Albesi, however, now talk of the *cru storici* (historic crus) when attempting to separate the traditionally valued sites from the minor vineyards and fantasy names that have mushroomed up in recent years.

The precise usage of the term 'cru' is further complicated by varying interpretations of its geographical significance. In Barbaresco, for example, both Gaja and di Gresy name their top wines after clearly mapped out single vineyards. Thus Gaja's Sori' Tildin comes from a particular plot in the Roncagliette area and di Gresy's Camp Gros from an individual parcel of his holdings at La Martinenga. Other producers label their wine according to the general name of a hillside, such as Vietti who bottle Barbaresco from Rabajà. Some would hold that Rabajà merely constitutes an important subzone of the commune of Barbaresco, others are happy to allow it the status of a cru proper. Our own sympathies lie with the latter, less pedantic school of thought; as in Burgundy the great crus of Barolo and Barbaresco are frequently extremely fragmented in their ownership.

Cesare Boschis of Giacomo Borgogno e Figli, based in the village of Barolo, believes that such confusion can only damage the name of Barolo. Despite owning land in some of the commune's prime sites, Borgogno are vehemently against making cru wines. Boschis claims that while in some years a wine from a particular site may show certain special characteristics, it can never be as complete as one made from a skilful blend of wines from the best zones. The legendary Luigi Pira, whom many remember as the greatest exponent of the old-school methods, made his Barolo from grapes grown on the four or five separate pieces of land he owned in the commune. Pira's argument in favour of the blended wine ran along the lines of, 'A cow knows where the best pastures in the village are, and produces its best milk as a result of grazing on all of them. It's the same with wine.' One well-known producer put it more bluntly: 'The good grapes have always compensated for the poor ones.'

The anti-cru lobby is, however, mainly made up of houses that rely on bought-in grapes, and whose reasons therefore have as much to do with the safeguarding of their sources of supply as with any firmly held convictions. Given the vast number of microclimates in the zone, the shortcomings in quality or quantity of a particular subzone in a lighter year are inevitable, while a blended Barolo may show a more consistent style. The blend, furthermore, has traditionally offered many larger producers the only way of producing saleable quantities of wine.

Today the motive for producing a cru is most likely to be a combination of authorial and commercial reasons. The most powerful argument remains the fact that most of the finest modern Baroli stem from the cru camp. Cru bottling is a logical progression for areas as small as Barolo and Barbaresco, whose combined production is a drop in the vinous ocean compared to regions like Bordeaux and Chianti. While there is still a strong case for generic Barolo, the area is ideally suited to 'limited production' wines.

MARKETING FOR BEGINNERS

The eagerness with which they have taken the cru concept to their hearts highlights another major issue confronting Albesi winemakers: the perplexing question of how to market their wines. The strenuous efforts taken to improve the quality of the product have in many cases yet to be matched by a clear understanding of how to sell it. The cru system has at least given producers the opportunity to present their wines as an attractive and exclusive package. The number of bottles produced is dutifully recorded on the carefully designed label, and the bottle gets taller, the glass thicker, the cork longer and the price higher. But for many producers the notion of marketing stops at the end of the bottling line. There is a general lack of interest or simple inability when it comes to investing similar efforts in the promotion of the product. A few larger firms with more substantial resources produce glossy brochures which are usually too full of what the Italians refer to as *poesia* to be of much use for export markets. So far only a handful of producers, notably the Ceretto brothers and Angelo Gaja, have come to grips with the idea of a dynamic marketing policy and the need to support it with their presence on an international stage.

The Profiles

The profiles are best seen as a series of snapshots: pictures of a particular place at a particular time in its development. Our study of the winemakers in the Langhe reflects the differing approaches that are currently typical in the zone, from the ultra-traditional to the ultra-modern, taking in most points in between. It also focuses on levels of production from the small-scale, 'one man band' style operation, through the medium-sized negociant house to the co-operative. The combination of these elements is intended to give a cross-section of winemaking in the Langhe today.

ELIO ALTARE: A Modern *Contadino*

Today's 'new wave' winemakers point to Angelo Gaja as their inspiration. He has shown them that the future lies with excellence and his own version of how it may be achieved. Eager to contribute something of themselves to the new identity for Albese wines, they continue their experiments. Waiting in the wings is a younger generation still – budding winemakers fresh from Enological School and young *contadino* farmers who, through the 1970s, grew up with the conflict between the 'traditional' and 'modern' schools of thought. They seem to have adopted a new mentor, a man still on the way up, with whom they can more readily identify: Elio Altare.

Elio, a small, wiry man with an impish grin, comes from a long line of *contadino* farmers. Records from the beginning of the nineteenth century show the Altare family's involvement with agriculture at Dogliani – where Elio was born in 1950 – just outside the Barolo zone to the south of Monforte d'Alba. The deeply rooted *contadino* mentality has had a profound effect on him. He remembers the bitter remark of his grandfather: 'You don't know what it feels like to be hungry' and learnt how he would light candles in church to give thanks for an 'abundant' harvest of 50 quintals per hectare. 'In those days,' Elio remarks, 'you couldn't be sure you'd have a harvest until you'd actually picked it. They had next to nothing to treat the vines with if anything went wrong.' The next generation remember how during the Second World War, the almost worthless copper coins were sold at a premium price so that they could be ground down and used as the basis for anti-cryptogamic treatments. In the 1950s a stability of sorts returned to the Langhe and even the smallest growers had access to the means of protecting their vines.

Elio's family moved to Cascina Nuova, a farm in the tiny village of Pozzo above Annunziata, when he was two months old. 'There are vineyards at Pozzo with tremendous potential,' Elio insists, 'but on the whole they've not been recognized yet. The *contadini* who farm them have to survive. They aim for a large harvest because the *commercianti* [traders] pay them so little for their grapes.' It is, not surprisingly, a subject very close to his heart. Elio studied agronomy for three years at Cravanzana in the alta Langa before beginning to take over at Cascina Nuova in 1976. He traded ideas with a group of like-minded young producers, Domenico Clerico, Luciano Sandrone and Roberto Voerzio, all of them looking for a way to put right the defects they saw in the Barolo they had grown up with. They decided to begin in the vineyards from the basis of top-quality grapes. 'We have to change the *contadino* mentality,' Elio maintains. 'If only the *commercianti* would pay a fair price for the grapes . . .' He added that as a grower he had approached some of the top negociant houses and offered to provide them with some of the best grapes they had ever seen, as long as they paid him the proper price for them. They refused.

In among his vines, Elio becomes a man possessed. His aim is to obtain the yields his grandfather realized half a century and more ago. He is certain that low yields are the basis of great wines and prunes

143

severely in order to achieve them. He leaves only one bunch to a shoot, usually the one closer to the base which receives more nourishment from the plant. Each vine, he claims, is capable of bearing no more than 1.5 kilos of great fruit. With barbera for example, for which he and his friends foresee a great future, Elio works with five or six buds per plant and anticipates a harvest of 20 quintals per hectare, giving him a final *resa in vino* of less than 15 hectolitres per hectare! 'I like concentrated wines,' he explains.

Elio identifies a need to reinterpret the old traditions. 'You see that hill over there?' he asks, pointing to Bricco San Biaggio which lies just behind his Arborina vineyard. 'You can see the trees on the crown of the hill, but do you know why they're there?' The roots of the trees, he explains, help to bind the soil together to lessen the effects of erosion after heavy rains. 'Our ancestors knew only that the *bricchi* should be wooded, they never stopped to wonder why.' Intuitive wisdom prevails still in the Langarolo's belief in *il terreno*. Elio notes the differences in terrain throughout Arborina and is constantly amazed how the wines from the different parcels vary. A more clayey soil, he has observed, gives a wine with denser structure, a patch of sand will produce a wine of great perfume but much less structure and colour, while the wine from one particular plot where there is a vein of sandy tufa with many stones, has a character all of its own. Elio cites the myriad differences in microclimate and terrain in the vineyards as the seat of the Langhe's greatness. 'By making great Cabernet and Chardonnay in addition to the great wines we already have here, Angelo Gaja has shown the world the true potential of the Langhe. We can do anything. There's no other region like it.'

Like many other growers these days, Elio has chosen to work the land without recourse to chemical fertilizers and toxic sprays – another reinterpretation of tradition. He thinks that his decision to have more respect for his environment may even have saved his life! Until the beginning of the eighties, the Altares farmed other kinds of fruit too. Elio recalls how at a particular time of the year he would suffer from a chronic throat complaint and a debilitating weight loss. The cause was eventually traced to an allergy to a particular type of spray applied to the family's peach trees. 'So I bought a chainsaw,' he grins.

Vinification still holds its mysteries for Altare. He does not exclude, for example, the possibility of other fermentations in addition to the alcoholic and malolactic ones: he notes that there is always an increase in bacterial activity in a wine at certain stages of the vineyard calendar, principally during flowering and the harvest. For this reason he is very careful about racking his wines off into wood at the right time.

Elio has launched himself into a period of intense experimentation as a result of the annual trip to Burgundy which he first undertook in the late 1970s. He has great admiration for Burgundian winemakers and their ability to produce wines that are balanced in their youth yet which have the ability to age well. Accustomed to Barolo which only began to drink after fifteen to twenty years, this was a revelation and provided the most important lesson in vinification he has learnt to date: 'A wine must be born with balance.'

His policy in the cellar therefore seems to be to leave no stone unturned. A barrage of new *barriques* containing Elio's 100 per cent nebbiolo *vino da tavola* 'Vigna Arborina' demonstrated the point. The wine was from a staggered harvest of four pickings over nearly two weeks: the wine from the grapes picked first was fresh with lively acidity and had perfumes of fresh fruits and flowers. It seemed as if every note on the scale was played down through to the wine from the final picking which had much more structure and perfumes of dried and preserved fruits. Elio felt the best result might be to blend and combine the various characteristics. He went on to explain that he was also trying out different kinds of wood to find out what effect that had and, furthermore, that some of the wines had undergone the malolactic fermentation in the *barriques* and some in stainless steel to see if that made a difference too! These restless probings reflect the perfectionist's need to understand every minor detail in his pursuit of the ideal form. What Elio learns from these experiments one year, he puts into practice the next, gradually refining his techniques from the experience.

There is less room for manoeuvre with Barolo, and Elio sticks to a more standardized approach. He feels that the winemaker has a basic choice between making a fresher, more perfumed wine or a richer, more structured one. At the moment he tends towards the former and aims to pick fairly early but has not ruled out the possibility of a staggered harvest here too. Where Vigna Arborina is fermented at between 22°C and 25°C, temperatures for Barolo will exceed this upper limit. Elio believes that the crucial part of the alcoholic fermentation takes place during the first 100 hours and although the process is fully complete after seven or eight days, he leaves the wine to macerate on the skins for a couple of days after that. The Barolo will then spend anything from one (strictly between ourselves that is!) to three years – depending on the vintage – in traditional oak *botti*.

Of Elio's other wines, Barbera has also been subjected to a battery of tests with different methods of vinification, including *ammostatura* (see p. 49). He seems, at least temporarily, to be happy with the system and the *barrique*-aged Vigna Larigi fully justifies his confidence: for such a concentrated wine it is remarkably polished and elegant. Similarly, Dolcetto appears to require little further finer tuning. As a wine with far greater uniformity of style throughout the zone, Dolcetto perhaps presents him with less of a challenge, although the vigour and easy charm expected of the variety seem to be overlaid with a distinctively suave and intense character in the Altare version.

Elio's total production is small: around 25,000 bottles a year made up of a few thousand of each style of wine. Having endured the customary apprenticeship of hardship and sacrifice, he is now in a position where the demand for his wines has begun to outstrip supply. They are eagerly sought after as far away as the USA. Elio seems less concerned with the burgeoning success than with making further improvements to the product. His eagerness to go on learning and his willingness to share his findings are almost unique in the Albese today. 'If we get together, we can help each other; we can taste together and learn from each other's experience.' Small wonder then that the next generation of Baroliste are already knocking at his door.

CERETTO: Taking on the World

'We would like to be known as great conservationists who make changes every day.' Bruno Ceretto pauses and smiles expectantly in anticipation of some acknowledgement that the irony implicit in his statement has not been lost. The carefully turned phrase reflects not only the Ceretto brothers' astute professionalism but also their burning desire to be recognized as leaders in the world of Albese wines.

Bruno and Marcello have done everything possible to see that ambition realized. Their investment has been massive: two extraordinarily impressive high-tech wineries, Bricco Asili and Bricco Rocche, in prime sites in Barbaresco and Barolo, a distillery in La Morra, a further winery and offices in central Alba, sole distribution rights for the Asti Spumante and Moscato d'Asti producers i Vignaioli di Santo Stefano and a huge warehouse/winery at Castellinaldo in the Roero complete with gleaming banks of state of the art autoclave for the production of their Arneis Blangé. However their latest project is the most spectacular by far.

La Bernadina is an 85-hectare estate close to the northwestern reaches of the Barolo zone just before the village of Gallo d'Alba. The estate dates back to 1880 and Vittorio Emanuele II. The property was built for his mistress La Bela Rosin and passed on to their son Conte Mirafiori.

The estate has been rented on a long lease from the present owner. The villa, which stands at the top of the hill, is not for the moment part of the plan, the brothers have rather turned their attention to the buildings (storehouses, cellars, stables, etc.) further down the hill. The interiors have been gutted to make way for new offices and another high-tech *cantina*. This has already become the new hub of their empire.

Following on from the trend in the zone towards 'mould-breaking wines', the brothers plan to turn La Bernadina into an experimental station, concentrating principally on white wines. The contours of the surrounding hills have been carefully bulldozed into shape and 30 hectares are to be planted with a roll call of hallowed grape varieties. Bruno read us the list from a magazine article on the project: '. . . cabernet sauvignon, pinot nero, merlot, chardonnay, sauvignon, viognier, semillon. . .'. Production levels will be kept small (5,000–6,000 bottles per wine style) from yields of around 40 quintals per hectare. *Barriques* may well be used 'for those varieties traditionally aged in them'. By late 1988, eight hectares of chardonnay, one hectare of cabernet and half a hectare of merlot had already been planted in preparation for what Bruno calls *il confronto* (presumably the wine world's equivalent of Judgement Day) when the brothers will be ready to take on the world with international as well as indigenous grape varieties. Masterminding vinification techniques at La Bernadina will be the up and coming enologist Donato Lanati.

Since they relinquished their interest in the Canale-based Arneis estate La Cornarea, the Cerettos have become increasingly involved with white wine production. 1988 was the fourth vintage for Arneis Blangé (the name, a common enough one around Alba, means 'baker's vineyard') and their growing confidence and expectations in this medium have led not only to the investment in La Bernadina but also to the plan to extend their existing 20 hectares of Arneis vineyards at Vezza. Their plant at Castellinaldo looks unpromising from the outside but the interior is a technological treasure trove. Each stainless steel autoclave is not only fully computerized giving complete control over the temperature, carbon dioxide pressure and sugar density during fermentation, but is also linked up to a VDU. This can display in the form of a graph exactly what is happening inside each vessel at any given moment and has an additional print-out option. Up-to-the-minute techniques like hyperoxidation have been looked at and abandoned (they felt it impoverished the must). Under the guidance of 25-year-old enologist Daniele Mauro – the Cerettos are surrounding themselves with youthful energy these days – they have opted for the 'modern classic' formula for white wine vinification: following a water-operated pneumatic pressing at 1.5 atmospheres – only the first run of juice is used – the must is clarified at 15°C with gelatine and silicates over eight hours and then racked clean. Any premature fermentation is prevented by the addition of 2 grams per hectolitre of sulphur dioxide. A proportion of cold-macerated must (40 per cent with the 1988) is added and fermentation started with the inoculation of a yeast culture taken from local grapes to ensure *tipicità*. Vinification takes place at 16–18°C (tests carried out with the University of Turin have led to the conclusion that a minimum of perfumes are lost at this temperature). The malolactic is avoided by careful filtration and the desired straw-yellow colour maintained by retaining a small proportion of polyphenols. Unfortunately, Blangé so far seems too much of a 'formula' wine and 'makes a virtue out of its neutrality' as one critic put it. This has not however stood in the way of a highly successful sales campaign.

Yet when we turn to Barbaresco and Barolo, Ceretto have clearly got the formula right. The hard work was put in during the sixties and seventies after the brothers had inherited the business from their father Riccardo. Since the mid-thirties he had been buying in grapes and wine and selling more in bulk than bottle. Bruno and Marcello set about selecting the right vineyards (esteemed names like Cannubi and Villero were tried and rejected) and Marcello, the winemaker, perfected a system based on the tenets of modern vinification methods for extracting the best out of the grapes. He was among the first to use stainless steel for fermentation, abandoned *cappello sommerso* in favour of frequent *rimontaggi* during a two-week maceration, and introduced induced *malo* followed by a minimal stay in large oak *botti*. Marcello is firmly opposed to the use of *barrique* for nebbiolo (there again he was sceptical of the virtues of planting cabernet and chardonnay in Alba a few years ago). The current range is extremely impressive. There are three cru Baroli and two cru Barbareschi:

Table 5

Vineyard	Size	Aspect	Altitude	Commune	Annual average production
Bricco Rocche	1.8 ha	SW	312–340 m	Castiglione F.	5/6,000 btls
Brunate	6.5 ha	S	276–342 m	La Morra	35/40,000 btls
Prapò	3 ha	SSE	310–370 m	Serralunga	13/15,000 btls
Bricco Asili	1.2 ha	SSE	260–320 m	Barbaresco	8,000 btls
Bricco Faset	1 ha	S	240–270 m	Barbaresco	7,000 btls

As Bricco Rocche and Bricco Faset have only recently come into production, it is too early to offer a realistic evaluation of them although signs are very promising. The others are all stylish and well-balanced wines, even in poorer vintages: Brunate, as befits its origins, tends to be a softer, more richly flavoured and accessible wine than the firmer, more structured and slightly austere (though still elegant) Prapò. The scented, supple and beautifully balanced Bricco Asili is arguably the finest wine the firm produces. In addition Ceretto market Barolo Zonchera which is based on the grapes from three growers in the *conca* between Brunate and Cerequio (though there are no prizes for guessing where Bricco Rocche ends up in less favourable vintages) and Barbaresco Asij (Piemontese for Asili) made from grapes grown 'further down the hill'. The other Albese wines Dolcetti Rosanna and Vigna, Barbera Piana and Nebbiolo Lantasco are also produced; from the 1989 vintage onwards they will be made at La Bernadina. The excellent sparkling moscato wines from partners i Vignaioli di Santo Stefano complete the Ceretto range.

One of the most durable contributions the brothers, and Bruno in particular, have made to the world of Barolo is through their presence in and effect on the marketplace. Few other wine personalities have attacked the question of marketing with such vigour; it is a subject most Albesi fight shy of. While in the early days Bruno's rhetoric may have been as subtle as a battering ram, it proved to be as effective, breaking down doors hitherto firmly closed on fine Italian wine. Owing to his typical Langarolo brusqueness, Bruno has had his fair share of critics but nowadays he seems to have mellowed, projecting a more benign exterior to the world and seemingly content with the epigrammatic utterance. The zenith of the new found magnanimity came in September 1986 when the brothers presided over a symposium on 'The Image of Barolo' attended by an international gathering of journalists and winemakers and a banquet dreamed up by some of the world's best known chefs, in celebration of the launch of Barolo Bricco Rocche Bricco Rocche 1982 (Bricco Rocche is a winery as well as a vineyard thus there is also a Bricco Rocche Brunate, etc.). Public relations on the grand scale had finally arrived in Barolo.

Marcello has, over the years, remained the quiet one. A small, dapper man, sensitive and serious, Marcello seems more at home in the company of fermentation vats and oak *botti* than *glitterati*. His work in the cellar is the foundation stone of the firm's success. Happily some of the other growers are beginning to benefit from his wisdom and look to the quiet man at the top of the hill (Marcello lives at Bricco Rocche) for help and advice on questions of winemaking technique.

Whether or not it is what they have actively sought, the Cerettos are becoming the 'new establishment' in Barolo. It is a perilous position, attained by setting themselves and their wines up as examples and therefore as targets to be tilted at. Other producers are beginning to gather for their turn. For the moment the pressure seems to be spurring them on to greater things: the La Bernadina project will long remain a major talking point. Its success or failure can ultimately reflect on only one thing: Barolo. All roads, however circuitous, lead there. The current view as expressed by Bruno is another masterpiece of overstatement:

> Barolo is like a beautiful, untouchable woman. Here in Italy she is rarely to be encountered between the sheets. . . But Barolo is a wine that needs to be drunk. Let us make 2 million bottles of great Barolo and call the rest something else. Otherwise confusion reigns.

CONSORZIO OF ALBESE WINES

Many producers belong to the Associazione Consorzi del Barolo, del Barbaresco e dei Vini d'Alba which nowadays operates as a single body. Founded in 1934, following a sixty-year gestation period after the first official attempt to compile a list of 'authentic producers of typical wine' in 1873, the present-day Consorzio is funded almost entirely by the contributions of its members. The Consorzio targets the domestic market for a revitalized sales drive. 'The home market can absorb a far greater share of our production,' insists Antonio Maggiore, the Consorzio's secretary. 'We must concentrate on the two areas of tradition and quality. There are few enough wines around today that are both classic and typical: we must reaffirm the excellence of our *vini storici*.' Promotion – advertising, trade fairs and press releases – accounts for between 40 and 50 per cent of the Consorzio's activities these days. The work has become easier of late according to Maggiore with the new breed of winemakers who have sought to highlight primary fruit flavours in their wines. 'We are still experimenting with different approaches to the art of winemaking. By the late nineties', Maggiore claims , 'we'll see a more unified style.'

The cultivation of the domestic market remains, for the moment, a very practical strategy – the Consorzio has neither the time nor the resources to carry out too many in-depth studies of foreign markets. With 140 members, ranging from the largest single source of Barolo, the Terre del Barolo cooperative, to the sort of one-man operation turning out less than 1,000 cases a year, their time is taken up with matters closer to home. While the list of members includes some of the zone's most celebrated names, Aldo Conterno, Bartolo Mascarello, Produttori di Barbaresco, Scarpa and Vietti, the Consorzio has never enjoyed the full support of all the region's winemakers. Individualists like Giovanni Conterno, the Ceretto brothers and Angelo Gaja will always prefer to pursue their own course. This does not, however, prevent the Consorzio from offering a valuable service, particularly to the small grower.

In addition to their promotional work, the Consorzio has two other principal functions: quality control and an advice and information service. The first runs parallel to the state control operated through the Ministry of Forestry and Agriculture. The Consorzio administers their policies, carrying out frequent checks on members' cellars to ensure official dictates are being adhered to, and sends out circulars notifying proposed changes in legislation. Samples for analysis and tasting allow them to monitor quality standards before the official Consorzio seal is granted to a wine and they are often approached to evaluate wines about to be submitted for DOC(G) approbation. This aspect of their work overlaps with their third consultative function which involves direct interpretation of the law. Members are advised on questions of winemaking and labelling within the particular DOC(G) discipline, as well as how to complete the necessary documentation to accompany wines destined for export. The Consorzio also possesses the sort of facilities that many small growers lack and maintain their own laboratory above the offices in central Alba; as vintage time approaches, they will monitor the ripeness of grapes from fifteen sites in Barolo and five in Barbaresco, keeping members fully updated with their findings.

Their ability to identify and advise on winemaking faults is much more of a grey area: there is often a thin line to be drawn between a fault and a preferred individual style, especially where the hard-headed Albesi are concerned. 'We always try to work with the producer to determine the cause of the fault in a wine. Normally we come to an agreement though at times it's difficult,' Maggiore admits. He is quick to add that there are fewer faults evident today now that producers take greater pains in their quest for a more elegant wine.

ALDO CONTERNO: Old but Young

If you were to spot Aldo Conterno on a Sunday afternoon, playing cards on the terrace of the café in Monforte's village square, you would at first assume him to be the typical Langhe hill-farmer. Aldo's short, wiry white hair and his brown, walnut-wrinkled face give away few clues to his open-minded approach to winemaking, but enthusiasm burns brightly in his eyes. Many would argue that this man is today the single greatest winemaker in Barolo.

As an English-speaking visitor to the Cascina Favot winery, perched on a bend on the high road between Castiglione Falletto and Monforte, you may be left to string together your meagre vocabulary of Italian for a good half-hour before Aldo gives you a taste of his generous and gravelly Brooklyn baritone. There is no doubt that a three-year term of military service spent in the USA in the early 1950s broadened Aldo's outlook on the world. The Conterno's family winery, Giacomo Conterno (p.157) run by grandfather Giovanni and then father Giacomo, was synonymous with the best in Barolo, particularly in the form of the legendary Monfortino *riserva speciale*. Aldo had planned to set up a new cellar in partnership with an uncle. However, the uncle died, and Aldo returned from America to work with his father and brother Giovanni. Giovanni was steadfastly sticking to the winemaking principles of the two previous generations. Aldo's desire to experiment and innovate sparked off an explosive

personality conflict. The younger returning soldier confronted the older brother, a farmer whose roots in the soil stretched as deep as a 100-year-old vine.

By the mid-1960s their father Giacomo had fallen ill. It was clear that there was no hope of synthesis, the only conclusion was division. In 1969 Aldo and Giovanni split the Conterno estate in half. Aldo took half of the family vineyards and half the wine stocks. Unlike the latter-day parallel of the Voerzio brothers, however, the cellar was not divided by a brick wall. Instead Aldo moved out of the village to build a new cellar, while Giovanni carried on in Monforte village with the established Giacomo Conterno name. Today both brothers are near the top of the tree, but Aldo suffered his share of cuts and bruises getting there. 'I had to start with a new name. Even being a Conterno it was not easy,' he says with characteristic understatement. The brothers still rarely talk to one another.

Aldo Conterno's estate now covers 25 hectares of vineyards, mostly in the prized Bussia zone of Monforte. Nine hectares are planted to nebbiolo, with five hectares each of dolcetto and freisa, another three of barbera, two newly planted hectares of chardonnay and one of arneis, as well as a pocket-handkerchief-sized plot of grignolino. The barolo vines date back forty years and produce yields of no more than

70 quintals of grapes per hectare. Aldo's approach in the vineyard is to use as little fertilizer as possible, to spray only with Bordeaux mixture and to reduce yields by pruning the new bunches of grapes in early summer to leave only one or two per branch. According to Conterno, this practice is traditional in Barolo, and has been carried out for as long as anyone can remember.

Vineyard owners have problems finding labour. 'It is hard to find people to work in the vineyard today, they have all gone to work in the factories of Miroglio or Ferrero in Alba. To get them back we would have to pay double.' Aldo can afford to pay a little above the average because he can sell his wine for higher prices, but he imagines it would be impossible for someone starting out. 'I produce 150–180 tonnes of grapes each year. If I bought them in rather than producing them myself, I would save 60–70 million lire every year.' The artificially low price of grapes is perpetuated by the *contadino*, the small farmer who works fourteen hours a day, seven days a week, and who may have his income supplemented by a pension.

The Conterno cellar is well equipped, with modern stainless steel, temperature-controlled fermentation tanks and spotless rows of *botti*. The ambient temperature is automatically kept at 15°C all year round. Aldo now regrets that the ageing cellar was built in concrete rather than brick, because the concrete dries out the air too much, causing even full *botti* to leak in summer if they are not doused frequently with water. A new brick maturation area is now being built on the hill at the back of the winery. The Aldo Conterno approach to vinification is summed up in his own words: 'The wine must always be kept clean, clean, clean!' Even the large oak casks are rigorously scraped to remove all tartrate deposits. Fermentation techniques are very flexible, the precise maceration period and temperature depending on the character of the grapes and the way the wine is intended to be aged.

Aldo's Barolo is made by fairly traditional methods, with *cappello sommerso* avoided in light vintages. He is adamant that a wine destined to be called Barolo must be made according to a traditional formula. 'Great Barolo must be made in a certain way, from certain vineyards . . . and the result may not be to everyone's taste.' Thus for Aldo, *barrique*-aged wines should never be called Barolo. Conterno's own small family of Baroli are grown on the superbly exposed slopes of the Bussia vineyard. They are wines that always display great complexity of perfume and flavour, supported by a taut chassis of tannin. Above all they achieve poise and balance; it would be unreasonable to demand greater finesse from so masculine a wine.

The Barolo is graded into three classes: Bussia Soprana is a selection from all Conterno's Barolo vineyards in the upper part of Bussia, while Vigna Cicala and Vigna Colonello are individual sites of just over one hectare and just under one hectare respectively. In special vintages Gran Bussia is made. Gran Bussia is a selection of the very cream from each cru. The selection is made in the cellar after careful study of the development of each cask, but the basis is always the wine from the Romirasco vineyard. Added to this are varying proportions of Ciabot, Cicala and Colonello vineyards. The assemblage takes place after three years age in *botte*, after which the final blend is kept for another three years in small 10-hectolitre stainless steel tanks where the wine matures as slowly as possible before bottling. This unusual technique is an updating of the traditional practice of ageing in demijohn for an intermediary period between cask and bottle. The end result is a wine of extraordinary depth and richness with an apparent capacity for unlimited maturation in bottle.

Aldo never tires of expounding his passionate philosophy: 'The wine should be old but *young*. It's like a person, you see. We get old anyway. The idea would be to slow down the ageing. A twenty-year-old girl may be beautiful. Well, that's nothing special, all twenty-year-old girls are good-looking. Now when you've got a forty-year-old woman who's beautiful, that's something special!' To prove that he was well on the way to discovering the vinous elixir of youth, Aldo showed us a 1974 Bussia Soprana that had been aged for about seven years in 12.5 litre bottles (a quarter *brenta*), stored under sand to minimize temperature fluctuation and rebottled in 75 centilitre size in 1984. The colour was surprisingly dark, the bouquet still floral and fresh with hints of aniseed, and the palate rich, spicy, and well knit. The only sign of the wine's true age was the way the tannin gave such an understated contribution on the finish.

Aldo Conterno's championing of 'traditional' Barolo does not mean that he is excluded from the fun of experimenting with *barrique*. In 1984, for example, he made no Barolo at all; all the nebbiolo was vinified with a brief maceration and transferred to *barrique* for between four and twelve months depending on the age of the individual cask. There are currently eighty French oak 225-litre casks in the cellar, and Aldo buys in more each year. The result is a *vino da tavola* called Favot, soft and accessible with well-controlled oak flavours. The other wine that goes into *barrique* is Barbera Conca Tre Pile, a wild success in Germany. Apart from an excellent Dolcetto, Conterno is famous for Freisa 'La Bussianella'. Dark, dry, ripely fruity and perfumed, the wine has a slight fizz and a sediment due to a second fermentation in bottle. Thankfully, strong local demand ensures the survival of this *avis rara*.

'The wine business is wonderful', says Aldo with a twinkle in his eye, 'because there are always surprises. So you should never stop trying.' It is hard to imagine that he ever will. The new Chardonnay is certainly worth looking forward to, and the 1985 Gran Bussia will doubtless be a new and monumental milestone. Aldo's sons Franco and Stefano have already graduated from Alba's Enological School, and will surely follow in their father's footsteps. It is hard to avoid suggesting that Aldo is the perfect embodiment of his own maxim, 'old but young'.

GIOVANNI CONTERNO (AZIENDA VITIVINICOLA GIACOMO CONTERNO): Intuitive Wisdom

Change happens slowly in the Langhe. The effect of the 'revolution' in winemaking which began in the late 1960s is only now starting to be felt in certain cellars in the Albese and seems to have bypassed others completely. Several old-school *Baroliste* of iron resolve have refused to deviate from the principles laid down by their fathers and grand-fathers. But the passion with which they uphold these customs is in itself an indication of how tenuous their position is: they are probably the last in line.

Where avant-garde winemakers like Elio Altare argue for a 'reinterpretation of traditional values', a hardy few continue to live those values out. Prominent amongst the last great defenders of the faith is Giovanni Conterno. Beneath the stern face and lean, sinewy

frame burn the passions of over two centuries of Langhe hill-farming tradition. His proud and determined commitment is matched by a frosty, rather severe manner. He is renowned for his bluntness, but it is often relieved by a touch of grim humour: 'Having an enologist in the *cantina* is like having a doctor in the house: it means there's something wrong!'

Conterno's approach to winemaking has the same basis as had his forefathers': a combination of intuitive knowledge and vast experience. It starts in the vineyard where Giovanni will time, where possible, his various viticultural tasks to coincide with the phases of the moon. As with his refusal to harvest any but the finest grapes grown on his 17-hectare Cascina Francia estate in Serralunga, the reasoning behind it is straightforward: 'We've always done it this way.' Conterno's mainly west-southwest facing vineyards overlook well-known Monforte sites like Ginestra across the valley of the Talloria di Castiglione. They are very steep in parts and wholly exposed to the vagaries of the weather. It is the way Giovanni wants it – arguing that in a well-ventilated site, there is less danger of humidity-related diseases – but he often has a terrible price to pay. To watch Giovanni pruning, arms outstretched as he reaches upwards towards the top wire of his 2-metre-plus-high trellis, he seems to be crucified on his vines. It is, however, not stones he attracts, but hail. Conterno lost his entire crop in 1986 during the famous storm at the end of May. In 1989, when some growers suffered a reduction of 25–40 per cent because of hail in the early summer, Conterno's nebbiolo vines were devastated once again and he expects to make no Barolo in this vintage either. As if that wasn't enough, he will sell off all his crop when the quality of the fruit falls below what he considers to be an acceptable level: he didn't make any Barolo in 1981 or 1984 for that reason. A minimal amount of copper sulphate solution is the only treatment he ever applies to his vines and the vineyards are fertilized solely before planting – clippings from the winter pruning are the only other source of nourishment to the soil.

Giovanni's obduracy is rather less apparent in the cellars. His new winery is built on the outskirts of Monforte just two minutes' walk from the village centre. His *cantina* is a remarkable contrast to the typical tiny, cramped cellars of the region. It is a spacious modern building with lofty ceilings and wide aisles between the rows of old *botti*; Giovanni's voice echoes all around as it rises to fever pitch in his defiant defence of the old system. But the concerned frown that continually wrinkles his forehead suggests that he too is beginning to turn over in his mind the wisdom of carrying on in this way. Computerized stainless steel fermentation tanks lining the walls of the brick and concrete cathedral confirm that not only the spirit of the law is being questioned.

For many years Giovanni resisted any form of compromise in the cellar. He relied upon his innate ability to recognize *il momento giusto* (the right moment) at which to draw the new wine off its skins (sometimes after a couple of months), or when to rack or bottle it. During the autumn he would doze the nights away beside the old fermentation tanks in case a sudden rise in temperature should threaten to send the bubbling must out of control. He would neither fine nor filter his wines nor use any sulphur on bottling them. Perhaps the most extreme measure of all was his policy on cask ageing. His Barolo Monfortino Riserva Speciale would spend ten, twelve or even fifteen years in wood (part, at least, of the 1970 vintage was not bottled until 1984). His perception of *il momento giusto* was guided solely by his palate: only when the tannins seemed to have reached the desired stage in their development would Giovanni consider a change of vessel appropriate.

Monfortino is the foundation stone of the Conterno family's fame. First made by his grandfather in 1912, the wine was conceived as an attempt to explore the limits of the possible with Barolo and thereby to set new standards for it. Monfortino was originally made from the best possible grapes grandfather Conterno could buy from the communes of Castiglione Falletto, Monforte and Serralunga (Giovanni no longer buys in grapes and since the mid-seventies has made wine from his Cascina Francia vineyard only). The grandfather – a tremendous influence on Giovanni – seems to have been quite a character. Armed with a hunting licence and a gun he would embark on a tour of the vineyards two weeks before the harvest. He never shot a thing: he was finding out who had the best grapes that year! It was quite an honour to sell your grapes to Conterno and if he'd bought some there was little difficulty in selling the rest.

There has been much conjecture about how Monfortino is made. Some of the more popular theories are that it is made from a proportion of later-harvested, semi-dried grapes or that it comes from a special selection of fruit from the best spots in the vineyard or from a staggered harvest. However it may have been made in the past, and Giovanni is notoriously reluctant to give away his secrets, it is nowadays solely a question of different fermentation techniques that distinguish Monfortino from Conterno's regular Barolo. The regular undergoes a 'linear' fermentation at a constant temperature of 26–7°C whereas Monfortino will be allowed to build up rapidly to a peak of around 30°C right at the beginning. Over the course of the next day or so, Giovanni brings the temperature back down to 24°C and finally allows it to climb gradually back to 27°C for the remainder of the fermentation. Where up to fifteen years in cask was once common for Monfortino, Giovanni contents himself with six or seven these days (the 1982 was bottled in the summer of 1989) and four years is now the norm for the regular, whereas it used to be considerably more.

Monfortino is made in lots of 7,000 or 8,000 bottles in only the better vintages (during the last twenty years, 1970, 1971, 1974, 1978, 1979, 1982, 1985 and 1987) out of a total of around 30–35,000 bottles of Barolo. Conterno produces three other wines: Barbera (20,000 bottles per annum), Dolcetto (32,000 bottles per annum) and a small amount of Freisa (3.5–4000 bottles per annum). In 1989 he made his first experimental batch of Chardonnay from bought-in grapes. 'If everyone else is doing it . . .' seems to be the new way of thinking.

Giovanni has never been one to theorize. 'Winemaking is not an exact science' is as much of an insight as he is likely to let slip. He describes himself as 'an old donkey' and seems to be looking forward to the day when son Roberto will take over at the helm. Roberto has inherited his father's stubborn streak but has a bright, enquiring mind: he will no doubt explore new directions for the Monfortino dynasty.

The Conterno wines are, like Giovanni himself, famous for their uncompromising character. They are precise reflections of their particular vintage; in 1985 both Barbera and Dolcetto were rich and concentrated wines of awesome structure, in 1987 they were forward, ripely fruity wines ready to drink as soon as they were bottled. The amount of time that the wines spend on the skins or in the cask depends entirely on the nature of the crop. With the exception of Freisa, all his wines are nowadays vinified at carefully controlled temperatures (a maximum of 27°C for Barbera and 25–6°C for Dolcetto) using *cappello sommerso*. Indeed this first concession to the new technology has persuaded him to continue making Monfortino – he once talked of discontinuing it owing to the risks involved with working at higher temperatures. The ability to exercise greater control over the fermentation process is something that even the most die-hard traditionalist welcomes. Giovanni is delighted with the way the 1982 has turned out, comparing it gleefully with the legendary 1971.

Tasting an older Barolo with Conterno, his 1958 for example, it is hard to see how the 'old ways' could be improved upon. Wines like that have earned him the sobriquet of 'Il Papa' of Barolo even amongst the more extreme modernist winemakers. Any change in the near future is likely to revolve around a 'reinterpretation of traditional values' as long as Giovanni is in charge. The severe expression on his lined and weatherbeaten face is more often replaced with a flashing smile these days. He is too much the crafty Langarolo to give up what he has fought so hard to preserve.

ANGELO GAJA: The Path of Quality

'Angelo Gaja è numero uno in Italia.' These words were uttered not by one of Alba's new breed of young winemakers who hold Gaja as their idol, but by the master of traditional Barolo, Bartolo Mascarello. Gaja's worldwide fame and success are not in question; what remains perhaps surprising to the person who has not met the man is how he has achieved so much while making so few enemies.

Gaja has created a position for himself that is at once lofty and accessible. On the deserted main street of the village of Barbaresco, facing the blank façade of the Gaja winery, whose solemn brass plate warns that unannounced visitors will not be admitted, you may be forgiven for thinking of Kafka's *Castle*. Once the massive electrically operated gates have parted you will cross a spacious, sober courtyard to Gaja's reception area. In this large, high-ceilinged, whitewashed concrete structure , furnished with futuristic armchairs of the Magistretti school, you could easily believe that you have wandered into a small gallery of modern art: abstract paintings and prints cover the walls.

Any feeling of coldness is dispelled on meeting Angelo Gaja, whose energy and enthusiasm are communicated by the lively, deep-set eyes and the expressive expanse of forehead which is continually arching in questioning curiosity or wrinkling in a frown of concentration. Gaja's *tour de force*, apart from his winemaking and marketing prowess, is his gift for communication. Watching the forceful gesticulations that are used to underline all important points, the first thing that comes across is Gaja's passion for wine. Then the power of the man's arguments becomes apparent. The Gaja philosophy is constructed on a rock-solid foundation of logic. Gaja's work with Barbaresco might be compared to that of a precision engineer. He has painstakingly dismantled Barbaresco, taking apart the nuts and bolts of vineyard and cellar technique, and most significantly the marketing approach. Every last part of the machine has then been put under the microscope and examined for flaws. If necessary, parts have been replaced with new ones, otherwise cleaned meticulously. Finally he has reassembled Barbaresco, and it looks different: gleaming, sleek and modern in Gaja's version, but still true to its traditional proportions. Ultimately the analogy is restrictive; if Gaja is an engineer, then he is one who writes sonnets in his tea break. For all their modernity, Gaja's best wines are not devoid of soul.

The reasoning behind Gaja's policy of innovation becomes clear when he talks of the problems faced by the current generation of Albesi. As the largest vineyard owner in the commune of Barbaresco with 31 hectares, Gaja could not afford to allow the public's growing apathy towards the famous Nebbioli go unchallenged. Gaja believes that the quality potential of 85 per cent of the nebbiolo vineyards in the Langhe is reasonably good. The problem lies rather in a discrepancy between production and demand. Gaja thinks that given a lack of agreement between producers, it is up to the individual winemaker to choose his own path. For Gaja the route is quality – the vagaries of climate and terrain prohibit the production of quantity. 'Listen! An absolute maximum of fifty producers (in Barolo and Barbaresco) are capable of selling their entire production every year. The others have to look for new markets. I don't know . . .' Gaja's discourse is punctuated by a typical shrug of the shoulders, '. . . maybe the moon . . .', Gaja's hand stretches toward the ceiling, 'or Russia?'

In brand-crazy Italy, it is the famous names who sell wine today. Gaja has marketed his own name heavily; on a plain, elegant black and

white label the word 'Gaja' is four times larger than the word
'Barbaresco'. With his plantings of French varieties chardonnay,
cabernet sauvignon and sauvignon blanc, Gaja has got the world
talking. The Chardonnay has been hailed by some critics as Italy's
finest. But in the end the small production of these internationally
styled wines is aimed to shed more light on Gaja's Barbaresco.

In 1988 Gaja staged another major publicity coup in buying 28
hectares of prime Barolo vineyards: the Marenca-Rivette cru in the
Serralunga valley. 'I never had a specific intention to enter Barolo',
says Gaja, 'but my father had always bought grapes from this area,
and I knew it was a unique opportunity.' From his first Barolo
vintage, 1988, some 2,000 cases will be produced. The figure is set
to increase to 5,000 cases when all the new plantings are in full
production. The rest of the Barolo vineyard will be planted to other
grapes: either arneis, barbera, chardonnay or cabernet. 'It will take
time to get to know the vineyard,' says Gaja. Doubtless, archrival
Ceretto will have a few sleepless nights before he tastes Gaja's
Barolo.

Gaja still sees Barbaresco as his major vocation, however. The path
of quality is made economically viable in two ways. Firstly, in lesser
years up to 50 per cent of his Barbaresco production is sold in bulk;
secondly, about 100,000 bottles' worth (or more in poor vintages) of
lesser quality nebbiolo grapes are vinified either as Vinot Novello,
bottle-fermented sparkling white Nebbiolo, or young Nebbiolo delle
Langhe *vino da tavola*. This compares with production of about
150,000 bottles of Barbaresco.

Gaja's road to quality has been one of gradual, logical experimentation and a perfectionist fervour to improve his wines. Complimenting
Angelo on the near-perfect balance and depth of flavour of his 1982
cru Barbaresco Sori' Tildin, the reply came back, 'Yes, it is good. But
wait till you taste the '85, our fermentation technology has improved
enormously since '82.'

The Gaja family firm was founded in 1859. While owning good
vineyards, the company was not known as one of the great names of
Albese wine until the influence of Angelo's grandmother was felt. Born
in France, Clotilde Rey married into the family in 1905. According to
Angelo, 'She had a big impact on the company's philosophy. She
pushed both my father and grandfather in the direction of quality.'

The grandmother is honoured in the names of two of Gaja's vineyards: Vignarey (Barbera d'Alba) and Gaia & Rey (Chardonnay). The feminine influence in the firm today is Angelo's wife, Lucia, a powerful character both behind the scenes and in the administration of the company. In the 1950s, under the direction of Angelo's father Giovanni, the company had a larger output than today; some grapes were bought in, including those for a generic Barolo. In 1960 Angelo graduated from Alba's school of enology where he received a grounding in traditional winemaking techniques. At this time his father gave him responsibility for managing the company vineyards. During the 1960s Angelo was a frequent traveller to France, studying at Domaine de l'Espiguette, an experimental winery near Montpellier, and also making occasional trips to Burgundy and Bordeaux. In the early 1970s he also began to visit California where he examined the use of new oak in more detail.

During the 1960s the seeds of future excellence were sown. In 1964 the company adopted a radically shorter pruning technique, using only ten buds per vine, to reduce yields. In 1969 Angelo's curiosity about the effects of small oak-cask ageing resulted in his first delivery of 225-litre *barriques*. In the same year a heating plant was installed in the *cantina* to help provoke the malolactic fermentation immediately after the alcoholic fermentation, thus stabilizing the wine at the earliest possible time.

In 1970 the reins were handed from Giovanni to Angelo, who at this time chose another Babareschite graduate of the Alba Enological School, Guido Rivella, as his enologist and collaborator. Experimentation with *barriques* continued until the 1976 vintage when Gaja saw fit to release a controversial Barbaresco partially aged in small oak casks. Trials with carbonic maceration meanwhile lead to the production of what is claimed to be Italy's first *novello*: Vinot. Other developments in the cellar included the use of nitrogen at all stages of production to banish any hint of oxidation. Angelo does not disguise his contempt for the worst, volatile, orange-coloured examples of 'old-style' Barbaresco. A major victory in his quest for cleaner wines was the installation in 1983 of a high-tech computerized fermentation system. This gives precise temperature control at all times, allowing maximum extraction of fruit flavours without an overload of harsh grape-skin tannins. Whereas the 1961 Barbaresco had spent some seventy-five days macerating on the skins, this had been reduced to a mere fifteen days for the 1983.

Gaja's wood-ageing practice for Barbaresco (also to be followed for Barolo) is to combine the best of *barrique* and *botte*, keeping the wine some six months in small oak before moving it on to the traditional large casks for another year. The aim is not to create a more oaky wine, but rather one of greater finesse. Only a third of Gaja's *barriques* are new, and these are first steamed to tame the aggression of the new wood. 'When I first considered using small barrels', says Angelo, 'my thought was not of new oak. Tasting the wines of my father, I had verified that wines kept in wood for four, five or six years had lost body and become harder.' The new generation of Gaja wines are held in bottle for one year before sale, and are designed to go on improving in bottle for decades. For Gaja, the *barrique* is only a step in the process of refinement, not an end in itself.

Gaja shares with all great winemakers the belief that the single most important factor in determining the quality of a wine is the state of the grapes. Vinification is rated by Gaja as second most important, with wood ageing contributing a maximum 10 per cent to the quality of the finished product. In the vineyard, the Gaja principle of elegance before power is applied. In 1986 the grapes for the cru Barbera Vignarey were harvested one week before their maximum ripeness, thus avoiding a rich but ultimately overpowering wine of 15 per cent alcohol. Similarly, the moment for picking cabernet sauvignon is now decided by tasting the grapes to check their flavour rather than just measuring their sugar level.

For all Gaja's innovations, he remains an admirer of tradition, particularly in Barolo where he cites the examples of Giovanni Conterno and Bartolo Mascarello. Gaja's warning to Barolo producers is 'be careful not to destroy this important monument' by radically altering the character of the wine. 'There are bad innovations, just as there are bad traditions,' he says with a smile. 'In Barbaresco perhaps it was easier for me to change. Barbaresco has always been a bit of an underdog, the parameters were less clearly defined than in Barolo where tradition is very strong.'

If there is one aspect of Gaja's logic that has attracted negative criticism, it is his pricing policy. Gaja's Barbaresco *normale* is double the price of wines from many other top-rated producers in the area.

The legendary cru Barbareschi – Sori' Tildin, Sori' San Lorenzo and Costa Russi – now retail for more than Bordeaux first growths of a comparable vintage. Gaja's adoption of an *en primeur* policy of selling futures of the best vintages reinforces the impression of a lofty, arrogant attitude. And yet in Italy, it is precisely this apparent élitism that has won Gaja the designer chic cachet: if you have made it, then a good way of letting the world know is to be seen to be drinking Gaja.

Not that the other producers are complaining. Gaja has attracted plenty of publicity to the Langhe, and most importantly he has virtually single-handedly elevated Barbaresco's international reputation. From the beginning Angelo Gaja has aimed to set himself above the competition, he has started from the top not merely in terms of price but also in the quality of his product. Behind the high prices lies a continual process of research, renovation and improvement in cellar and vineyard. Gaja's PR efforts also involve considerable costs. Currently he spends some two or three months each year in the USA, his most important export market. His method of promoting his wines is not that of a salesman, but rather that of a chess grand master turned showman. With endless patience Gaja expounds the concepts behind his wines, rehearsing aloud the steps in the great plan.

While he continues to sell all his wine, Gaja must be judged a highly skilled interpreter of the market. It is rumoured that his real profits come not from wine making, but from his upmarket Italian wholesale division, Gaja Distribution. Gaja Distribution has a well-conceived portfolio of luxury agencies including Domaine de la Romanee-Conti, a selection of Bordeaux first growths and Sauternes, various California boutique wineries, Riedel glasses and Screwpull corkscrews.

And why has Gaja made so few enemies? While he could not be called modest, Angelo nevertheless avoids a dogmatic mentality. He will press the palm of one hand to his chest, raising the other arm in a shrug, while the lines on the great forehead arch, 'I don't know, this is what I think, you may think differently . . .'

MAURO MASCARELLO: A Tradition Without Defects

The 1970s were the formative years for 'modern' Barolo. The wine grew up amidst much confusion and change: production was increasing, consumption declining; negociant houses beleaguered their traditional lines of supply with demands for ever lower prices; some growers reacted by deciding to go it alone and make wine for themselves. As domestic sales tottered, the new winemaking techniques propounded by men like Renato Ratti appeared to hold the key to the more sophisticated international markets. Many producers abandoned the old ways: the days of 'traditional' Barolo seemed, for a while, to be numbered.

Mauro Mascarello took control of the family business in 1967. The almost inevitable arguments with his father ensued, as he too, at the turn of the decade, followed the guidelines of the modernist doctrine. As his steely eyes suggest, Mauro is a single-minded character and was determined to find his own way. He cut back the period of maceration on the skins (down to six days in 1974) and started to give his wine less time in wood. By 1978, however, Mauro had bucked the trend. He looks back on his experiments dispassionately: what he learned from the experience he puts into practice, but nowadays fervently expounds a 'tradition without defects'.

The main lesson of the 1970s for Mascarello was the necessity of temperature control during fermentation. The *cantina* his grandfather had bought in Monchiero lies 3 metres below the level of the Rea stream, providing a naturally cool and constant environment. (The building was constructed at the end of the seventeenth century and the cellar once used to conserve ice). Until 1982 when modern refrigeration equipment was finally installed, Mauro had to rely heavily on the ambient conditions of his cellar. In milder vintages he would still pump the wine through pipes immersed in cold water and out into clean, pre-cooled vats, while in the warm autumn of 1971, he was forced to take cruder steps, lowering lumps of frozen CO_2 into the fermenting must.

The legacy of the 1970s is evident today in atypically cool fermentation temperatures for barbera and nebbiolo (24–5°C) though Mauro opts for a more typical 22–3°C for his dolcetto. Otherwise his vinification methods reflect more closely a born again traditionalism: maceration on the skins for three weeks and more, the use of *cappello sommerso* (even, in some vintages, for dolcetto) followed by fairly lengthy cask ageing for Barolo and Barbaresco (around three to four years is usual for Barolo even in lighter vintages, the exact time depending on the nature of the crop). Mauro loves the traditional wines, their weight, substance, structure and tannin, and insists that Barolo should not pander too readily to modern tastes but strive to preserve its own identity.

In the dimly lit cellars, rows of oval-shaped *botti* of Yugoslavian oak line the walls. Most of them date back to the late fifties and early sixties, a time – Mauro remembers – when you could actually go there and choose the wood for yourself (preferably in the hillier western part of the country where the wood was harder and less porous). The thick staves cut down on loss through evaporation and even their oval shape performs a useful function, minimizing ullage space at the top and allowing for a more efficient settling of deposits at the bottom. The barrels are cleaned every year while the wine is being racked and, with proper maintenance, Mauro anticipates that they could last for up to a hundred years.

There is nothing remarkable about Mascarello's approach to vinification: it follows a fairly simple and typical traditional pattern. It is his concern for the excellence of the raw materials that enables him to produce some exceptional wines. He believes that the basis of a fine wine is a small crop of healthy grapes and, like other top growers, Mauro reduces yields through extensive summer pruning. However, he is convinced that to achieve the desired balance between perfume and structure, the right site is crucial. Mauro shares the popular Albese belief in *la terra*; even during our tour of the cellars he was rummaging through various sacks for lumps of soil to show us how the ground changes between the neighbouring vineyards of Monprivato and Villero. The different terrains, he argues, play a fundamental role in determining the nature of a wine's balance. Some parts of Barolo produce a wine overloaded with hard tannins while the great vineyards – through a combination of soil type and exposure – give a wine with, amongst other things, much softer, sweeter tannins. Analysis of the soil in Monprivato shows a good, active limestone content and the presence of various macro- and micro-elements including iron, boron and manganese; it also benefits from an excellent southwest exposure. According to Mauro, only grapes grown under such conditions provide the elegant perfumes and well-balanced structure that characterize great Barolo. Vinification enters the equation as a question of interpreting the raw material, with the winemaker's intuition and experience dictating when to rack, bottle, etc. 'You can't work miracles in the cellar,' he says, his rather ascetic face breaking briefly into a broad smile.

Monprivato is the centrepiece of the Mascarello range. His grandfather acquired a farm there in 1904 and though the family subsequently moved the business to Monchiero, they kept the land in Castiglione Falletto. Mauro chose to follow at least one piece of his father's advice – the Monprivato wine had always formed the backbone of the family's Barolo and his father's counsel was to continue the policy and, beyond that, to buy good grapes. The opportunity to expand their holdings in Monprivato finally arrived in 1985 when Mauro bought a further couple of hectares (and a piece of Villero) from Violante Sobrero. He now owns almost all of the 6-hectare site. Mauro added his own impetus to the family tradition when, in 1970, he first vinified the wine separately. He generally allows Monprivato a little longer in wood than his other Baroli simply because it tends to be a more concentrated wine: his magnificent 1978, for example, was made from yields of just under 16 hectolitres per hectare.

Monprivato and Villero form the core of production but Mascarello makes other cru Baroli from bought-in grapes in certain vintages – for example, Dardi (Monforte) in 1982 and Francia (Serralunga) in 1984. He buys the grapes for his exotically perfumed Barbaresco from Treiso's Marcarini. Of the two Barbere (both from Monforte), Santo Stefano is a weighty and structured wine, Ginestra by comparison is plummy and fairly forward. Dolcetto from old vines in the Gagliassi vineyard of Monforte has a remarkable structure needing time in cask and then in bottle to reach its peak, often several years after the harvest. Having bought grapes from Gagliassi for many years, Mauro was furious when the owner recently sold the land to someone from outside the zone.

At a recent vertical tasting of Monprivato going back to 1970, the wines from Mauro's experimental phase had held up well, but the real stars, 1978 and 1982, came from the period after the full turn of the circle back to the time-honoured approach. Mauro seems to have a 'tradition without defects' within his grasp.

PRODUTTORI DEL BARBARESCO: Hard Work and Humility

Think of an Italian winemaking cooperative, and the chances are that an image of the sun-baked south will spring to mind. Your next thought may be of the 'wine lake', vast quantities of unwanted and undrinkable wine whose production is sponsored by Alice in Wonderland subsidies from state and EEC alike. There are numerous cooperatives whose entire production is destined to go no further than the nearest distillery. This is certainly an excessively harsh generalization about the *cantina sociale*. Scattered throughout Italy are notable exceptions to mediocrity, and the paradigm of these is the Cantina Produttori del Barbaresco.

In Italy cooperatives enjoy significant subsidies and tax concessions from the state. Given the right company structure, these benefits allow the cooperatives to invest in the latest technology without putting up the price of the wine. The disadvantage is that as a cooperative, you cannot refuse to buy in grapes from your members, even when they have overcropped or the vintage is poor. The private negociant, of course, has the advantage of being able to pick and choose both quality and provenance of his grapes. Few *cantine sociale* seem to have resolved this problem. Many prefer to ignore it by blindly mixing good grapes with bad and ending up with a mediocre wine (doubtless very competitively priced).

At the Produttori del Barbaresco, they have the answer. Through rigorous selection of the grapes even before they arrive in the cellar, it is possible to grade the production in a systematic fashion. This logic is extended through the entire production and marketing process. Although only small fry in the sea of cooperatives, the Produttori have a thing or two to teach their big brothers.

In the tiny pond of Barbaresco, however, they are a rather bigger fish. Just a few doors up from Angelo Gaja, the Produttori's cellars are always open for the sale of a few bottles of Barbaresco. The relaxed, easy-going façade of the operation belies the seriousness with which it is run. In its present form, the cooperative dates from 1958 when it comprised a group of nineteen growers. Today there are sixty members who between them own 110 hectares of vineyard, of which ninety produce nebbiolo for DOCG Barbaresco. The Produttori account for some 20 per cent of the total production of Barbaresco. The vast majority of their vineyards lie within the commune of Barbaresco itself, with only 16 hectares in the commune of Neive and a token fifth of a hectare in Treiso. Unusually, the *cantina* specializes exclusively in the vinification of nebbiolo. Where a producer grows dolcetto or barbera, he will either sell them to a negociant, or vinify them himself. In 1987 the Produttori's production of Barbaresco was 3,250 hectolitres.

In the offices and cellars the helm is guided by a blend of youth and experience. President of the Cantina Produttori is Celestino Vacca, a patient man who has an endearing openness and ease with strangers. The young man in the cellar is Gianni Testa, a bright and confident character whose enological expertise has given the Produttori a more refined style of wine. Testa is a good example of the pragmatic new breed of winemaker in the Albese. 'We have always tried to follow a traditional system', he says, 'but always making small improvements to produce a finer wine.' In fact, Testa's method of vinification is a healthy compromise between tradition and modernism. At every stage measures are taken to ensure a clean wine with no defects. Fermentation temperatures for Barbaresco are kept down to around 26–7°C to emphasize aroma, and the duration of maceration is dependent on the quality of the vintage. In light vintages the wine may remain in contact with the grape skins for thirteen to fourteen days, while in a great year this may be extended to a month. Testa also has a sensible policy for *cappello sommerso* – it is only brought into play in the best years and then only for the last week of maceration to boost tannin levels discreetly after flavouring and colouring elements have already been extracted from the grapes. Another sign of the modern approach is the encouragement of the malolactic fermentation by heating the cellars immediately after the alcoholic fermentation is finished. The wine is racked three to four times in the first year to avoid any possible off-flavours from contact with the lees. After the first year in stainless steel or cement, the Barbaresco is transferred into 50 hectolitre *botti* or some spectacularly large old *tini* (the vertical casks that are a rare sight in the Langhe nowadays).

The policy of separating grapes of different quality means that there are three routes which a nebbiolo grape can follow once it has arrived at the cellar. Grapes are judged by their appearance and sugar levels. If of the top quality, they will be vinified alone as a single vineyard wine. Normal quality grapes will be blended into the generic Barbaresco, while lower quality fruit will make a table wine called simply Nebbiolo delle Langhe.

The Cantina Produttori's Nebbiolo delle Langhe is a good example to many other growers of how to make a good simple wine from lesser raw materials. The other benefit is that the quality of the prestige wine, Barbaresco, is not compromised by blending together the entire production. The recipe for the sweetly fruity and fragrant Nebbiolo is certainly individual. The must is fermented at a very cool 23°C using selected yeasts, and macerated for nine to ten days. The partially fermented wine is then racked off the skins into vitrified cement tanks. At this point the equivalent of some 30 per cent of uncrushed, healthy, whole nebbiolo grapes is added to the wine. These grapes undergo a type of carbonic maceration and after a week, when they have burst, the wine is pressed and racked clean again. Testa compares this system to the traditional *governo all 'uso toscano* of Chianti. It is a secondary fermentation which, he claims, underlines the perfumes and primary fruit qualities in the wine. According to Testa, this technique is traditional in the Langhe, but has fallen into disuse. Malolactic fermentation takes place immediately, and the wine is stored in stainless steel during the winter to stabilize tartrates, then bottled in June for consumption from October onwards. The result is an elegant wine with little of the tannin and aggression associated with nebbiolo.

The core of the Produttori's work, of course, is their Barbaresco; in particular their cru wines. In the best vintages single-vineyard *riserva* accounts for some 40 per cent of production – an extremely high percentage. This policy goes back to 1967 when their first cru was bottled separately. Unfortunately, in recent years the added cachet of a cru designation on the label has fostered misuse of the term. Even a badly situated vineyard has a name, so in the absence of an official classification, what guarantee exists for the consumer that a cru wine will be of superior quality? In the case of the Produttori del Barbaresco the answer is twofold. Firstly, the majority of the crus that they bottle are those which are historically recognized as producing the best grapes. Some sites, such as Ovello, have only more recently been considered worthy of elevation to the top rank. The second part of the answer is that only a selection of the best grapes from the vineyard will be used in the cru wine.

The fascination of the cru wines from the Produttori del Barbaresco is that they give an opportunity to compare side by side all the famous vineyards of Barbaresco, all vinified in identical fashion. Those who argue against the cru concept, who claim that apparent nuances of character between one vineyard and the next are more due to the enological whims of different winemakers than to variation of soil and microclimate should study the wines of the Produttori.

Tasting the full range of nine crus from the excellent 1982 vintage, we found marked variations of character. The wines fell into groups, firstly the lighter, more delicately structured and faster-maturing wines: Moccagatta and Porra. Then there was a middle band of more complex but still very elegant wines that for many are quintessential Barbaresco: Rabajà, Pajé and Asili. Finally we tasted the heavyweights from vineyards in the north of the commune, wines with a rich, earthy, masculine quality more commonly associated with Barolo: Montefico, Montestefano and Ovello. Rio Sordo fell between the refined and earthy styles. We had our own favourites (Asili stood out as the most complete wine on the day), but all were very good to excellent wines with distinct individual personalities. Proving as ever that beauty lies in the eye of the beholder, Testa said that among their clients, loyalties are fairly evenly divided between the crus.

Unlike some of their more fashionable neighbours, the Produttori produce wines that are consistently excellent value for money. 'We have always had a humble policy', says Celestino Vacca, 'to offer the best quality at a reasonable price.' Indeed, the members of the cooperative are paid the same price for their grapes whether they end up as cru or *normale*. Thus the benefits are shared by all, although individual growers receive their little bit of glory on the back label of the cru wines where their names are listed.

In 1987 a mere 26 per cent of their production was exported, some 46,000 bottles of which were drunk by the canny Germans. Surely before long the rest of the world will latch on to this unpretentious blend of hard work and humility.

PRUNOTTO: Honest Tradition

There is no sign of whimsy at the Prunotto winery at San Cassiano on the outskirts of Alba. The high vaulted ceilings, immaculate gleaming wood and perfect brickwork are more reminiscent of a modern church than a cellar. The impression of seriousness is reinforced on meeting owner Giuseppe (Beppe) Colla. His lean, ascetic face and quietly patient demeanour give him an almost saintly aura. Beppe is respected as one of the most reliable authorities on Albese wine. His status was officially recognized when he was appointed President of the Barolo Consorzio during the mid-eighties.

Beppe Colla took over the Prunotto concern in 1956, after Alfredo Prunotto retired for health reasons. In 1922 Prunotto himself had bought the Vini delle Langhe cooperative which had been established in Alba since 1904. 'The old cellars were very inconvenient,' says Colla 'up, down, all over the place.' Colla began building the new *cantina* at San Cassiano in 1969 and moved into it in 1972. As he points out, it is one of the first modern cellars in the zone to be built according to a logic of vinification.

There is an impressive array of nineteen vitrified cement fermentation vats, 3,500 hectolitre capacity of stainless steel storage tanks and sixty-three oak *botti* of various dimensions. The centrepiece of the winery is a magnificent temperature and humidity-controlled underground cellar for the maturation of bottled stock. This facility for storing 450,000 bottles in perfect conditions is virtually unique in Alba.

Today Colla is definitely seen as a winemaker in the traditional mould, but in his day he was an important innovator. In 1953 Beppe made experiments with *barrique*, but rejected the results as unsuitable for Barolo and Barbaresco. With a wry smile he suggests that 'from a commercial point of view it would now be a good idea to use *barrique*: people have got *barrique* on the brain.' Colla's major contribution to the development of Albese wine has been to support the marketing of wines from individual crus. After a period of experimentation to determine which were the right crus, Prunotto came out in 1961 with Barolo from Bussia, Barbaresco from Montestefano, Dolcetto Valmaggiore and Freisa Ciabot del Prete. We were invited to taste some early releases together with Beppe Colla and his younger brother Tino (also an enologist, who joined Prunotto only in 1986). The wines, dating back to a 1964 Barbaresco, all showed a good, ripe character and had aged well. The Prunotto house style shows a preference for well-ripened grapes, fermented to obtain a good colour and plenty of tannin. The crus produced today in the best vintages are Dolcetti Mosesco and Gagliassi, Nebbiolo Ochetti, Barbera Pian Romualdo, Barbareschi Rabajà and Montestefano, Baroli Cannubi and Bussia. Tino Colla explained the Prunotto thinking on cru wines:

> It is only worth vinifying a cru separately when a certain position gives a wine of a well-defined individual personality. There are many zones where good Barolo and Barbaresco are grown, but there are only a few areas which show distinct personalities year in year out. Apart from these crus it is logical to make a blend of different zones, aiming for a fairly consistent product.

Prunotto has always followed the policy of a traditional negociant, producing only the classic Albese red wines in both *riserva* and cru bottlings. Total production of around 20,000 cases puts them amongst the larger cellars in the area. Owning no vineyards, they buy in grapes (not wine) from small farmers; the grapes for the cru wines are bought in on a regular contract basis.

Vinification is along traditional lines, using submerged cap fermentation with a maceration period of a maximum of fifteen days for Barolo. Temperatures are controlled where necessary with a heat exchanger. Malolactic fermentation is encouraged by raising the cellar temperature. There is lengthy wood ageing of up to four years for Barolo. Nebbiolo and Barbera spend under one year in *botti*, while Dolcetto and Roero are stored in stainless steel. Bottle ageing of over one year for Barolo and Barbaresco offers a fine example to other producers.

An interesting and unusual feature of the Prunotto winery is the facility for the production of their own grape-must concentrate. Tino Colla explains the advantages of using his own concentrate in the lighter vintages: 'With the normal rectified concentrate you dilute the must a little – you increase the sugar content, but not the other components. With our own concentrate we also increase the extract.' It also offers the benefit of using concentrate from the appropriate grape variety. In contrast to the commercially produced concentrate, Prunotto's version is worked slowly and heated as gently as possible to avoid any cooked flavours. As the cru wines are not vinified separately in lesser vintages, they are not subjected to concentration.

Prunotto's new series of plain, elegant labels do more justice to their wines than the heavy, old-fashioned designs they replace. The labels eloquently portray the dedicated, professional approach of Prunotto. As Beppe Colla himself says, 'A good producer is one who maintains the character of his base product while adapting to the demands of the market.' Prunotto are honest supporters of the best aspects of Langarolo tradition.*

---

*In late 1989 the Tuscan-based house of Antinori acquired a majority shareholding in Prunotto.

ROERO: A New Discipline

Travelling north from Alba across the river Tanaro, you are immediately in a different landscape. In contrast to the severe majesty of the slopes of Barolo, the Roero has a more homely feel. Although vineyards are still often planted on vertiginous slopes, the hills are smaller and more curvaceous. Above all, the colours are different. In summer the Roero is bathed in a dusty, orange light reflected off the pale sandy soil. To visit the Roero is to gain a glimpse of how Barolo and Barbaresco would have looked two centuries ago, before the vine was planted to the virtual exclusion of all other crops. On the left bank of the Tanaro, mixed farming – *coltura promiscua* – is seen at its most attractive. Vineyards occupy the best, south facing, high slopes, while northern expositions remain heavily wooded. Lower down in the valleys is a cornucopia of fruit and vegetable production: peaches, strawberries, apples, fields of maize, and the ubiquitous hazelnut. The *contadino* is in his element in the Roero: vineyard ownership is fragmented, and few farmers depend solely on the vine for their livelihood. In 1988 a total of 195 vineyard owners cultivated a mere 153 hectares of DOC Roero.

Examining the work of two typical producers, Deltetto and Negro, many of the typical trends and attitudes in the Roero come to light.

Antonio Deltetto

The young, dynamic face of the Roero can be seen in producers like Antonio 'Tonino' Deltetto. Tonino has the serious yet gentle face of a young scientist. Indeed the level of technical sophistication he has introduced to the family cellar is impressive. The operation has a brisk, businesslike feel to it. Until 1978, when Tonino graduated from Alba's Enological School, father Carlo only sold in bulk. Production was restricted to red wine and included Barolo and Barbaresco. Today a balance of 70 per cent white wine production shows an astute assessment of both local and international markets (a rare talent amongst Langhe producers). Nearly all Deltetto's production is of local wines from bought-in grapes, although there are likely to be imminent additions to the 3 hectares of vineyards presently owned by the family. The presence of Gavi, Piemonte's best-known white, on the list is perhaps surprising given that the grapes come from a growing area over 50 miles away, but reinforces the company policy of specialization in white wine. About 35 per cent of Deltetto's annual 110,000 bottles are Arneis.

In a very short space of time Arneis has become a trendy drink in northern Italy. Many examples do not stand up to close examination; Arneis is often a rather insubstantial white wine, very low in acidity and with little keeping power. The best Arneis is a different proposition, its unique aniseed, nutty flavour and ripeness are a tonic to the bored Chardonnay drinker. However, in 1989 arneis grapes were fetching double the price of nebbiolo from Barolo. The bubble looks ripe for pricking.

The reasons for the wine's success lie partly in the aura of mystery surrounding the variety. This in turn is enhanced by the scarcity of product. In a sea of red wine production in the Albese, a few rock-pools of white will always be drunk thirstily by locals.

Deltetto's Arneis is made with the aim of retaining as much freshness and primary fruit flavour as possible. After destalking, the grapes are cold-macerated at 3–5°C for twenty-four hours to extract

extra flavour from the skins, and then pressed softly in a Vaslin device. Sulphur dosing is kept low (40 milligrams per litre) when the grapes are healthy, and a cool fermentation temperature of 16–18°C maintains the delicate perfumes intact. The wine is kept in stainless steel on its lees for one month to develop complexity. Acid levels are maintained by complete avoidance of the malolactic fermentation. Bottling of 40,000 bottles of both Arneis *normale* and a weightier cru San Michele begins early, in February and March, doubtless spurred by the clamorous demands of the Italian market for wine of the latest vintage. Deltetto also produce a curiosity from their arneis grapes – 5,000 bottles of a sweet *passito* wine from the Bric' Tupin vineyard, made from grapes whose sugar content has been boosted by being left to dry on mats in the open air for six weeks. The wine is still at an experimental stage, part is fermented in *barrique* and part in stainless steel. The lack of acid in the variety would, however, appear to mitigate against the possibility of ever producing a really well-balanced Arneis dessert wine.

Favorita has had a less meteoric rise over the last ten years, although Tonino Deltetto claims that demand for favorita grapes is always greater than supply. If truth be told, Favorita is often an anaemic, neutral white wine. Deltetto's, by contrast, is attractively delicate and aromatic, his cru from San Michele showing a little more complexity. He claims that the grapey character is a component of the variety rather than the result of any discreet blending of aromatic wine such as Moscato or Riesling. However, we have yet to encounter another Favorita which backs up Deltetto's assertion.

Red wines from the Roero occupy an even more tenuous perch. Despite the official blessing of DOC bestowed on Roero in 1985, there is not yet much unity of style, and standards are highly variable. Deltetto's Roero DOC is made in a style that many would wish to see as the norm. Pale red, raspberry perfumed and refreshing: what the English would call a 'luncheon wine'. This light style of Nebbiolo, vinified using a short maceration of up to one week at 25–8°C, with no wood ageing and further softened by the addition of between 2 and 5 per cent Arneis, would appear to suit the modern taste for more delicate drinks, even though at around 12 per cent the alcohol level is not slight. Certainly the product has more hope than its ugly sister DOC of Nebbiolo d'Alba.

On the export market, Roero DOC has a simple problem: price. It is already hard enough to sell the most basic level of Barolo in most markets, and to market Roero at the same or a slightly higher price is an absurdity. Production levels are still only 750,000 bottles per annum, but the growth rate is over 25 per cent.

Tonino Deltetto sees a positive future for the development of red wines in the Roero. He is interested in experimenting with ultra-montane varieties such as sangiovese, and recognizes the sleeping potential of local varieties freisa, ruchet and, in particular, barbera. In the Roero much barbera has now been replanted with arneis. Barbera has an image problem, agrees Tonino, but if the right sites are used and the yields reduced, great wines can result, he argues.

Deltetto is dedicated to making good wines with commercial clear-sightedness and willingness to experiment. The family company appears to have a bright future.

Angelo Negro

Angelo Negro proudly represents his village, Monteu Roero, as mayor. He also represents the modern spirit of winegrowing in the

Roero: moving through a phase of transition, building on peasant traditions towards a future on a wider market.

Angelo's ruddy cheeks and cheerful greeting are to be found at wine fairs all over Europe. Although he looks more at home with a pair of wellingtons and a tractor, Negro is also a busy missionary for the wines of the Roero.

The Negros have deep roots in the Roero. Local archives show the family owning land at Perdaudin (apparently a corruption of 'Prato di Audino di Negro') since 1670. By 1974 Angelo had outgrown the family farmhouse near his arneis vineyards at Perdaudin, and Cascina Riveri was built near the road to Monteu in 1974. Until 1976 Negro sold his grapes along with his numerous other fruit crops, then, like so many others at the time, he took the plunge into vinification and bottling. Subsequently vineyard holdings were increased to about 15 hectares over the next ten years, and other vineyards at Canale are now rented to augment production.

Negro's total annual production of about 100,000 bottles is dominated by Arneis which contributes 50 per cent of the total, including 12,000 bottles of the cru Perdaudin. Another 12,000 bottles of Favorita are made, and the rest is red wine. Roero amounts to 20,000 bottles at present, with half as much Barbera and a mere 3–4,000 bottles each of Bonarda from the Bric' Millon vineyard and a rare aromatic dry Brachetto.

As a winemaker, Angelo has been growing in confidence with every vintage. Aided by enologist Gianfranco Cordero, his white wines are now made to the most modern recipe. The modest cellar now boasts plenty of stainless steel and computerized temperature-control equipment. Arneis is cold-macerated on the skins and fermented in autoclave with selected local yeasts at very low temperature (15–16°C). Malolactic fermentation is avoided to accentuate freshness, and a little residual sugar remains in the finished wine (particularly noticable in the cru Perdaudin) to give a touch of aromatic perfume.

Negro's Roero DOC from the Prachiosso vineyard is made with a relatively long maceration of fifteen days on the skins, including the final week with *cappello sommerso*. Prachiosso also benefits from an unusual technique related to Tuscany's *governo*. The nebbioli on five rows of vines (about 5 per cent of the total) are left to ripen beyond the normal harvest and then added to the wine after the normal fermentation is over. The subsequent refermentation, according to Negro, adds perfume and finesse to the wine. Up to six months' wood age is used to knock the edges off all Negro's red wines.

Angelo sells most of his wine in Italy, but he is keen to develop on the export market. Bruno Giacosa was the first to open the door for Arneis in Germany and Switzerland, and producers like Negro now find their wine easily accepted in German-speaking markets. As his wines reach consistent levels of quality, Angelo Negro and other small farmers like him feel ready to make the leap from being mayors of their local villages to international ambassadors for the Roero.

RENATO RATTI: The Father of Modern Barolo

When Renato Ratti died in late 1988, the Barolo zone lost more than just an exceptional winemaker. It was largely his vision which brought Barolo kicking and screaming into the modern world. The full extent of his influence has perhaps never been acknowledged locally. Where Angelo Gaja has shown a whole generation the glittering success one individual is capable of achieving, Ratti campaigned ceaselessly on behalf of the region as a whole. As president of the Consorzio of Albese Wines and later of the Consorzio per la Tutela d'Asti, his concern was to promote the overall image of the wines and not the determining role he had chosen to play in their future. Nowadays there is much talk of 'leaders' in the Langhe, those people who are pushing back the boundaries of vinification, viticulture and marketing and increasing public awareness of their efforts. The concept dates back no more than a couple of decades to when Ratti was the original and undisputed leader in the zone.

Ratti was born in 1934. By the time he had graduated from Alba's Enological School his precocious talents were already evident from the papers he had compiled on all aspects of wine production. He started work in 1953 for the famous Canelli-based firm of Contratto. A year later he joined Cinzano and was employed by them for the next ten years. In addition to making vermouth, Ratti travelled extensively in France (Cinzano had the concession for selling Cognac Otard in Italy) and Brazil. This was really the gestation period of his vision. It became clear that the excellent raw materials available to the Langaroli were not, in contrast to the more enlightened approach to winemaking he had witnessed, above all, in France, being used to their full potential. Ratti returned to Italy in 1965, determined to prove that his beloved Langhe hills were capable of producing wines equal to those he had found anywhere else.

Although born and bred in the Langhe, Ratti did not come from a wine-producing background. This, he felt, was a distinct advantage: he was not steeped in, and therefore blinkered by, tradition. Similarly he saw that the taste for the old marsala-like wines was directly dependent on years of familiarity with that style. Taking his inspiration from the French, Ratti resolved to create a new style of Barolo by building a platform for the future founded on the ethos of the past.

Ratti revitalized the principles of the pre-1930s period. His formula for the new style of vinification restated traditional values while employing the benefits of modern technology. In an ideal world, soft pressing would have replaced the harsh crushing machines, frequent *rimontaggi* ousted *cappello sommerso* and the bottle taken over from the cask as the principal vessel for ageing the wine. Lack of funds meant a gradual changeover: Ratti was able to buy his first Vaslin press in 1971, while stainless steel fermentation vats did not arrive until the end of the decade. In 1969 Ratti was joined by his nephew Massimo Martinelli. Martinelli had graduated from Alba's Enological School in 1963 and then worked for five years in Switzerland absorbing the technical know-how already much in evidence there. Like his uncle, he is also grateful for not being hidebound by tradition. As Martinelli gradually took over the responsibility for the day-to-day running of the *cantina*, Ratti was able to spread his message further afield.

Not surprisingly, the missionary did not at first receive a rapturous welcome. His ideas on winemaking were greeted with scorn and the maps he drew to show the great historical growing zones of Barolo and Barbaresco were received with outrage. It is a measure of the man's diplomacy that by the early eighties he had become president of the Consorzio of Albese Wines; the revolutionary had won acceptance at last. His message to the winemakers of Barolo remained the same, to return to the traditional values of their grandfathers' time. He wanted

to see bottles and not *botti* in their cellars. Early bottling, he insisted, preserves the unique fragrance of Barolo, emphasizing the relation of wine to vine. Furthermore he unravelled the mysteries of the malolactic fermentation for his fellow *Baroliste* and gave the cru bottling movement a broader base, encouraging producers to vinify the individual vineyards separately and to record the numbers of the reserve on the label. At the same time Ratti began to travel the world to speak of the virtues of Albese wines: that the rise in consumer awareness of Barolo dates back to this period is no coincidence. Somehow Ratti also found time to pay homage to the zone's winemaking roots by creating a fascinating wine museum (usually if you've seen one. . .) in the fifteenth-century desanctified Benedictine monastery above his winery. His scholarly gifts were realized in the form of a series of books on the history of Piemontese wines.

By the mid-eighties, Ratti had drawn up a list of the top crus of the two DOCG zones. Together with people like Angelo Gaja, he was working hard on obtaining official recognition for the prototype classification. Angelo pays tribute to the influence of his great friend and ally: 'The project will probably come to fruition in fifteen years' time. If Ratti had lived on, he could have done it in five.'

Martinelli, along with Ratti's son Pietro, has now taken charge of the Abbazia dell'Annunziata winery. He too is a talented winemaker, determined to carry on the work of his mentor. The winery's range is not large, in keeping with the basic principle that the zone's fine wines are produced in restricted quantities. The firm buys in some of its grapes, the rest comes from their own vineyards mainly in and around the Marcenasco area of Annunziata (named after the village of Marcenascum where vines surrounded the ancient castle as long ago as the twelfth century).

Barolo Marcenasco: 25–30,000 bottles per annum (grapes bought in from five growers owning some 5 hectares of south and east facing vineyards at altitudes of between 250–300 metres).

Barolo Marcenasco Conca: 3–5,000 bottles per annum (this 1.5 hectare vineyard owned by the Ratti family is the amphitheatre of vines lying just below the winery. It is mainly east to south facing.)

Barolo Marcenasco Rocche: 6–8,000 bottles per annum. (This south-southwest facing 'grand cru' vineyard lies just over the brow of the hill to the west of the winery. In addition to their own small plot of vines, they buy in grapes from two other growers.)

Barbaresco: 5,000 bottles per annum (from bought-in grapes).

Nebbiolo d'Alba Occhetti: 12–15,000 bottles per annum. (A famous south facing vineyard – 280 metres – at Monteu Roero where there is a long-standing agreement with a local grower.)

In addition the firm produces Barbera d'Alba (15,000 bottles per annum) and Dolcetto d'Alba (20–25,000 bottles per annum) at the La Morra winery. Abbazia dell' Annunziata are also exclusive distributors for the wines of two small *aziende agricole* both associated with branches of the Ratti family.

Azienda Agricola Colombé is based at Mango and produces exclusively Dolcetto. Dolcetto d'Alba Colombé (15–16,000 bottles per annum) and Dolcetto d'Alba Ca' Colombé (3,000 bottles per annum) both come from high – 500 metres – southeast facing vineyards in one of the optimum dolcetto zones. The Ca' Colombé Dolcetto is a *tête de cuvée* wine.

Azienda Agricola Villa Pattòno produces 8,000 bottles per annum of a unique *uvaggio* (80 per cent barbera, 15 per cent freisa and 5 per cent uvalino) from east to west facing vineyards near Costigliole d'Asti. The wine is aged in wood for twelve months split evenly between *barrique* and *botti*.

187

Although all the wines are good examples of their types, it is the Barolo that really stands out, and in particular, Conca and Rocche. Conca tends to be the softer and more accessible of the two, while the firmer, more structured Rocche is the longer lasting. Both share that expansive spectrum of aromas that quickly became Ratti's hallmark. The Colombé Dolcetti are fine modern examples of this varietal.

The last time we saw Ratti was just a couple of months before he died. He was very thin but his glittering eyes had lost none of their intensity and the acute awareness that inspired so much respect remained undiminished. He uncorked a bottle of Marcenasco 1971. In deference to the ceremony that must always surround fine wine, we chatted about Barolo while the wine had a chance to breathe. Forbidden alcohol by his doctors, Ratti drank in the wine through its perfumes. 'Smell those truffles! That licorice! The flowers! The mint!' The old flame rekindled, it seemed almost as if he were discovering Barolo for the first time. Anyone who would suggest that Barolo is not capable of delicacy and subtlety cannot have tasted a mature Ratti wine from a great vintage.

Renato Ratti was a graceful and gracious man; he could none the less liven up the dullest moment with his broad, infectious smile and gently sardonic aside. We shall all miss him.

TERRE DEL BAROLO: The Other Side of The Coin

Where the Cantina Produttori di Barbaresco serves as a model of excellence to other cooperatives throughout Italy, with Terre del Barolo we come back down to earth again. There is a tremendous difference in size and therefore manageability between the two. With just sixty members, the former can implement and monitor more easily a number of clear-sighted strategies. With 550 members and between 30 and 35,000 hectolitres of wine to look after, life is that much more complicated for Terre del Barolo. They are not taking any new members.

While today's great *Baroliste* may disagree about most things, they speak from a relatively secure position brought about by buoyant demand for their wine. There is, however, one fact about which they all agree: there is simply too much Barolo. While an annual average of 6.5 million bottles is very small, there are too few truly 'vocational' vineyards, they argue, to support this level. The zone's prime sites were by and large well established by the time that the area under vine almost doubled following the arrival of DOC in 1967. Slopes traditionally planted to other grapes, or even other crops, were quickly brought into production and nebbiolo was forced more and more to act out the ill-suited role of cash crop. What could not be sold on quality had to be sold on price. In today's contracting, quality-conscious market, the legacy of that era is the grim reality of a mini Barolo lake.

There is a stark contrast between the zone's typical small, family-run winery and Barolo's cooperative. Just inside the gates at Terre del Barolo, a weighbridge standing ready to measure the size of the latest vintage is immediate confirmation of an operation on a very different scale. Every year Terre del Barolo process 6–7,000 hectolitres of Barolo, 12,000 hectolitres of Barbera and 10,000 hectolitres of

Dolcetto. The balance is made up of the area's other red grapes, freisa and grignolino, plus a small amount of pelaverga from Verduno, Roddi and La Morra. Seventy per cent of this wine is sold as DOC(G) and much of the rest to private customers who come armed with their own demijohns. Between 25 and 30 per cent is exported, with the UK as the number one foreign market followed by Germany, Switzerland and Belgium. The Dutch and Americans take very small quantities. The winery has a total capacity of 80,000 hectolitres: 12,000 in *botti*, 20,000 in stainless steel and the rest in cement.

Terre del Barolo was founded in 1958 with just forty members: today their 550 growers work vineyards in all eleven Barolo communes. Some have tiny plots of land – less than half a hectare – but the overall average is closer to the zone's norm of around one hectare. According to Roberto Scatizzi, commercial director of the enterprise, they all receive the same message: prune short. Growers are encouraged to cultivate good raw materials and the advice to prune for quality rather than quantity of fruit aims to keep production levels under control. Scatizzi explained how the policy works: 'If the growers follow our advice, they produce better grapes with higher sugar levels and are paid more for them. If sugar levels are low, we pay less. If this happens, they normally return the following year with a much better quality crop.'

The location of his vineyards can also have a bearing on price: the better the area, the more a grower stands to earn. For many of today's small *contadini* growers, with the *mezzadria* system and the hungry years following the Second World War still fresh in their memories, it is a very hard lesson to learn. Although the *cantina sociale* pays above the going rate on the open market, a small high-quality harvest must still seem to many of them an incomprehensible luxury.

In return for the security he is offered, a grower must undertake to sell all his grapes to the cooperative and also leave 10 per cent of the value of his production in the communal coffers for three years, generating capital for the business to finance itself.

As with the Cantina Produttori in Barbaresco, different gradings of the grapes give rise to a number of different lines. In the great vintages, Terre del Barolo market cru Baroli: Rocche (from Castiglione Falletto's best-known vineyard) and Castello (from the vineyard below the castle at Grinzane Cavour). Barolo Brunate has also been produced. In 1986 a new strategy was introduced: vinification by commune. Barolo di Serralunga and Barolo di Castiglione represent an attempt to bring marketing policy into line with consumer demands for wines with a more clearly defined identity. However while their ability to react to these trends shows a certain insight, they have yet to upgrade the quality of their production to match. Even a Barolo *normale* 1985 tasted in summer 1989 was already well past its prime: a pale and thin apology of a wine. After the generic Barolo, the final selection of grapes is destined to become Nebbiolo delle Langhe. This, Scatizzi believes, allows them to upgrade the quality of their Baroli. 'Every year our members produce Nebbiolo di Barolo; our job is to find a way to sell and market it.' The policy is also extended to Barbera and Dolcetto: with Dolcetto for example, there is a Dolcetto d'Alba di Monforte DOC, a regular Dolcetto d'Alba DOC and Dolcetto delle Langhe.

Giuseppe Veglio, the technical director who also sits on the DOCG tasting commission, oversees a broadly traditional approach to vinification. Nebbiolo, for example, undergoes a reasonably short fermentation on the skins at temperatures up to 28°C with twice daily *rimontaggi* (the cap may be submerged for the final few days). During its first year the wine is racked four or five times and once a year thereafter. The new Barolo will then spend a minimum of two years in *botti* – some of which are enormous, up to 150 hectolitres – which may be extended up to four or five in vintages like 1978, 1982 and 1985. Barbera is fermented at similar temperatures for a shorter period with only the *superiore* version seeing any wood. Dolcetto undergoes the shortest maceration of all (five or six days) after maximum colour has been extracted. The malolactic fermentation is induced for these early-drinking style wines.

Terre del Barolo aim to popularize Barolo by selling it at a fair price. 'Barolo used to be put on an altar,' Scatizzi says. 'Today's wines are rounder and less tannic and the lighter vintages can be consumed younger with all types of food. It's only the great vintages that you need to keep for game.' He cites the high mark-ups that restaurateurs take as one of the reasons for declining consumption, adding that Barolo continues to sell well in the off-trade where people seem content with more realistic profits.

Terre del Barolo's average annual output accounts for a sizeable proportion of the zone's total production. Around 4,500 hectolitres of Barolo is sold in bottle, the rest in bulk. Almost one out of every six bottles of Barolo therefore passes through the cooperative's hands. Their responsibility not only to their own members but to every producer of Barolo is enormous and they have a major part to play in determining the wine's future. A wine's image in our realistic times depends a lot on quality at the basic level as well as the high-performance models at the top of the range. The Cantina Produttori di Barbaresco's story is thus one of the most heartening to be told about winemaking in the Langhe today. A visit to Terre del Barolo in late 1988 clearly revealed the other side of the coin: rows of *botti* full of wine going back to the 1980 vintage. The evidence is there for all to see: there is simply too much Barolo.

VIETTI: Enlightened Traditionalism

The series of labels on the Vietti wines seem to promise something old but new, rustic yet sophisticated with a gentle sense of humour. There are bright colours, careful drawings depicting a ladybird climbing an ear of corn, a snail contemplating some woodland flowers or a tumbling pile of almonds, hazelnuts and grapes. The Vietti wines are not a disappointment: made with care and precision, they propose solid Langhe traditions with generous fruit and style.

Alfredo Currado, born in 1932, is a well-built man with severe but warm eyes. He often seems rather a reclusive character, and would prefer to leave public relations to son-in-law and commercial director Mario Cordero. With a glass of wine in his hand, however, Currado can be persuaded to relax. He says that he only became a Barolo producer by chance. Having trained in enology in the early fifties, Alfredo was introduced to Luciana Vietti on a blind date by his friend Renato Ratti when both were working in Canelli. Luciana Vietti's family were *contadini* who had farmed grapes and made wine since the early part of the century. Most of the family vineyards in Castiglione Falletto were sold during the war, but the cellar which tumbles down the north side of the village was still intact in the fifties. Currado's first

vintage in 1960 was fermented in the old-fashioned open topped *tini* and made to a traditional recipe.

The year 1961 was the first in which wine was bottled under the Vietti label, and in 1963 the first cru designation appeared. Currado cites Beppe Colla of Prunotto as being the other pioneer of the cru, and remembers the objections raised at the time by the French to prevent the word 'cru' from appearing on a Barolo label. 'I have always just put the geographical attribution of the wine on the label,' he says. The first Vietti cru was Rocche, the famous Castiglione vineyard where Vietti own one hectare. Rocche has always been the flagship Barolo for Currado, because he feels the vineyard produces wines of exceptional balance and structure that are capable of ageing well. Villero, where Vietti also have just under one hectare, is for Currado a 'second growth' with wines high in alcohol and acidity that need time to mature. The other owned vineyards are 3.5 hectares at Scarrone in Castiglione, which are mostly planted to barbera. The initially bewildering range of other crus produced by Vietti varies from year to year, depending on the quality of grapes produced by the *contadini*. Barolo sites that have appeared on Vietti labels include Meriondina in the 1960s, Bussia in the late 1970s, and now Brunate from 1985. Barolo from the Briacca vineyard (a part of Rocche in Castiglione) had been a minor legend in being a unique example of a wine made from 100 per cent nebbiolo of the rosé subvariety. The fifty-year old vines were replanted in 1986.

While Barolo will always be the heart of Vietti's 80,000-bottle production, the wide range of other wines is equally worthy of attention. In Barbaresco there are now two crus, a ripe, perfumed Rabajà having recently been added to the more robust wine from Masseria. Dolcetto and Barbera mainly come from the best vineyards in Monforte: Bussia (Dolcetto and Barbera), Disa (Dolcetto), Sant'Anna (Dolcetto) and Pian Romualdo (Barbera). These wines are amongst the most dense and concentrated Dolcetti and Barbere produced anywhere in the Albese. Fioretto is the name of Vietti's *uvaggio* from Scarrone: a blend of nebbiolo, barbera and the almost extinct neyrano, partially aged in small oak casks. The total production of this wine is around 200 cases. The two Nebbiolo d'Alba from San Michele and San Giacomo are among the best of their kind: elegant and perfumed Nebbiolo. In 1964 Vietti were among the very first to vinify Arneis: the few hundred cases they produce each year are always sold out within a few days. Vietti even make a little Moscato d'Asti at the Cascinetta farm under the care of Mario Cordero.

With this plethora of wines from tiny vineyards, Currado appears to have covered virtually every niche that the fanatical lover of Albese wines could imagine. As a pioneer of such specialization, it is a surprise to hear Currado talk about turning his hand to producing blended wines. The first reason he offers is romantic and enigmatic: 'Because I like old-fashioned things.' But it seems the deeper motivation for this change of heart is disillusionment with the way the single-vineyard concept has latterly been exploited by producers all too eager to slap any old vineyard name on their labels. 'Crus are in an inflationary state,' says Alfredo, 'we have to go back and concentrate on the historic crus.'

Both in their own vineyards and those from which they buy grapes, Vietti favour a virtually 'organic' approach: fertilization of the soil every three years with animal manure, ploughing every three years, cutting of grass rather than use of weedkiller, minimal chemical treatments. Pruning of the second bunch of grapes on every cane keeps yields low. Currado believes that since 1984 there has been a leap in the average quality of Barolo, and puts this down to lower yields and greater readiness to declassify wines. In his opinion the maximum yield for good quality nebbiolo is 60 quintals per hectare rather than the 80 quintals allowed by DOCG.

Similarly in the cellar, Currado adopts a careful traditional approach. His daughter, Elisabetta, has for years been a major influence in the way the wines are made. She trained at Alba's Enological School and then worked for a year at various wineries in California. In 1989 Betta took charge of running Ornella Muti's new winery in Ovada, Abazzia di Vallechiara. Her younger brother Luca has now graduated in enology at Alba, and is hoping to spend a year in Bordeaux before settling down to work in Castiglione Falletto.

The Vietti vinification policy involves temperature-controlled fermentation in stainless steel, long maceration times and use of *cappello sommerso* for nebbiolo. The Vietti Barolos of 1982 stayed in contact with the skins for forty-five days, although thirty days is more typical. Currado is dismissive of the problems of *cappello sommerso*: 'Of course there are risks. It's like crossing the road: if you don't pay attention, it's dangerous.' Currado is not a man to compromise on the style of his wines, and he accepts that for the British-trained palate, they may be difficult to understand. He cites the principle characteristic of Albese wines as being their tannin. Malolactic fermentation is encouraged immediately after the alcoholic fermentation, and Barolo is kept in *botti* of about 30-hectolitre capacity for about two years. After wood ageing the wine may be held in stainless steel tanks for a period before bottling. None of the Vietti red wines are filtered (from 1989 even Dolcetto is only fined). Currado sees bottle ageing as a crucial factor in appreciating Barolo, and aims to extend the one-year period that his wines are held in bottle before sale.

Currado sees a bright future for his own brand of enlightened traditionalism. He claims that after the initial euphoria of those converted to the *barrique* has died down, many producers are returning to traditional winemaking techniques. He also sees an increased demand from the public for a well-made traditional style of wine. In recent years, the most important market for Vietti wines has been the USA, but now Italy itself is waking up to the genuine quality offered by the Currado family. There are very few competitors in the Albese who can honestly claim a similar tradition of excellence stretching back thirty years.

ERRATA (*Barolo* by Michael Garner & Paul Merritt)
The publishers appologise for the following omissions:
the graph which should appear on p52

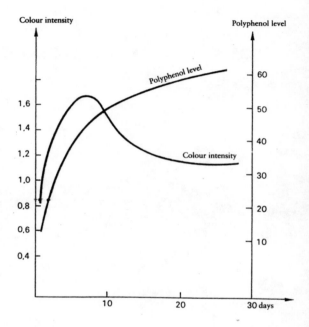

7

WHO'S WHO IN
THE LANGHE

Accademia Torregiorgi

In a tiny cellar behind the Contea restaurant in Neive, around 7–8,000 bottles of Barbaresco are bottled each year. The winery was founded in the seventies by the Milanese, Mario Giorgi. The grapes come from several growers in the Messoirano vineyard. These wines receive long cask ageing after a brief maceration period, and are nearly always labelled *riserva*. A small amount of Barolo Arnulfo is also produced.

Azienda Agricola Lorenzo Accomasso

A link with the past in their vinification methods, Lorenzo Accomasso and his sister Elena macerate their Barolo on the skins for an extraordinary length of time. The results would not please a modernist palate, but there is no doubt that the small family vineyards in La Morra's Rocche, Rocchette and Rocchettevino are tended with great care. The Dolcetto too is in a rustic mould.

Fratelli Alessandria

A 6 hectare estate in Verduno, producing a cru Monvigliero Barolo. Attractive, early maturing wines in a traditional style. Production includes the rare Pelaverga.

Elio Altare

See p. 142.

Arione Vini

Bruno Arione is based at Castiglione Tinella and makes good Moscato d'Asti San Giorgio and Dolcetto d'Alba Il Paolo from his five hectares of vineyards. Production spans the full range of Albese wines including generic Barolo and Barbaresco.

Giacomo Ascheri

Lightweight, fruity wines from a winery in Bra that produces many of its wide range of wines from grapes grown in its own vineyards. The family's 17 hectares are scattered throughout the Langhe. Since Giacomo's death in 1988, young Matteo Ascheri is in charge.

Azienda Agricola Azelia

The maximum annual production of Lorenzo Scavino's winery in Castiglione Falletto is about 45,000 bottles of Barolo and Dolcetto. The family vineyard, Bricco Fiasco, lies adjacent to that of cousin Enrico Scavino. In the best years, the vineyard on the crown of the hill is vinified separately as Bricco Punta. Since 1982 the Barolo has been made to a modern, elegant and fruity design by son Luigi and his wife Lorella.

Fratelli Barale

Young Sergio Barale has a heavy burden of responsibility, running one of Barolo's oldest family firms since the recent deaths of his uncle, father and his brother Carlo. Founded in 1870, Barale remains a traditional company, despite its small production of an unremarkable Pinot Chardonnay (sic) and Arneis Perdaudin. Lengthy cask maturation, followed by ageing in demijohn, produces wines that are fast maturing. The Barolo is made mainly from grapes grown in the Castellero cru in Barolo, while Barbaresco comes from the Rabajà vineyard. Production c. 100,000 bottles, of which one-third is normally Barolo.

Produttori del Barbaresco

See p. 171.

Bel Colle

A 10 hectare estate in Verduno founded in 1978 and producing some 150,000 bottles each year. At present enologist Paolo Torchio is most noted for his spicy Pelaverga, but other wines such as Barolo 'Monvijé' may well be worth watching in future.

Azienda Agricola Fratelli Bera

The young Bera brothers, Walter and Attilio, are highly respected producers of Asti Spumante and Moscato d'Asti from their 18 hectares of vines at Neviglie.

Bersano

A large, old, established company, based at Nizza Monferrato. Recent changes of ownership have no doubt prevented their wines from attaining consistent quality levels despite some good vineyards in Serralunga. About 50,000 cases of run-of-the-mill Albese wines are made out of a total production of 350,000 cases.

Azienda Agricola Luigi Bianco e Figlio

A tiny *contadino* producer in Barbaresco producing a total of around 10,000 bottles of three separate crus: Rabajà, Faset and Ronchi.

Bianco Mauro (Cascina Morassino)

Small family-run winery owning some 4.5 hectares of vines in the
Ovello district of Barbaresco. Good, fruity Dolcetto Vincenziana and
less impressive Barbaresco plus a range of *vini da tavola*.

Giacomo Borgogno

The large Borgogno cellar has dominated the village of Barolo since
1848. Today, the younger members of the Boschis family are carrying
on their ancestors' traditional styles of winemaking. A feature of the
company is their policy, unique in the zone, of putting away stocks of
good vintages in bottle and releasing them some twenty years later,
after decanting and rebottling. Important landowners in the Barolo
area with some 20 hectares of vines. Annual production is around
300,000 bottles, of which about half is Barolo.

Borgogno Serio e Battista

The Borgogno brothers' neat, white cellar stands in a prominent
position midway along the Cannubi hill overlooking their three
hectares of vines. In addition to their cru Cannubi, they also produce
Barolo and Barbaresco from bought-in grapes. Traditional winemaking methods result in rustic, heavyweight wines.

Azienda Agricola Gianfranco Bovio

Bovio manages to combine the profession of restaurateur at La
Morra's highly rated Belvedere with that of winemaker further down
the hill in his Gattera vineyard. The Barolo Gattera expresses the
elegance and perfume typical of this zone. The approach to vinification tends to the modern, with relatively short maceration and cask
ageing. Also a good Dolcetto Firagnetti and from 1985 Barolo
Arburina (*sic*).

Azienda Agricola Brezza

Another catering/winemaking operation. The new cellar is below the rebuilt Hotel Brezza in Barolo, where Giacomo and Oreste vinify Barolo, Dolcetto and Barbera in a sturdy rustic style. In some years, Sarmassa and Castellero are vinified apart.

Bricco Maiolica

A small producer in Diano whose cru Sori' Bricco Maiolica is exemplary in its simple, grapey fruit. Good Dolcetto *normale* and Barbera, but the Moscato so far lacks style.

Azienda Agricola Fratelli Brovia

Miss Brovia is one of the great personalities of the Langhe, tirelessly beavering away at her one-woman PR campaign. In their cellar in Castiglione Falletto her brother works diligently away from the spotlight. In the best vintages a selection of their Rocche Barolo is made as 'Rocche dei Brovia', a good example of healthy traditionalism. Other wines include an extraordinary, overblown Dolcetto of nearly 15 per cent alcohol called 'Solatio', and Barbaresco from Rio Sordo.

Commendatore G. B. Burlotto

Marina Burlotto carries on traditions such as fermenting in open *tini* in this historic company founded in 1850. The results are no doubt authentic, but seem out of touch to a modern palate. Production at Verduno includes Barolo, Dolcetto and Pelaverga of about 80,000 bottles per annum.

Ca' Rome'

This small winery is located above the Rabajà vineyard in Barbaresco.

Owner/winemaker Romano Marengo produces tiny quantities of different *cuvées* of Barolo and Barbaresco in good vintages only. Barbaresco *normale* and 'Maria di Brun' (in honour of his mother) are joined by Barolo from the Carpegna vineyard in the Sorano district of Serralunga. Old-fashioned wines of uneven quality.

Dott. Giuseppe Cappellano di Teobaldo Cappellano

One of the last true examples of Barolo chinato is made by Teobaldo Cappellano. Chinato is a bitter-sweet drink of tonic properties made by adding old Barolo to an infusion of alcohol, quinine and various aromatic barks and herbs. It even has its own DOC. This small winery also makes Nebbiolo d'Alba, Barbera and a regular Barolo in the traditional Serralunga mould.

Tenuta Carretta

Since 1985 Carretta has been owned by Alba's massive textile and clothing manufacturer, Miroglio. Previously the Veglia family had built up sizeable vineyard holdings throughout the Langhe, but particularly in the Roero. Carretta's Arneis and Roero show signs that the new bosses are investing in quality, so the Barolo Cannubi may be worth watching in future.

Cascine Drago

Alba's well-loved pharmacist, Luciano de Giacomi, is none other than the Grand Master of the Order of the Knights of the Truffle and the Wines of Alba. As such he created Piemonte's first regional *enoteca* at Grinzane. His winemaking activities take place at San Rocco Seno d'Elvio, the zone which lies between Diano and Barbaresco. The range of products is large and eccentric, but Bricco del Drago itself (especially the Vigna del Mace selection made in the best years) is a very successful *vino da tavola uvaggio* of Dolcetto (85 per cent) and

Nebbiolo (15 per cent). Total production of about 40,000 bottles, of which a third is Bricco del Drago.

Castello di Neive

The Stupino brothers of Turin purchased the castle, vineyards and ancient cellar in 1959. The Castello's wine was winning prizes in London as long ago as 1862, when Louis Oudart supervised production. The estate still extends over 25 hectares of Barbaresco, taking in crus Santo Stefano, Gallina, Messoirano and Basarin. The house style of Barbaresco is usually quite austere and tannic, yet always refined and elegant. Good Dolcetto from Basarin and very fine Arneis *vino da tavola*.

Castello di Verduno

This is the castle in Verduno which King Carlo Alberto bought to experiment with Barolo production. The winery is now owned by the Burlotto sisters, who produce both Barolo and a well-structured Pelaverga.

Fratelli Olivio e Gildo Cavallotto

The Cavallotto brothers own some 16 hectares of prime vineyards at Bricco Boschis in Castiglione Falletto. Three separate Barolo crus are produced: San Giuseppe, Colle Sud Ovest and Punta Marcello. Punta Marcello, from the highest point of the vineyard, is the biggest wine and benefits from extra wood age. Maximum potential production of Barolo is c. 38,000 bottles, plus a further 50,000 bottles of Dolcetto and Barbera. These are attractively tarry, warm and generous wines; old fashioned due to their lengthy spell in *botte*. Vintages from the end of the eighties appear to have been vinified after a more modern formula, so a change in style should be expected.

Ceretto

See p. 146.

Azienda Vinicola Fratelli Cigliutti

A highly reputed *contadino* producer of a maximum of 25,000 bottles of Barbaresco, Barbera, Dolcetto and Freisa, Renato Cigliutti is based at Bricco di Neive. He is slowly updating his careful and conscientious traditional winemaking methods and the first signs in the form of a ripe and perfumed Barbaresco Serraboella (*sic*) 1985 show great promise.

Azienda Agricola Domenico Clerico

Domenico is a clear-thinking modernist, but with deep roots in the soil of Monforte. His Barolo Ciabot Mentin Ginestra combines strength with an extraordinary range of perfumes; while in their precise flavours, both his Freisa and Arte (a *barrique*-matured *vino da tavola* Nebbiolo/Barbera) demonstrate great skill in the cellar. A small jewel of a winery, founded only in 1976 with a capacity of 900 hectolitres and 7 hectares of vineyards in the Monforte area.

Cogno-Marcarini

Jolly Elvio Cogno masterminds the annual production of between 50–60,000 bottles of some excellent, traditionally made wine. Business partner Anna Marcarini is the great granddaughter of Cav. Tarditi, one of the most important producers of Barolo at the end of the last century. Their low, vaulted cellars lie off Piazza Martiri, and Elvio explains how in Tarditi's time, this part of La Morra was 'a hill of wine'. The grapes arrived at the press houses on the street leading up to the town's main square and, after fermentation, the wines were racked down to the next level of the hill (the present cellars) for ageing. They would then be transported away to their eventual destination from a collection point on the road lying below the winery. These days things happen on a much smaller scale! Up to 15,000 bottles of Barolo Brunate, slightly less of Barolo La Serra and, from 1987 onwards, 5,000 bottles of Barolo Canun are fermented at low temperatures (not exceeding 25°C) with a long maceration on the skins (five or six weeks) and spend two to three years in wood. These rich, soft, perfumed and velvety wines are archetypal examples of the La Morra style. Production also includes the unique Dolcetto Boschi di Berri from a small plot of pre-phylloxera vines and further cru Dolcetti Fontanazza, Nassone and La Serra (around 22,000 bottles in total), plus some 1,500 bottles of Barbera Fontanazza.

Tenute Colue'

Purchased by his family in 1864, the Colue' estate is today owned by Massimo Oddero. The 15 hectares of vineyards are principally in Diano, but also in Barolo's Cannubi and Treiso's Rombone. Oddero's top Dolcetto site is Vigna Tampa; he also makes a *normale* version, and has recently planted chardonnay.

Confratelli di San Michele

This 'fraternity' is a small and reliable cooperative of Barbaresco producers based at Neive.

Aldo Conterno

See p. 153.

Giacomo Conterno

See p. 157.

Conterno Fantino

The company is owned and run by two generations of the Conterno family: father Lorenzo who supervises the vineyards at Ginestra in Monforte, and sons Diego and Claudio together with their brother-in-law Guido Fantino (ex-*cantiniere* at Prunotto) who manage the cellars and the administrative side of the business. The current production of 70,000 bottles is shortly to be increased to 100,000 with the purchase of new vineyards at Bricco Bastia for dolcetto and chardonnay. Small quantities of impressive Barolo come from two plots on the same hillside: Sori' Ginestra and Vigna del Gris. An early-drinking Ginestrino Nebbiolo delle Langhe and Barbera Vignota are also produced. A *vino da tavola* Mon Pra' (50 per cent barbera and 50 per cent nebbiolo), aged in *barrique*, is in its early stages of development.

Giuseppe Contratto

A historic spumante house at Canelli, whose production includes Barolo and Barbaresco.

Cornarea

One of the first estates to specialize in the production of Arneis in the Roero, Cornarea's vineyards occupy some of the best sites in Canale. After Ceretto sold his interest in the company, the quality was sometimes variable, but now enologist Luigi Bertini together with owner Francesca Rapetti has put Cornarea's Arneis and Roero right back on course.

Azienda Agricola Giuseppe Cortese

A dedicated, small *contadino* producer in Barbaresco with vineyards in the Rabajà cru. Giuseppe Cortese also grows dolcetto and barbera in the nearby Trifolera vineyard. Total production of 32,000 bottles of well-made, traditional wines.

Deltetto

See p. 180.

Tenuta Denegri/Cantine Ca' Bianca

The small Denegri estate in La Morra was sold to Ca' Bianca in 1985. Ca' Bianca is owned by a young Italo/Swiss partnership which may bring some new life to the winemaking in future.

Fratelli Dogliani

Dogliani wines are nowadays marketed as the 'Sette Cascine', seven farms which include some prime sites in Barolo, La Morra and Serralunga. A large firm producing a lot of dull wines.

Redento Dogliotti e Figli (Azienda Agricola Caudrina)

Redento Dogliotti has a long-standing reputation as a fine Moscato d'Asti producer. Today his son Romano continues the tradition with all the benefits of modern technology, aided by brothers Pierfranco and Claudio. The family owns 15 hectares of vines at Castiglione Tinella, making a small amount of Dolcetto and Barbera as well as the gloriously balanced Moscato, a little of which is now also made as cru Galeisa.

Dosio

A very small grower with vineyards high in the hills at the back of La Morra. Cru Barolo Fossati and Dolcetti from Bricco Dente, Nassone and Serradenari are produced in tiny quantities to reliable standards.

Cantina Duca d'Asti/Michele Chiarlo

A well-known firm producing an eclectic assortment of Piemontese wines including oaked and unoaked Gavi and various experiments with *barrique*-aged Nebbiolo/Barbera blends (Barilot and l'Airone). Until recently the Moscato d'Asti was the pick of their rather ordinary

Albese wines, but Michele Chiarlo has introduced Barolo (Rocche di Castiglione Falletto) and Barbaresco (Rabajà) from the 1982 vintage, so better things may be on the way.

Poderi di Luigi Einaudi

Einaudi was Italy's first postwar president in 1948. His family's winery in Dogliani has a tradition of Barolo production going back to 1897. The company owns 25 hectares of vineyards in the Langhe and produces an old-fashioned Barolo from the San Luigi vineyard.

Vignaiolo Elvio Pertinace

Named after Alba's Roman Emperor, this cooperative was founded in 1973 by twelve growers in Treiso owning 100 hectares of vineyards. Reliable producers of Dolcetto and Barbaresco, also growing barbera, moscato and chardonnay.

Fenocchio Giacomo e Figli

A small estate with 6.8 hectares of vineyard producing about 2,000 cases annually of traditional Barolo from Bussia Sottana and Cannubi Boschis.

Azienda Agricola Pianpolvere Soprano di Riccardo Fenocchio

Traditionally made Barolo and Barbera of a weighty style. Young enologist Ferruccio Fenocchio may gradually modernize vinification. Cru wines from Bussia and Pianpolvere.

Maria Feyles

A serious, small negociant winery in Alba who produce rugged, old-style Barbaresco and Barolo Ginestra.

Tenimenti di Barolo e Fontanafredda

This impressive estate has a virtual monopoly on the vineyards of the Serralunga valley, owning 110 hectares. Founded as a winery in 1878 by the son of King Vittorio Emanuele II and Bela Rosin, the Tuscan bank Monte del Paschi di Siena became owners in 1931. Employing about 100 people, Fontanafredda produce 5 million bottles each year. Unusually for a large winemaker, they have succeeded in vinifying a range of cru Baroli in the best vintages. The crus are mostly from the Serralunga zone and exhibit subtle variations due to different soils and expositions. The Barolo crus produced first in 1978 were: La Rosa, San Pietro, Garil, Gallaretto, La Delizia, Bianca, Lazzarito, Gattinera, and from the commune of Barolo, La Villa. Apart from a full range of traditional Albese wines, Fontanafredda are noted for their spumante production, especially an elegant Asti Spumante and a good *metodo classico* wine Contessa Rosa (available as Brut or Pas Dosé) and the 100 per cent pinot noir single vineyard Gattinera Brut.

Franco-Fiorina

Giuseppe and Elsa Fontana own no vineyards, but run a respected negociant winery in Alba with a capacity of 7,000 hectolitres. Production covers the full range of traditional Albese wines plus Chardonnay Favorita and Pelaverga. Enologist Armando Cordero produces a middle-weight, elegant style of Barolo and Barbaresco that has good keeping powers. Founded in 1925, Franco-Fiorina have been bottling wine since 1947.

Gianni Gagliardo

Owned by Paolo Colla, this La Morra-based winery produces a wide selection of soundly made wines, including some rather uninspiring cru bottlings.

Gaja

See p. 162.

Casa Vinicola Bruno Giacosa

Bruno Giacosa is one of the landmarks of Albese winemaking. Like the man, the wines are austere, monumental and unyielding. Barolo crus Rocche and Villero in Castiglione Falletto and Falletto and Vigna Rionda from Serralunga, as well as Barbaresco from Santo Stefano (grapes purchased from Castello di Neive) have become legends in their own lifetime. Believing in minimal interference with the wines, Giacosa may leave them in wood for up to seven years. His genius lies in selecting the finest grapes, a talent learnt from grandfather Carlo. Apart from Cascina Falletto in Serralunga, the family owns no vineyards. Production at the Neive cellars runs to some 300,000 bottles per annum, including a large proportion of a soft, slightly sweet Arneis that is hugely popular in Germany.

Fratelli Giacosa

The other Giacosas in Neive are the brothers Valerio and Renzo. They are an unpretentious negociant winery with no vineyards of their own, buying in grapes to make a range of *normale* plus cru wines from Roncaglia in Barbaresco and Pira (Castiglione Falletto) in Barolo. A *barrique*-aged Barbera from Mango, available under either Maria Gioana or Alto Mango label, shows promise.

Giovannini Moresco

The legendary 12 hectare Podere Pajoré Barbaresco cru in Treiso is now owned by Gaja, and no longer bottled under the founder's label.

Cantina del Glicine

Stylish, vigorous and fruity Barbaresco from crus Cura' (10,000 bottles) and Marcorino (2,000 bottles) is produced by Adriana Marzi and Roberto Bruno in their fine old cellar in Neive. Similarly small quantities of Dolcetto and Barbera are made, as well as Glicinello, a pink wine made from nebbiolo and freisa fermented *in bianco*, and a good, fresh Arneis.

Azienda Agricola Elio Grasso

Until he was forty, Elio Grasso worked in a bank. Then he returned to farm his father's vineyards in Monforte and began bottling his own production in 1978. Production of Barolo amounts to only 2,600 cases, firstly from Gavarini (1.67 hectares) which is divided into small sub crus: Runcot, Chiniera and Grassi. The family's other Barolo vineyard is a 2.46 hectare section of Ginestra named Casa Mate'. Grasso's remaining production is divided between Barbera (1,160 cases) and Dolcetto (450 cases). The style of wines has been a little heavy and even coarse in the past, but recent vintages show some improvements in finesse.

Tenute Cisa Asinari dei Marchesi di Gresy

The aristocratic di Gresy family have entrusted young Alberto with the running of their Martinenga estate. Amongst the 12 hectares are some of the finest vineyard sites in Barbaresco. Vinification is in a relatively modern style, with the wine fermented at 28°C, a fifteen day maceration, short cask ageing and plenty of bottle age before release. From 1985 the Gaiun cru is initially aged half in Allier *barrique*, half in stainless steel, before the whole is married in *botte* for a brief period. Gresy's top Barbaresco cru is Camp Gros. Good Dolcetto Monte Aribaldo and interesting Chardonnay come from another 9 hectares of Treiso vineyards. New plantings of 2.5 hectares of chardonnay, sauvignon and barbera have been made below Martinenga. Gresy's Moscato is made for him by Rivetti, while he is also experimenting with a *passito* version flippantly labelled 'L'altro Moscato', the 'other' Moscato.

Malabaila di Canale

The noble estate of Malabaila encompasses an impressive 22 hectares centred around a castle at Canale. Roero *normale* and cru Bric Volta are produced as well as Nebbiolo d'Alba and an Arneis cru Pradvaj.

Azienda Agricola Malvira' dei Fratelli Damonte

Roberto Damonte is one of the most respected winemakers in the Roero. His 4 hectare Malvira' estate at Canale produces delicate Arneis, Favorita and Roero.

Marchesi di Barolo

The Falletti family were the originators of Barolo in the early nineteenth century. The Marchesi's properties became Opera Pia Barolo when the family line came to an end, and in 1919 were purchased by the present owners, the Abbona family. The well-equipped cellars in Barolo produce a wide range of Piemontese wines every year, including a Barolo *normale* and in good years 70,000 bottles of six different cru wines from their 35 hectare holdings in the commune of Barolo. The vineyards are Sarmassa (1.94 hectares), Brunate (3.34 hectares), Costa di Rose (1.32 hectares), Cannubi Muscatel (2.74 hectares), Cannubi (0.98 hectares) and Valletta (3.34 hectares). New enologists are being employed to modernize the style of the wines, and the cellar also benefits from the inspiration of *cantiniere* Luciano Sandrone.

Bartolo Mascarello

Old school *Barolista* Bartolo Mascarello is a tradition in his own right.

A genial man rarely seen without his favourite flat cap, Mascarello is the local oracle to be consulted on all matters relating to the history of Barolo and its wines. Owning land in the Cannubi, Rue' and San Lorenzo (Barolo) and Torriglione (La Morra) vineyards, he produces around 30,000 bottles of wine annually. They are made to traditional specifications: his Barolo (up to 20,000 bottles) is a blend from these four plots of land ('If I made a cru,' he quips, 'it would only cost more') and is macerated on the skins for around four weeks followed by up to three years in cask. *Conoscenti* consistently place it in the top rank. The balance of production is made up of Dolcetto and a tiny amount of Freisa. The 'secret' of Mascarello's ripe, perfumed Barolo lies in the low yields of his vineyards: he leaves just one bunch of grapes per shoot. In the absence of any successors willing to carry on the family business (his daughter apparently does not like wine), young enologist Alessandro Fantino is pledged to carry on in the great man's footsteps. One 'modernization' everyone hopes he will make, is to install a telephone in the *cantina*!

Giuseppe Mascarello

See p. 168.

Massolino Giuseppe (Azienda Agricola Vigna Rionda)

One of the few small grower/bottlers in the Serralunga valley, with vineyards in Vigna Rionda, Parafada and Margheria (bordering the Marenca-Rivette estate). An individual approach to fermentation (starting off at low temperatures and building up in a crescendo to over 30°C) plus lengthy barrel ageing gives densely structured wines in the old-fashioned Serralunga style. Regular Barolo and cru Vigna Rionda, plus Dolcetto (Vigneto Barilot) and Barbera (Vigneto Margheria) and Nebbiolo delle Langhe.

Moccagatta

A tiny Barbaresco producer making wines from the eponymous cru in a traditional style.

Azienda Agricola Monfalletto di Cordero di Monte-zemolo

The 22 hectare Monfalletto estate in La Morra is dominated by a magnificent cedar of Lebanon, visible the length of the valley. Since the death of Paolo Cordero in 1988, his sons Giovanni and Enrico are in full charge of the firm. The family are noble descendants of the Falletti clan. Both Barolo and Dolcetto are fermented at low temperatures (22–3°C) to emphasize the more perfumed character of La Morra wines. Enrico VI, a 2 hectare cru in Castiglione Falletto's Villero, exhibits a fuller, more structured style.

Tenuta Montanello

An *azienda agricola* just north of the village of Castiglione Falletto run by the Monchiero brothers. Traditional vinification and lengthy barrel ageing result in full-bodied, weighty Barolo.

Angelo Negro

See p. 182.

Fratelli Oddero

A traditional family company dating back to 1878, Oddero own 20 hectares of vineyards. These are mostly spread throughout the best crus of the Barolo zone (Barolo accounts for half of their 180,000 bottle annual production), but also in Barbaresco. In charge is enologist Luigi Oddero, assisted by his niece Cristina. At present only blended wines are produced to a high standard, but a cru Barolo from Vigna Rionda is rumoured to be on the way. Dolcetto is also recommended.

Parocco di Neive

This small, chaotic cellar is run by Neive's parish priest Don Giuseppe Cogno with the help of brother Achille. Barbaresco, Barbera and Dolcetto are produced from the Gallina and Basarin vineyards. The ripe, forward fruit which the regular Barbaresco Gallina shows in good vintages tends to be muted by extra barrel age in the *riserva* version.

Azienda Agricola Pasquero

Father Secondo and sons Giovanni and Silvano maintain high standards on their tiny Barbaresco estate at Bricco di Neive. Their cru Barbaresco is Sori' Paytin, made with temperature-controlled fermentation and about one year's age in *botte*. Total production of 40,000 bottles includes Dolcetto, Barbera and a new Chardonnay.

Azienda Agricola Pelissero

Small *contadino* producer of around 40,000 bottles of Barbera, Barbaresco, Dolcetto, Freisa and Grignolino based in Treiso. Barbaresco Vanotu (8,000 bottles) and Dolcetto Munfri'na (15,000 bottles) show some promise.

Pio Cesare

This famous negociant house is based in the heart of Alba and was founded in 1881 by Cesare Pio. The present owner Pio Boffa has turned tradition on its head by introducing an increasing proportion of *barrique*-aged wine into his Barolo from 1978 onwards. The

60,000 bottles of Barolo produced annually are always a blend of grapes from different sites, although predominantly from the family's own vineyards at Ornato in Serralunga. Of the other wines made, the oak-aged Chardonnay from Treiso, Piodilei, is perhaps the most significant.

E. Pira e Figli

After the death of Luigi Pira in 1980, the tiny cellar and remaining 1.5 hectares of vineyards (in Cannubi and other crus in the commune of Barolo) were purchased by the house of Giacomo Borgogno. Chiara Boschis, now in charge, does not promise to resurrect all the historic vinification techniques, such as crushing by foot, but the cellar would seem to be in good hands. Recent vintages have given a subtly aromatic style of Barolo.

Cantina della Porta Rossa

Luigi Artusio, former winemaker at Fontanafredda, makes Dolcetto from Diano that resembles his own larger than life character. Particularly the crus Praedurent, Piadvenza and Bruni, these are wines to demonstrate the masculine side of Dolcetto. The cellar is owned by Domenico Berzia and Artusio's wife, Marilisa Rizzi. They own no vineyards, but buy in grapes. Barolo from Serralunga's Delizia cru and Barbaresco from Faset are made in a tannic, archtraditional fashion.

Prunotto

See p. 176.

Azienda Agricola Punset

This Neive-based firm founded in 1968 is owner of 20 hectares of vineyards in Barbaresco, producing so far unimpressive Barbaresco, Chardonnay, etc.

Azienda Agricola Fratelli Rabino

The Rabino family at Santa Vittoria are amongst the longest-established winemakers in the Roero. The brothers today produce some 80,000 bottles including an unusually rich and concentrated Nebbiolo d'Alba and a Roero of real promise.

Ratti/Abbazia dell' Annunziata

See p. 184.

Azienda Agricola Battista Giuseppe Rinaldi

Battista Giuseppe Rinaldi, one of the zone's elder statesmen, graduated from Alba's Enological School in 1937. Rinaldi owns land in the Barolo section of Brunate, Ravera and Le Coste (which surrounds the ancient winery). His winemaking methods are ultra-traditional: a proportion of the wine is still fermented in open *tini*, and in great vintages, following lengthy cask ageing, the *riserva* is kept in 2-litre *bottiglioni* for further maturation. These bottles are then kept upright before being decanted by hand into regular bottles before release. While modernists might dispute the validity of his methods, the rugged *normale* and Riserva Brunata (*sic*) are wines of phenomenal concentration and longevity. And that, maintains Rinaldi, is what his customers are looking for.

Francesco Rinaldi e Figli

Amongst his 12 hectares of vineyards, three hectares of Cannubi and 2.3 hectares of Brunate are vinified individually by Luciano Rinaldi much in the style of his forebears. The company offices and warehouses are in Alba, and the cellar Palazzo is at Cannubi. Though the wines generally have a good reputation, recent vintages have been disappointing.

Alfredo Roagna (I Paglieri)

The heartening story of a small *contadino* winery that came good. Wines made by Alfredo Roagna – a leading figure of the modern school – are much sought after by fashionable *enoteche* and restaurants. His singular Opera Prima *vino da tavola* is a blend of different vintages of Nebbiolo aged in *barrique*. Alfredo seems to prefer such individual flights of fancy to the official sanction of DOCG, and markets his elegant Crichet Pajé as a *vino da tavola* rather than the Barbaresco it is perfectly entitled to be. His less inspiring regular Barbaresco, Dolcetto *novello* and new Chardonnay seem strangely out of place in this company. Father Giovanni helps out in the vineyards.

Azienda Agricola Rocche Costamagna

Claudia Ferrarese Locatelli, together with her husband and son, runs this tiny estate in La Morra. Barolo from various tiny parcels in the Rocche and Rocchette vineyards is produced in a light, austere style.

Podere Rocche dei Manzoni

Former restaurateur from Piacenza, Valentino Migliorini now owns one of Monforte's most impressive cellars. Certainly the sight of some 500 *barriques* will be a shock to the traditionalist. The nebbiolo/barbera blend Bricco Manzoni was amongst the first successful new-oak-aged wines in the Langhe. Today Migliorini also uses new oak for his Baroli, both Riserva and Vigna 'd la Roul. His white wines, including Chardonnay, are much less interesting.

Cantina Gigi Rosso

At the time of writing, Gigi Rosso is president of Barolo's *consorzio*. His cellar produces 300,000 bottles of a range of Albese wines including a respectable Barolo from Serralunga's Arione vineyard, a

rich, alcoholic Barbera and a good Dolcetto from Diano, Moncolom-
betto.

Azienda Agricola Luciano Sandrone

This tiny winery close to Barolo's village centre was established only in
1977 when Luciano Sandrone realized his dreams by buying just over
one hectare of land in Cannubi. With the help of daughter Barbara and
agronomist brother Luca, Sandrone produces an average of only
23,000 bottles a year, though he plans to acquire new vineyards in the
near future. Believing in a 'hand-crafted' approach, winemaker
Luciano shows remarkable talent. Dolcetto (13,000 bottles) is rich,
grapey and concentrated. Barbera Paiagallo (3,000 bottles first
produced in 1988) shows a deliciously round, juicy ripeness. The jewel
in the crown is Barolo Cannubi Boschis. Made from low yields (40–5
hectolitres per hectare) and harvested early to retain perfume and
freshness, the wine is matured in 7-hectolitre *fusti* of French oak to
bring it to an early peak. Luciano insists that there is a tradition of
using smaller barrels in the village, and finds French wood very similar
to the now unobtainable local oak. Sandrone is one of the zone's most
promising small producers, and his Barolo is now amongst the finest
examples of Cannubi.

Saracco

Respected Moscato producer in Castiglione Tinella, now also making
a version from late harvested grapes. A rich but firm, unoaked
Chardonnay Prasué was first produced in 1988.

Mario Savigliano e Figlio

This Diano producer makes 25,000 bottles a year of a delicious
Dolcetto from the Bartu' vineyard.

Scarpa

Mario Pesce runs the Scarpa winery with obsessive perfectionism. Although based in the Asti zone at Nizza Monferrato, the house has a tradition of producing Barolo and Barbaresco going back 100 years. The results today are amongst the most refined of Albese wines. A pioneer of cru bottlings since 1961, including Barolo from Tettimorra (La Morra) and Le Coste (Monforte) (the latter presently out of service for replanting), and benchmark Barbaresco from Tettineive and Barberis.

Azienda Agricola Giorgio Scarzello

A 5 hectare estate in the commune of Barolo, shortly due to produce a cru Merenda Barolo.

Azienda Agricola Giovanni Scarzello

In the best traditional style, Giovanni Scarzello believes in interfering with nature as little as possible when producing his 6,000 bottles of Barolo in the vintages that permit. His faith lies in the quality of his grapes from Mosconi in Monforte.

Paolo Scavino di Enrico Scavino

Enrico Scavino applies the same meticulous care to his work in the cellar at Castiglione Falletto as he does in the vineyard (see p. 37). The cleanliness shows through in all his wines, whether Dolcetto, Barbera, Barolo *normale*, Barolo Cannubi or the pinnacle of Scavino's efforts: Bric' del Fiasc'.

Sylla Sebaste

Mauro Sebaste is a dynamic young winemaker who in 1985 took over the reins of the family business begun by his mother Sylla in the mid 1960s. Sparkling wine giants Gancia now hold a 50 per cent stake in the company, but appear to have left Mauro a free hand. A graduate from Alba's Enological School, Mauro Sebaste has constructed an impressive modern winery with banks of stainless steel autoclave and rows of *barriques*. His approach to winemaking is thoroughly modern. Production levels are to be maintained at around 150,000 bottles per annum, with between 20–50,000 bottles each of Arneis, Freisa, Dolcetto and Barolo (cru Bussia and Barolo di Monforte). All are well-made and consistent wines. The balance of the production is made up of a *barrique*-aged Barbera/Nebbiolo blend Bricco Viole and a *novello*-style Dolcetto. Mauro's hard work in the promotion of his products and insistence on holding prices at a reasonable level set a fine example to other young producers.

Aurelio Settimo

A 7 hectare estate in the Annunziata part of La Morra producing Barolo Rocche and Dolcetto. A family company where daughter Tiziana assists father Aurelio. Traditional methods produce an early maturing style of wine.

La Spinona di Pietro Berutti

In some markets the terrier has disappeared from the label and the wines are marketed as La Ghiga. Hearty, old style, tannic Barbaresco including a cru Faset. Berutti also produces a rather neutral Chardonnay.

Terre del Barolo

See p. 188.

Giuseppe Traversa

An eccentric miniature winery at Bricco di Neive that has a 100-case production of a cru Barbaresco where each case contains twelve different pictorial labels! Each depicts suggested foods to accompany the wine (ducks, mushrooms, etc.). Other wines include a dry white Favorita/Arneis blend and a rich Moscato d'Asti.

Valfieri

A large Asti-based company owned by Riccadonna producing a range of mediocre Albese wines amongst its annual 90,000 cases.

Azienda Agricola G.D. Vajra

Aldo Vajra's Cascina San Pionzo is located high in the hills above Barolo in the hamlet of Vergne, with vineyards nearby in Coste, Fossati and Bricco delle Viole. Aiming for a totally organic method of cultivation, Vajra freely blends traditional and modern ideas in the cellar. Barolo cru Bricco delle Viole receives long maceration on the skins, but relatively brief cask maturation. Vajra's most inspired wines are his intense Barbera from Bricco delle Viole and a dry Freisa from Costa di Vergne which in good vintages has a fabulous bouquet of honeysuckle and roses. Total production is no more than 60,000 bottles.

Azienda Vitivinicola Giovanni Veglio

The three Veglio brothers produce some 40,000 bottles a year of full-blooded Dolcetto grown in Diano's Talloria valley.

Viberti

Very small production of good, clean, fruity (but traditional) Barolo

(c. 8,000 bottles per annum) from the hospitable *padrone* of Il Buon Padre trattoria high up in the Vergne district in the commune of Barolo. Barbera and Dolcetto are also made.

Vietti

See p. 192.

Vinicola Piemontese

Major owners of La Morra's Cerequio vineyard, which gives about 40,000 bottles of a rich, soft, traditionally styled Barolo and 3,500 of Barbera. Dolcetto and Barbaresco are made from grapes purchased in Treiso and Barbaresco. One of very few producers with stocks of older vintages of Barolo.

Gianni Voerzio

Gianni's production since he parted ways with brother Roberto majors on Dolcetto, Barbera and a perfumed, fresh Nebbiolo, Ciabot della Luna, from his 6 hectares in La Morra. Very small production of a full-bodied aromatic Barolo from La Serra above Brunate and a fine Arneis from grapes grown in Castellinaldo.

Artigiano Vignaiolo Roberto Voerzio

Roberto is a controversial modernist (hence the disagreement with his brother) who makes a wide range of the classic Langarolo wines in an exciting and individual manner. He describes himself as an *artigiano vignaiolo* – an artisanal *vigneron*. Experiments with lower yields, longer skin contact and less sulphur for his Dolcetto would seem to smack of born-again traditionalism, yet the relatively short maceration and wood ageing for his Barolo La Serra put him firmly in the modernist camp. In 1988, Roberto rented vines in Brunate and

Cerequio to produce about 3,500 bottles of each of these crus. His aim is to reduce the tannin content of Barolo and produce a more accessible wine. Style and elegance are the key words for a range which includes Freisa, a fine Arneis, and a slightly drier style of Moscato d'Asti. Roberto's new purpose-built cellar in La Morra will allow him more space to express himself with wines such as the new Vignaserra *barrique*-matured Nebbiolo/Barbera blend.

8

LA CUCINA

TARTUFO BIANCO

The most evocative symbol of the rich and earthy cooking of the Langhe is the white truffle: *tartufo bianco d'Alba* in Italian, *trifula* in dialect, and to the botanist *tuber magnatum*.

In late October on a Saturday morning, weaving through the market stalls along Alba's narrow Via Maestra, your nostrils will be assailed by an extraordinary volatile, penetrating, decadent perfume. In the Mercato del Tartufo, rugged characters with rough hands huddle together and look shiftily about, as if expecting an imminent raid by the vice squad. Wearing berets and straw hats, they smoke their cigarettes from cupped hands. There is much conspiratorial conversation. The arrival of a buyer will prompt the jealous unveiling of their treasures from the earth: dull lumps resembling potatoes or Jerusalem artichokes. If a deal is made, the sums of money changing hands may well be into seven figures (of lire that is). In 1989 the price for a good specimen was in excess of £600 per pound.

For the *trifolau*, the truffle hunter, a morning's work can feel like winning the national lottery. The rewards are almost as great for those who bring inferior specimens from hundreds of miles away in the Abruzzi or Umbria and pass them off as local truffles. Between the beginning of September and the end of December the *trifolau* will set off at dawn with his dog to the secret locations where he hopes to

unearth the culinary jewel. The truffle lives in symbiosis with the roots of trees, particularly the oak, and a clue to its presence is often the absence of any surface vegetation near the base of a tree. For it to flourish, the ideal conditions are dampness and rain. So it is said that a good vintage and a good truffle season are mutually exclusive; but either way the farmer has means of richly consoling himself.

The only tool required by the truffle hunter is a slice of bread ready to jam into the dog's slavering mouth as it unearths the truffle. At Roddi there is even a university for truffle hounds (favoured breeds are poodles and terriers) whose graduates have included dogs from as far afield as Canada.

The truffle must be eaten while its perfume is most intense. The tinned version is usually a very expensive disappointment, while the extra virgin olive oil flavoured with truffle shavings accurately retains the pungent aromas. A few drops of this oil can be sprinkled on one's pasta without the need for prior consultation with the bank manager.

The white truffle's fabulous value (the black type, as celebrated in Perigord, is treated with disdain in Alba and sold for a tenth of the price) is no doubt due in part to its magical and aphrodisiac reputation. In 1368 the Duke of Clarence took an Italian wife whose dowry included the Langhe truffle hills. Unfortunately his excessive consumption of *trifule* at his wedding feast meant that he did not live to test their reputation that night. Savonarola was doubtless not seeking an aphrodisiac effect, but nevertheless complained that the truffle was hard to digest. The twentieth-century 'King of Truffles' was Giacomo Morra (1889–1963) who succeeded in tinning and exporting the tuber. His public relations efforts were considerable, every year gifts of fresh truffles were sent to the famous all over the world. The largest recorded specimen was sent to President Truman – it weighed in at over 2.5 kilos!

The paradox of the truffle, essentially earthy and elemental, yet in the theatre of the grand restaurant elevated to the role of *prima donna*, is shared by *langarolo* cooking as a whole. The hordes of wealthy Milanese who pile into La Belvedere restaurant in La Morra every weekend in autumn perceive the Langhe table as a cornucopia of gourmandise and excessive richness. Of course there is a tradition of great feasts at weddings and holidays, but historically, the everyday reality of the Langhe has always been the simple and robust style of rural poverty.

POLENTA AND BAGNA CAODA

From the days when work in the vineyards and cellars was far more physically demanding than today, there remains the legacy of hearty dishes rich in calories. For the modern city dweller a feast in the Langhe should be approached with caution and patience.

Giorgio Rocca, chef and owner of Il Giardino da Felicin in Monforte, can remember when workers would congregate in the village square to fortify themselves mid-morning with mugs of tripe soup and beakers of Dolcetto. It is important to remember that in Italy wine has always been considered a food, a source of calories. In these days of low alcohol and low calorie obsession, it is easy to doubt the future for strapping great red wines.

In the same way, there are a growing number of restaurants in the Langhe whose style of cooking is evolving in parallel to the new styles of wine, using traditional local ingredients, but with smaller portions, more delicate flavours and new techniques adapted from *nouvelle cuisine*.

As in many parts of Italy, it is very difficult to understand fully Piemontese cooking solely by visiting restaurants, however excellent or typical they may be. Inevitably in a restaurant meat dishes play a far greater role than they ever would at home. Since the sixteenth century the peasant staple in the Langhe, as in many hilly zones of northern Italy, has been *polenta*. The coarse yellow maize flour is laboriously stirred in a large copper pot to make a sort of porridge which is then eaten in a communal fashion from a large board in the middle of the family table, its blandness enlivened with a slice of highly aromatic home-made salame.

The other great collective dish of the Langhe and Monferrato hills, also impossible to eat properly in a restaurant, is *bagna caoda* (literally 'warm bath'). The *bagna caoda* itself is a gently bubbling pot of olive oil flavoured with salted anchovy and garlic, which sits in the middle of the table and into which you dip a selection of raw vegetables. The vegetables may include a wide range of textures and flavours, such as capsicum, Jerusalem artichoke, onion, celery, cabbage, radish, fennel. However, according to tradition, the indispensable vegetable is the *carda*. The cardoon resembles a broad-based, coarse celery and has a pronounced bitter flavour. Of course, the *bagna caoda*, which is normally a complete and leisurely autumn evening meal *in famiglia*, is hard work on the digestive system. The after-effects are notorious, but can be softened by first removing the garlic's green heart and boiling it in milk for fifteen minutes before adding it to the bubbling oil and anchovy. A red wine with plenty of acid is needed to accompany *bagna caoda*, ideally a weighty dry Freisa, or failing that a good young Barbera.

ANTIPASTI

The Albesi are famous for the long succession of tiny portions of starters that are commonly served in their restaurants. In most traditional hostelries there is no written menu. You will be served from the menu of the day, which may include up to ten different *antipasti*, followed by a *primo piatto* of pasta, and then a *secondo piatto* of meat, then by cheese and/or dessert. The golden rule is to take your time.

The *antipasti* are normally variations on a number of conventions. Fish are not common in the hills, but dishes of cold, cooked and marinated eel or carp from the Tanaro are traditional.In summer it is common to serve various fried meats *in carpione*: with a sharp vinegary dressing that does no favours to wine. Various *funghi*, wood mushrooms of all sorts, are almost worshipped in the Langhe. The king of mushrooms are *porcini*, large *Boletus edulis* which can be served in many ways, even deep-fried as a *secondo*, but are particularly delicious raw with oil and lemon.

Carne cruda (raw meat) is ubiquitous both in restaurant and home. Raw veal fillet is served in two different ways. In the first it is sliced very thinly in the fashion of *carpaccio* and served with oil and lemon and shavings of parmesan cheese (and when available white truffle too). The other method resembles steak tartare, where the ground meat is briefly marinated, and this is known as *insalata di carne cruda*. We find the former style more digestible.

Vegetarians will be more at home with the *frittata erbetta*, which, being cooked long and slowly, resembles a tortilla more than an omelette. Other *antipasti* may include green and yellow peppers served with the oil, anchovy and garlic accompaniment of *bagna caoda*, various pâtés and flans, and flights of fantasy such as stuffed zucchini flowers.

Rather than bread, delicious home-made grissini are more common. Those unevenly shaped, metre-long wands of golden crunchiness bear not the slightest resemblance to their factory-produced namesakes.

The wine that will go with all these things is, of course, Dolcetto. Dolcetto, because of its supple fruitiness, is the wine for all foods, *vino da tutto pasto*, and will commonly be drunk from beginning to end of a meal.

PRIMI PIATTI

At this stage in the meal, you will probably have to make a choice. It sounds easy, because there are normally only two alternatives. In fact the decision can be agonizing, because both are so wonderful in their own way.

Both sorts of pasta are classics of the Langhe. If there are truffles about, you will probably opt for *tajarin'*. These are similar to *taglierini*, but must be home-made from a hard dough of only flour and egg, rolled and cut into very fine strips by hand. Giorgio Rocca has an unusual inspiration for cutting the *tajarin'* every morning, rocking his knife back and forth to the strains of boogie-woogie jazz. The delicacy and apparent weightlessness of this dish is supported by a sparse and light meat sauce containing little or no tomato. If you have the resources to plump for truffles, the waiter will pre-weigh the specimen and shave it onto your pasta at table, using a sort of miniature mandolin. After he has reweighed it, some L30,000 per head may well be added to the bill. Don't worry, the heady perfume will dispel all your anxiety.

The other great pasta dish is *ravioli* (sometimes known as *agnolotti*), little parcels filled with a subtle meat and vegetable stuffing, and served with butter. The Langhe variety is traditionally larger, while nearer Asti they are often quite small and may be *col plin*, which means they are pinched and twisted together rather like a sweet wrapper.

At this stage in the meal you may remain happily with the Dolcetto, but equally it is a good time to begin drinking your Barolo or Barbaresco.

SECONDI PIATTI

The *secondo piatto* is often less daunting than might be supposed. In a good restaurant, when you are already rather full from the pasta course, it will be a small portion of well-flavoured meat or poultry.

The most common dish is *brasato al Barolo*, a joint of lean beef stewed slowly for many hours in Barolo and served sliced thinly with a little highly concentrated sauce.

Game is naturally popular in such a wooded, hilly region such as the Langhe. Wild boar are hunted still in the alta Langa. Their powerfully flavoured meat is normally stewed slowly. At Il Falstaff in Verduno, the young chef Franco Giolitto serves a tender, perfumed fillet of *cinghiale*, cooked pink. Game birds, particularly pheasant (*fagiano*) are often casseroled rather than roasted.

In truffle season, *fonduta* is a common dish that may be served as either *primo* or *secondo*. This is in origin an alpine dish of melted fontina cheese with a little milk and egg, that resembles swiss fondue. *Fonduta* makes a superb blank canvas on which to show off white truffles.

Traditional dishes of Rabelaisian proportions which involve a great selection of meats are declining in popularity. These encompass both the *bollito* (boiled) and *fritto* (fried) *misto*.

FORMAGGI

Piemonte offers a fine selection of local cheeses. The Langhe speciality is definitely *robiola*, also known locally as *töma* (pronounced 'tu-ma'). This small round cheese of sheep's or occasionally goat's milk was fêted by Pliny. Made of unpasteurized milk, every cheese seems to be unique in flavour. It may be eaten very fresh, served with a little olive oil and ground pepper, or matured into a strong flavoured cheese.

Three other richly flavoured matured cow's milk cheeses from the pastureland west of the Langhe are Castelmagno, Bra and Raschera, all of which enjoy DOC status.

Bross is another local speciality. Not a cheese for the faint-hearted, it is matured to the point of putrefaction and sometimes even fortified with grappa.

DOLCI

With such abundance of savoury flavours, perhaps it is not surprising that sweet things take a back seat in the Langhe.

The pudding most often encountered is *bönet* (often *della Nonna*), usually a rather dull, chocolate (sometimes with coffee), milk and egg pudding.

More promising is the Albesi's use of their superb local hazelnuts in *torta di nocciole*. This may resemble a cake or a tart according to the recipe. Its slightly dry texture cries out for its natural accompaniment: a rich, grapey Moscato d'Asti. Moscato itself is used in *zabaglione al moscato*, the pudding made from heated egg yolks.

Production of *torrone* is a small local industry. There are numerous styles of this slightly brittle nougat; the best is the hazelnut version, made with the famous local variety *nocciola tonda gentile*. Watch out for your fillings!

DIGESTIVI

After the meal, the restaurant owner will usually attempt to persuade you of the digestive properties of a small measure of grappa. Grappa is the distillate of grape skins left over after pressing, and may vary in style from firewater to an ultra-refined *eau de vie*. Most grappa made in the Langhe is a white spirit with no wood age. The current fashion is for single grape variety grappa, even from a single vineyard. Grappa made from moscato can be extraordinarily aromatic, staying true to the unmistakable perfume of the variety. Nebbiolo often gives a more earthy style of grappa, although the best examples have richness and subtlety. Top small-scale specialist producers are Fratelli Marolo in Alba and Fratelli Rovero at San Marzanotto near Asti. The only wine producer with its own distillery is Ceretto, who produce a number of single vineyard bottlings. Most other winemakers have their own grappa distilled and bottled for them at one of the local distilleries. One grappa specialist worth looking out for is the eccentric Romano Levi in Neive. The hand-torn and drawn labels depicting 'La donna selvatica' (the wild woman) are to be seen in all the finest restaurants.

A SELECTION OF RESTAURANTS

Alba

Daniel's, Corso Canale 28; tel. 0173/43969. Closed Tuesday.
A smart restaurant with good service offering a slightly lighter style of traditional cooking. Good wine list.

La Capannina, Borgo Moretta; tel. 0173/43952. Closed Monday.
A rustic atmosphere prevails at La Capannina, run by the Gallina brothers just outside Alba. Portions are for those with a good appetite. Good wine list.

Osteria dell'Arco, Vicolo dell'Arco 2/b; tel. 0173/363974. Closed Sunday.
Simple regional cooking in a small, smart, modern trattoria. Encyclopaedic wine list.

Il Vicoletto, Via Bertero 6; tel. 0173/363196. Closed Monday and Sunday evening.
Carefully prepared traditional food in a simple but tasteful setting. Good choice of wines.

Barbaresco

Vecchio Tre Stelle, Frazione Tre Stelle; tel. 0173/638192. Closed Tuesday.
The young Scaiola brothers are bringing enthusiasm and new ideas to an old-established restaurant. Very good value and a fine selection of Barbaresco on offer. Tre Stelle is a few kilometres south of Barbaresco on the road to Alba.

Barolo

Hotel Brezza, Via Roma 33; tel. 0173/56191. Closed Tuesday.

In its modernized form, Hotel Brezza has lost a little of its old world charm, but remains one of the few places to stay in the vineyards. Traditional restaurant with a wide choice of wines including Barolo and Dolcetto from Brezza's own vineyards.

Del Buon Padre, Via Narzole 50, Frazione Vergne; tel. 0173/56192. Closed Wednesday.
Giovanni Viberti and his wife run a friendly little restaurant that offers the genuine taste of Langarolo home cooking; generous portions and rich flavours. Giovanni's own Barolo is also recommended, the cellar is under the restaurant.

Castiglione Tinella

Trattoria Moscatel da Palmira, Piazza XX Settembre 18; tel. 0141/ 855176. Closed Tuesday.
Palmira is the great character in the kitchen at this traditional trattoria. She still cooks many of the almost extinct Langarolo peasant dishes such as *tartra'* (a sort of savoury egg custard) and *batsua'* (pigs' trotters). Good selection of wine.

Grinzane

Al Castello; tel. 0173/62159. Closed Tuesday, booking advisable.
Grinzane's noble castle houses not only a fascinating *enoteca*, but also this elegant restaurant with panoramic views over the Langhe. Traditional cooking and vast choice of wine.

La Morra

Belvedere, Piazza Castello 5; tel. 0173/50190. Closed Sunday evening and Monday, booking advisable.
Gianfranco Bovio is one of the region's most charming hosts (not to mention talented Barolo producers), and his sister Maria Vittoria cooks textbook examples of the classic regional dishes. A smart yet

relaxed restaurant that gets very crowded at weekends in truffle season. Fine selection of wines.

Trattoria Veglio, Frazione Annunziata; tel. 0173/50717. Closed Thursday.
An unassuming little trattoria on the winding road down the hill towards Alba. Good home cooking at very modest prices.

Monforte

Il Giardino da Felicin; tel. 0173/78225. Closed Wednesday, booking advisable.
Giorgio Rocca's cooking can be inspirational. He brings a light touch to many of the Langhe's most serious dishes. The counterpoint to his gruff humour is the elegance of his wife Rosina and the passion of his son Nino for all things vinous. Excellent food in smart surroundings with a stunning choice of wines. There are simple rooms above with a view of the vineyards. A popular choice with Swiss and German visitors.

Trattoria della Posta. Piazza XX Settembre 9; tel. 0173/799120.
An unpretentious trattoria serving ample portions of serious country food. Wines from the best local producers.

Hotel Grappolo d'Oro, Piazza Umberto; tel. 0173/78293.
A simple, friendly hotel in the village square. Good, honest cooking. Good wines from Monforte growers.

La Collina, Piazza Umberto 13; tel. 0173/799297.
Family-run bar and restaurant serving traditional dishes. Sound choice of wines.

Neive

La Contea, Piazza Cocito; tel. 0173/67126. Closed Monday, booking advisable.

In this intimate restaurant Claudia Verro cooks dishes of daring and fantasy using the great traditional raw materials of the Langhe. Long and dazzling menus with a fine selection of wines from the top producers.

Roddi

La Crota, Piazza Principe Adameo 1; tel. 0173/615187. Closed Tuesday, booking advisable.
Popular traditional restaurant.

Serralunga

Trattoria del Castello, Via Baudana 49, Frazione Baudana; tel. 0173/53375. Closed Tuesday.
Good traditional cooking in a rustic setting just to the north of the village. The Zunino family produce their own wines.

Treiso

Osteria dell 'Unione, Via Alba 1; tel. 0173/638303. Closed Monday and Tuesday.
Intimate trattoria with a simple, totally reliable, classic Langarolo fixed menu cooked by Pina Bongiovanni. Good choice of wines. Fine value.

Vezza d'Alba

Trifula Bianca, Via Torino 9, Frazione Borbore; tel. 0173/65110. Closed Wednesday.
Good value traditional cooking in a rather unatmospheric setting. Sound selection of wines.

Verduno

Il Falstaff, Via Comm. Schiavino 1; tel. 0172/4592443. Closed Monday, booking essential.
Young chef Franco Giolitto's enthusiasm brings a fresh approach to Albese traditions. Well-balanced menus of more delicate flavours. A rising star. Good choice of more unusual wines.

CONCLUSION

Winemaking in the Langhe stands at a crossroads. Since the 1970s more and more Piemontese winemakers have been asking questions about their own wines, in terms of how the grapes are grown, how the wines are made, and most importantly who they are sold to. The enthusiasm and innovation of young, small-scale growers has woken up the whole trade in Alba. The complacency of long-established negociant houses has been shaken as more and more small farmers have begun to vinify and bottle their own products.

The reaction of the bigger privately owned houses such as Fontanafredda and Marchesi di Barolo has been to put more marketing emphasis on an increasingly large selection of upmarket single-vineyard wines. This trend, combined with the diminishing availability on the open market of grapes from the best traditional sites, means that every year it is harder to make good generic wines.

Why has Barolo, Alba's flagship, become difficult to sell? For the top single estate producers there is little problem, but for the medium-sized negociant and the cooperative it is hard work to avoid stockpiling. The short and painful answer is that the wines are not good enough. The traditionalist producer would say his wines were not understood – the old cry of 'That's my Barolo, take it or leave it' (hydrogen sulphide and all). By the beginning of the 1970s the Italian market had lost faith in Barolo; it had become a product impossible to sell for nine months of the year, the sales only seasonally redeemed by the wine's long-standing function as a Christmas gift. Barolo's image had become entangled in a mesh of cobwebs, and many producers still made a product to match, tasting of dank, dirty cellars. Wines were being made for a market that no longer existed, despite the revealing fact that in Italy good, fruity Dolcetto was, and remains, a much easier selling proposition than Barolo.

Today's reality is that the average standard of wines is being raised. Albese wines are being made in a cleaner, fresher, more fruity style: one that is easier to appreciate for the man who doesn't have a plate of wild boar in front of him. The Piemontesi are an inherently conservative breed, and they will never entirely abandon the concepts of tradition which simultaneously support and undermine the progress of winemaking in the Albese. It is easy to become sentimental about a rural area many of whose centuries' old traditions are in danger of dying out, but survival is about adapting to new circumstances. While the zone's potential for superb quality wines has been demonstrated as never before with the 1985 vintage wines from top producers, the 1990s will be crucial in redefining the image of Albese wines.

The shortcomings of Italy's DOC system, established in 1963, are widely recognized. In effect, it only guarantees the origin and approximate style of a wine, giving no real indication of the quality level. The introduction of the superior classification of DOCG for Barbaresco and Barolo was a unique opportunity to put the record straight. Instead it only went half way, tightening up on the movement of stocks to put an end to the arrival of the tanker from Puglia in the middle of the night, and ensuring that all wines were subjected to the approval of a tasting commission. Given some of the poor quality products in circulation that have been certified as 'typical', one is entitled to question the value of a tasting panel who have strong commercial interests in the region and are reputed to reserve their rejections exclusively for the smaller producer with no political clout.

DOCG has done little to reassure the consumer of the class of Barbaresco and Barolo, and nothing at all to help him grasp the concept of a wine which can cost anything from L4,000–40,000 per bottle ex-cellars and yet still have the same basic denomination. There is an urgent need to raise the public image of the great Nebbioli, particularly on the export market. The surest route would be to introduce a new, officially sanctioned three-tier system of appellation:

generic, commune and cru. The Burgundian model of a pyramid of quality can be applied to Barolo and Barbaresco in a logical and true fashion. The three levels would be:

Generic: e.g. Barolo DOCG
Commune: e.g. Barolo di Castiglione Falletto DOCG
Cru: e.g. Barolo di Castiglione Falletto Vigneto Monprivato DOCG

In the absence of any unified campaign to restructure the law, a simple and successful marketing strategy has evolved which has helped producers sell their best wines: the use of the cru. The cru concept, although rooted deep in Alba's history, was first commercially developed in the early sixties by the likes of Prunotto and Vietti. Since then tiny producers owning only one vineyard have seized on the idea, making a virtue of necessity. The marketing potential of cru labelling was elaborated and championed for the public in the 1970s by Luigi Veronelli and Renato Ratti. While there will never be a simple answer to which sites are the greatest in Barolo and Barbaresco, there is now ample information to classify the proven outstanding crus. Factors of microclimate and the variation of soil within a single vineyard site may prevent such a precise classification as achieved in Burgundy, and there will always be those who argue that a blended wine is potentially greater than the sum of its crus.

Products such as Monfortino and Gran Bussia demonstrate that in absolute terms a generic wine can be the equal of any cru. Small but prestigious growers such as Domenico Clerico are now even talking of returning to the blend for its greater potential balance. As the smaller *aziende agricole* become more successful, their holdings may be expanded throughout the various communes, and the ultimate dream of a perfectly balanced Barolo become a reality. But for the moment the cru is in fashion. To justify its place (and its price) the cru must be able to demonstrate its own individuality. As in the rest of Italy, the Langhe has its share of 'crus' of dubious merit waiting to be weeded out by a strict official classification. If you look hard enough, almost every vineyard in Italy has a name of some sort!

The cru has become a vital selling tool for producers of Barolo and Barbaresco. By giving it official status, and introducing an intermediary level of communal classification, the developing structure of the market would be reinforced and made comprehensible to the outside world. The Langhe's profile would be raised overnight, and with luck and hard work the quality of the lower end of the market could be pulled up to a level of respectability. As we write, the region of Piemonte has decided to undertake an official classification of crus, but there is not the slightest indication that this is ever intended to be married into the DOCG rules. The major potential obstacle to the restructuring of the law is the vested interests of the big and powerful, who, whether private or cooperative, far too often prevent the administration of the curative medicine. In Italy, regional, commercial, *consorzio* and cooperative politics can be relied on to fudge the issue with excessive bureaucratic delays. In the cold light of day, an average annual total of 2 million cases of DOCG red Albese wines is not a lot to sell throughout the world if one compares the 43 million-case production of red Bordeaux. An even more pointed comparison is that between Barolo's 540,000 cases and the annual figure of a single Bordeaux commune, such as the highly prestigious Pauillac which makes an average 630,000 cases. The obvious conclusion is that there is no room in the Albese for bad wines.

The revolution in the cellar has affected nearly all producers in one way or another – with every vintage fewer faulty wines are made. Contributing factors include improved temperature-control facilities at fermentation, earlier and better controlled malolactic fermentations, improved cellar hygiene and shorter cask ageing. Nor is the revolution over. The fervour for experimentation (and investment in stainless steel and *barrique*) is as strong as ever. We hear reports of some cellars reintroducing the now controversial submerged cap system in a new high-tech Australian-derived form!

Progress in the vineyard is a slower affair; the intuitive wisdom of the *contadino* is not easily dismissed by agricultural scientists. Serious research work in the fields of clonal selection and choice of rootstocks has hardly begun. Inevitably changes are hampered by the absence of a vital young work force in the vineyards. Vineyard owners now talk of using imported labour from Africa and the Third World. Following the lead of Gaja in his new plantation such as Darmagi, more producers are experimenting with the potential benefits of the extra sunlight exposure afforded by planting in vertical, rather than the traditional horizontal rows. Individual experiments by small growers like Elio Altare and Enrico Scavino have proved the dramatic effects of deliberately reduced yields, but the message remains incomprehensible to the average *contadino*. The vicious circle created by artificially low prices for nebbiolo means that overproduction (often beyond the DOC norms) is the only means of survival for the farmer selling his grapes. The responsibility for improving the quality of fruit lies not just with the negociant and the cooperative, but also with the importer, retailer and, ultimately, the consumer. If the world shows no sign of appreciating a better product and only wants to drink a familiar name at an affordable price, then the future is bleak.

Pointing the way ahead are the rich Swiss and German markets, which consume plenty of generic Barolo but also shows an unquenchable thirst for the cream of the Langhe's crus. The USA is receptive to quality, while Britain seems reluctant to look beyond the lowest prices. The fickle Italian market, dominated by fleeting concerns of modishness, has begun to re-evaluate Barolo and Barbaresco, thanks to the new lustre conferred by the 'designer' houses of Gaja and Ceretto. In Italy Dolcetto d'Alba is the belle of the ball, its uncomplicated fruit widely appreciated; while the majority of Barbera d'Alba remains undeservedly in the dog house, remembered only for a mean acidic streak. The disappearance of the lowest level of Barolo and Barbaresco would leave a convenient gap for Alba's other varieties to step into the edge of the limelight. Nebbiolo d'Alba and Roero have further to come, but there is room for the best examples. Some of Alba's most exciting red wines are now being released as *vini da tavola*. These limited production wines are vital to Alba's success on the wider market. They are the stars that will add the necessary glitter to the scene.

The significance of Alba's white wines will grow enormously over the coming years. In response to a newly white-thirsty domestic market, almost every grower appears to be planting new vineyards of white grapes as fast as possible. It is too early to assess the ultimate quality potential of the zone for white wines but the signs are good for wood-aged Chardonnay. Arneis is in a boom period, and there are indications that the quality is beginning to justify some of the hype. To be sure of long term success, Arneis producers will have to tie a few heavy weights to the price balloon. Moscato d'Asti, the original low-alcohol wine, is surely destined to follow in the wake of Asti Spumante's international success.

The corner has been turned, the journey is being undertaken with the energy and spirit of a strong community. 'Siamo sulla strada giusta' is beginning to ring true.

VINTAGES

At the beginning of the 1990s growers are questioning the habits of a lifetime. In the late 1980s summers have been getting hotter and drier, while snowless and rainless winters have made their own contribution to a lack of moisture in the ground. Whether these factors can be attributed to global warming, sun spots or a temporary aberration in the climatic balance, the reality is that grapes are ripening earlier and with less acidity. The resulting wines have high pH levels, and, particularly in the case of Nebbiolo, may lack the traditional structure despite the attractively ripe style they display in their youth. One group of growers is so concerned that it is petitioning for the law to allow 10 per cent barbera to be added to Barolo to readjust the acidity.

1989

Weather Patterns

Despite a cold winter where periods of sunshine alternated with heavy fogs, there was no snow for the second year in succession. The dry spell continued throughout the early spring with temperatures climbing towards the end of March for bud-break in the better exposed sites. April, however, was wet and foggy and though the temperatures continued to rise, stormy weather brought hail at the end of May and beginning of June. The communes of Barolo and Serralunga suffered the worst and dolcetto, in particular, was badly affected. Fortunately humidity levels remained fairly low and the diminished crop healthy.

The weather turned around in the middle of June with a succession of warm, dry days and though violent hailstorms hit the Roero in the second week of July, the rest of the month was very hot and dry. Although a little variable to start with, most of August enjoyed warm and dry conditions. The beginning of September was disappointing and retarded the development of a crop which, up till then, was very advanced. The second half of the month was very fine for the dolcetto and barbera harvests and the nebbiolo crop was in perfect shape when picked in early October.

Summary

1989 must be classified as an exceptional vintage; some growers are already, and perhaps prematurely, claiming it is superior to 1985. Hail reduced the size of the crop at a very early stage but thereafter climatic conditions were excellent with little humidity-related disease. Unprecedentedly high sugar levels for nebbiolo (over 22° Babo) have been reported but they were balanced by excellent acidity: some Baroli had arrived at 15 per cent alcohol following fermentation. Initial signs are of superbly balanced, deeply coloured wines brimming over with sweet, ripe fruit: early optimism appears to be well grounded.

1988

Weather Patterns

Following a mild, dry winter, the first rains fell at the end of March. Spring was rather variable but, because of the generally moderate conditions, budding took place early – in Cannubi nebbiolo buds were already open by 9 April. The uneven weather continued throughout May with heavy rains during the second week. Towards the end of the month, the weather had turned cloudy and rainy with fairly high humidity.

The nebbiolo vines began to flower towards the end of May but the variable start to June delayed the other varieties. After some mid-month hail, the rest of June was wet and stormy with high humidity.

Following a patchy start, July enjoyed much better, hot and dry weather though humidity levels rose towards the end of the month. Similarly the first three weeks of August were hot and dry with more uneven weather in the final week. The start of September saw a drop in humidity levels and the return of cool night temperatures. Most of the rest of the month was fine and the grapes in a very healthy state heading into the final phase of the vintage. October started well but fairly heavy rains between the 10th and 16th dashed hopes of a truly great vintage in Barolo (though by now most of the crop had been harvested in Barbaresco). However, the sun returned immediately afterwards, quickly drying the grapes out again for a medium-sized harvest of good if not great quality.

Summary

Despite the poor late spring and early summer, some excellent weather in July, August and September helped the grapes to ripen well. The week of rain just prior to the harvest did not prove disastrous as the immediate return of good weather kept the grapes healthy.

Wine Styles

Cask samples of Nebbioli have shown a forward, ripe and elegant style of wine not overloaded with tannins. They should provide excellent early to medium-term drinking. In general those who picked early made the best wines. Similarly the early-ripening grapes (barbera, dolcetto and the white varieties) produced some first class wines.

Production Figures for DOC(G) Wines

Barolo: 6,710,533 bottles
Barbaresco: 2,361,466 bottles
Nebbiolo d'Alba: 1,497,200 bottles
Roero: 756,400 bottles
Barbera d'Alba: 5,874,666 bottles
Dolcetto d'Alba: 7,889,600 bottles
Dolcetto di Diano d'Alba: 795,066 bottles
Moscato d'Asti: 32,455,466 bottles

1987

Weather Patterns

After a fairly warm, dry autumn, winter arrived with a vengeance in mid-January with heavy snows and cold temperatures which continued throughout February and March. The first week of April was cold and wet but conditions improved with warmer weather for bud-break at the end of the month. The first half of May was cooler with rain towards the end of the third week but the end of the month saw drier, brighter weather.

Highish humidity and frequent rain made a miserable start to June and flowering took place in cool and damp conditions around the middle of the month. July started bright, clear and very warm. After a patch of stormy weather mid-month, temperatures rose and remained high through into the first week of August with winds keeping humidity levels and the risk of disease down. Apart from some light rains at the start of the final week, temperatures and humidity stayed quite high. September, by and large, was warm and dry and, up to this point, the grapes were very healthy. (Peronospera had appeared briefly at the end of July and there had been little problem with oidium).

The beginning of October was fine too but the weather became very miserable with heavy rains in the middle of the second week during almost exactly the same period as in 1988, but conditions this year stayed humid until the end of the month.

Summary

The vintage looked promising until the heavy rains and high humidity arrived just before the nebbiolo was fully ripe in Barolo. Again Barbaresco fared rather better, but 1988 looks to be a superior vintage for both wines.

Wine Styles

On the whole 1987 lacks some of the ripeness and accessibility of 1988, producing rather leaner-framed wines. However they have good aromas and fair balance though will not be wines for very long ageing. Barbera was probably the most successful variety though some good Dolcetti were also made.

Production Figures for DOC(G) Wines

Barolo: 6,317,600 bottles
Barbaresco: 2,577,733 bottles
Nebbiolo d'Alba: 1,427,333 bottles
Roero: 593,600 bottles
Barbera d'Alba: 5,778,000 bottles
Dolcetto d'Alba: 7,239,467 bottles
Dolcetto di Diano d'Alba: 782,667 bottles
Moscato d'Asti: 31,444,993 bottles

1986

Weather Patterns

A cold winter with some snow in late January, during the second half of February and mid-March. Spring weather was very variable but seemed to be picking up in May when disaster struck in Barolo at the end of the month – on the 29th – with a violent hailstorm. The higher and more exposed sites were particularly badly hit and some growers were forced to resign themselves to a total loss of their crop. Barbaresco escaped the storm. Flowering was delayed by low temperatures at the beginning of June. The month ended with warm, sultry weather.

July's weather was very inconsistent with bouts of rain and high humidity but picked up for the final week. The brighter spell continued throughout most of August and into the first week of September. Thereafter the weather was humid and rather cool, but brightened up at the start of October and continued fair for the harvest.

Summary

Very variable weather for most of the year. The hail at the end of May wrought havoc with the size of the harvest in Barolo, but a good August helped to save the remaining crop. Peronospera was to be quite a problem because of the humid early summer but the good bout of weather at harvest time was beneficial.

Wine Styles

The hail affected some areas more than others, leading to a very uneven vintage. On the whole, the wines are quite ripe and perfumed but even in Barbaresco (which was spared the hail), high humidity was a negative factor and the wines lack the intensity and concentration of a truly great vintage. Many wines will provide very good medium-term drinking none the less. Some classic Dolcetti.

Production Figures for DOC(G) Wines

Barolo: 3,710,933 bottles
Barbaresco: 2,665,866 bottles
Nebbiolo d'Alba: 1,344,533 bottles
Roero: 437,867 bottles
Barbera d'Alba: 4,557,467 bottles
Dolcetto d'Alba: 5,484,533 bottles
Dolcetto di Diano d'Alba: 850,800 bottles
Moscato d'Asti: 30,530,667 bottles

1985

Weather Patterns

A rather cold winter with some heavy snows. Temperatures stayed cool throughout March and most of April but there was little rain. May was much warmer and much wetter with heavy rains in the middle of the month that slowed down the vegetative cycle of the vines. A glorious summer began at the start of June and lasted almost without interruption until the nebbiolo harvest. Brief showers of rain on 25 August and 15 September were particularly beneficial for the later ripening grapes while the cool nights and warm days from the beginning of September onwards helped to keep the ripening process on an even keel. The vintage started quite early with a largish crop of outstanding quality.

Summary

A truly exceptional vintage with near-perfect weather patterns.

Wine Styles

The vintage of the decade for Barolo and Barbaresco. The wines show outstanding balance of perfumed and concentrated fruit, fair acidity levels and ripe, sweet tannins. The rich fruit and soft tannins of the nebbiolo wines make them approachable quite young but they have the balance and concentration to age well. Many growers consider 1985 the best vintage for Barbera since 1947: some of the wines will age superbly. Some of the Dolcetti are excellent, concentrated wines, again with the ability to sustain several years' bottle age, though a few have proven to be a little over-ripe and their lowish acidity has resulted in a rather overblown style. Excellent Moscato (though only the *passito* versions will still be worth drinking).

Production Figures for DOC(G) Wines

Barolo: 7,260,533 bottles
Barbaresco: 2,662,000 bottles
Nebbiolo d'Alba: 1,532,133 bottles
Roero: 337,066 bottles (first year of production)
Barbera d'Alba: 6,182,000 bottles
Dolcetto d'Alba: 7,120,533 bottles
Dolcetto di Diano d'Alba: 763,200 bottles

1984

Weather Patterns

The first three months of the year were cool with some snow, especially in February. Although conditions improved in April, May was cold, cloudy and misty with very heavy rains – a difficult period for bud-break. The weather was variable for the first half of June and delayed flowering by between two and three weeks in Barolo (up to two weeks in Barbaresco). The second half of June was much warmer but the rain and heavy dew at the end of the month pushed up humidity levels.

The generally dry, clear and warm July weather continued into the first week of August but there was a wet spell in the middle of the month and high humidity caused problems with grey rot. September started off wet but in the cool temperatures that followed, while the danger of rot receded, the ripening process of the grapes slowed right down. The start of October was again wet, cool and humid but clear and warm conditions quickly returned and the weather remained stable for the nebbiolo harvest.

Summary

A very difficult year with rain and humidity problems at various key stages of the vine's growing season. The better weather which began in early October was of immense benefit for Barolo though came too late for Barbaresco and the earlier-ripening varietals.

Wine Styles

Those growers in Barolo who harvested later than normal and made a careful selection from their crop salvaged some good wines. While much mean and hard Barolo was made, the best are clean and well balanced with good, if highish, acidity, moderate tannin levels and fairly promising aromas. The vintage could prove to be something of a 'sleeper' in a few cases. 1984 was prematurely written off as a total disaster, in fact the better examples are probably more successful and certainly more typical than the 1983s (Barolo only). A poor vintage overall for Barbaresco and the other varietals with some very mean Barbera and Dolcetto.

Production Figures for DOC(G) Wines

Barolo: 4,310,400 bottles
Barbaresco: 1,405,733 bottles
Nebbiolo d'Alba: 809,733 bottles

Barbera d'Alba: 4,193,066 bottles
Dolcetto d'Alba: 5,930,666 bottles
Dolcetto di Diano d'Alba: 598,933 bottles
From 1984 onwards, the last four wines had to be bottled in 75 centilitre bottles in keeping with EEC directives.

1983

Weather Patterns

A fairly mild winter with no snow (a worrying sign for many growers who believe a snowy winter does the nebbiolo nothing but good), followed by a wet March. Although the start of April was again wet and cool, the weather picked up as the month went on. Bud-break occurred at the normal time but a variable May delayed flowering, though good weather towards the end of June gave excellent conditions for the setting of the grapes.

July was a warm month without rain but rather high humidity levels. The start of August was also warm but the weather turned sultry with rain in the middle of the month. High humidity returned and caused the onset of grey rot in the final week. September began well but the variable weather in the middle of the month made for autumnal conditions which continued into the start of October. The weather for the harvest was, however, much improved.

Summary

A very patchy vintage with a lot of humidity-connected disease. Rot was quite common and thus careful selection of the grapes was vital. The good spell of weather in June, when the grapes set, created a large crop.

Wine Styles

A large and rather disappointing vintage. The Nebbioli started off quite well, showing a forward, round and accessible style, but because of the low tannin and acidity levels, they are ageing very quickly. Many examples of Barolo and Barbaresco are now feeble wines characterized by a rather coarse floral/vegetal smell indicating that they will not develop any further. Obviously there are plenty of exceptions and the vintage on the whole was more successful in Barbaresco than Barolo, but even the best wines should be drunk soon.

Production Figures for DOC(G) Wines

Barolo: 7,467,533 bottles
Barbaresco: 3,216,133 bottles
Nebbiolo d'Alba: 2,398,055 bottles
Barbera d'Alba: 6,316,389 bottles
Dolcetto d'Alba: 6,946,389 bottles
Dolcetto di Diano d'Alba: 747,917 bottles
Moscato d'Asti: 33,214,675 bottles

1982

Weather Patterns

The cold, foggy, wet start to the year improved with clearer, warmer weather in March. April had similarly fine conditions building up into a warmer and drier than average May. June and July were hot months with hardly any rain at all. August too was very dry with consistently high temperatures: by now many parts of the Albese were suffering serious drought problems. In a year such as this, a clay-based subsoil will retain moisture and remains – via the deep base roots – the sole source of water for the vines. Light rains on 9 August provided a brief respite to the hot, dry summer. It was one of the hottest Septembers on record (overall average temperatures of 20.5°C – a good couple of degrees above the norm). The first half of October was also warmer than usual, though light rains in the second half of the first week caused no problems at this stage. The grapes were in a superb condition for an early harvest and, thanks to the wonderful summer, the crop was large as well as very healthy.

Summary

An excellent vintage overshadowed only by 1985 over the course of the decade. If anything, the summer was perhaps a little too hot and, though memorably rich, ripe and concentrated, the only question mark about the wines' long-term future hangs over their slightly low acidity levels. None the less 1982 produced some truly superb Barbaresco and Barolo.

Wine Styles

Wines of splendidly rich and ripe fruit underpinned by a firm and impressive structure of sweet, ripe tannins. They will provide wonderful drinking throughout the 1990s becoming velvety and sumptuous during the second half of the decade. The great wines will go on improving into the next century. Some excellent Barbera is still drinking well.

Production Figures for DOC(G) Wines

Barolo: 7,479,466 bottles
Barbaresco: 3,042,000 bottles
Nebbiolo d'Alba: 2,424,028 bottles
Barbera d'Alba: 6,675,972 bottles
Dolcetto d'Alba: 6,116,528 bottles
Dolcetto di Diano d'Alba: 714,444 bottles
Moscato d'Asti: 30,292,987 bottles

1981

Weather Patterns

A cold winter with snow in February. The spring was very variable with mild temperatures but lots of rain. This pattern continued throughout June and July with higher than average temperatures and rainfall with dangerously high humidity. Peronospera was rife throughout the hot, damp and clammy summer with rot setting in towards the end. September's weather was marked by a slight improvement, and a warm and humid first three weeks of October gave growers a glimmer of hope before a downpour towards the end of the month and even a brief snowstorm during the final week.

Summary

A very problematic vintage with heavy rains and much humidity-related disease. Once more a rigorous selection of grapes was the only possible way of making decent wines.

Wine Styles

A small crop of light-to-medium-bodied wines even the best of which are now fully mature.

Production Figures for DOC(G) Wines

Barolo: 6,233,866 bottles
Barbaresco: 2,760,133 bottles
Nebbiolo d'Alba: 1,712,222 bottles
Barbera d'Alba: 5,123,056 bottles
Dolcetto d'Alba: 4,260,833 bottles
Dolcetto di Diano d'Alba: 477,083 bottles
Moscato d'Asti: 22,396,623 bottles

1980

Weather Patterns

Winter was fairly mild with above-average temperatures though some snow in January. Spring was mild but wet, leading to a cooler than average June and July with a wet spell right in the middle. The weather improved throughout August and September with temperatures reaching fairly high levels and, although rainfall in August was above the average, September was quite dry. October started with a warm spell, but steady rain during the second week compounded the problem of a pretty damp vintage.

Summary

A large but rather dilute crop of reasonably healthy grapes. There was simply too much rain throughout the year to produce wines of real concentration and backbone though the cold nights from the beginning of October were beneficial for nebbiolo.

Wine Styles

Average quality for both DOCG wines – though lacking some intensity and structure. Rather forward but quite perfumed wines most of which are now fully mature: some indeed are starting to dry out. Baroli have lasted better than Barbareschi.

Production Figures for DOC(G) Wines

Barolo: 7,238,933 bottles
Barbaresco: 3,142,400 bottles
Nebbiolo d'Alba: 1,948,194 bottles
Barbera d'Alba: 7,374,028 bottles
Dolcetto d'Alba: 6,804,306 bottles
Dolcetto di Diano d'Alba: 776,528 bottles
Moscato d'Asti: 20,162,597 bottles

1979

Weather Patterns

A cool start to the year with widespread frost, mist and some snow. April and May were much milder months with less rain than usual and some bright, clear weather. June began well with warm, dry weather for flowering though there was some rain at the end of the month. July was quite hot and dry and the good weather continued throughout August interrupted by a few light rains. Temperatures in September were higher than average with a few showers in the middle of the month. The problem with 1979 was a wet October with steady rain for most of the month.

Summary

Initially a promising year with good weather up until the end of September. The wet start to October rather diluted a potentially excellent vintage.

Wine Styles

A fairly large crop of rather soft-centred wines, many of which were delicious in the mid-eighties but which lack the concentration to give them true staying power.

Production Figures for DOC Wines

Barolo: 7,387,917 bottles
Barbaresco: 3,229,028 bottles
Nebbiolo d'Alba: 2,592,638 bottles
Barbera d'Alba: 11,036,250 bottles
Dolcetto d'Alba: 6,922,778 bottles
Dolcetto di Diano d'Alba: 818,194 bottles
Moscato d'Asti: 24,264,675 bottles

1978

Weather Patterns

The first two months of the year were cold and damp. Spring too had lower than average seasonal temperatures and frequent rain – April and May were particularly wet months. Not until the second half of June did the weather pick up, too late for the flowering which took place in very wet conditions causing a significant reduction in the crop even at this early stage. Although July and August were much drier, temperatures were cool for the time of the year and there were problems with peronospera in the rather humid conditions. After light rains at the beginning of September the weather suddenly turned right around and the rest of the month was hot and dry with a marked difference between day and night-time temperatures. The dramatic improvement continued through until the end of the nebbiolo harvest during the third week of the month.

Summary

A wet, cool spring and rather poor summer gave way to a wonderful autumn which saved the tiny, remaining crop.

Wine Styles

Some extraordinarily good Barolo and Barbaresco was made: the best are wines of phenomenal concentration and backbone with a deep core of rich and intense fruit beneath the rather forbidding exterior. Others however have proved to be less successful and that kernel of fruit has not held up beneath the fearsomely tannic structure, resulting in unbalanced wines which have already begun to dry out. The stars are real long-distance runners and in some instances may outlast the 1982s.

Production Figures for DOC Wines

Barolo: 4,413,750 bottles
Barbaresco: 2,005,972 bottles
Nebbiolo d'Alba 1,102,639 bottles
Barbera d'Alba: 5,114,583 bottles
Dolcetto d'Alba: 2,613,194 bottles
Dolcetto d'Alba: 289,861 bottles
Moscato d'Asti: 19,520,909 bottles

Other Vintages Worth Looking Out For

1974

A cold, snowy winter with spring coming late. Summer was hot and dry and a mild autumn allowed the grapes to ripen fully. Overall weather patterns (including summer droughts) have parallels with 1982 and the wines were similar in many respects too, being fairly firm and tannic with lowish acidity but good, rich fruit. Now fully mature.
Barolo: 7,252,916 bottles
Barbaresco: 3,049,027 bottles

1971

An icy-cold winter continued through into April, then hail in May and June reduced the size of the crop. The clear, hot summer lasted through into a perfect, warm, dry October giving a smallish crop of wonderfully rich and concentrated wines of exceptional balance and elegance. The best still have plenty to give. The vintage of the decade.
Barolo: 5,500,000 bottles
Barbaresco: 1,569,026 bottles

1970

Another cold, snowy winter retarded the vegetative cycle of the vines but the rest of the growing season was very favourable with generally warm and dry conditions. Although overshadowed by 1971 and perhaps lacking some of its structure and concentration, 1970 produced some superbly balanced and perfumed wines which are now fully mature.
Barolo: 4,552,500 bottles
Barbaresco: 1,842,222 bottles

Good Earlier Vintages

1967 (a fairly large crop of ripe, balanced wines) and 1964. 1961 was the best vintage in living memory for some producers (e.g. Prunotto) and 1958 was also exceptional. Though now almost impossible to find, 1947 was magnificent. Wines from the best producers, if stored well, are easily capable of lasting this long.

GLOSSARY

Acciaio inossidabile	Stainless steel
Acino	Grape or pip
Ammostatura	Fermentation process involving addition of whole grapes to must
Aratura	Ploughing
Autoclave	Pressure-controlled sealed vat
Azienda agricola	Company producing wines exclusively from grapes grown in its own vineyards
Barolista	Specialist Barolo producer
Borgata	Small, outlying village or suburb
Botte	Large horizontal wooden cask (may be from 10–200 hectolitres)
Brenta	Traditional wooden pannier for transporting wine or grapes on a human back. Also a measure of volume equivalent to 48 litres
Bricco	Prime hilltop vineyard site
Cantina	Cellar
Cantina Sociale	Cooperative cellar
Cantiniere	Cellarmaster
Capo a frutto	Fruiting cane of a vine
Cappello	Cap (mass of skins and pips on surface of fermenting must)
Cappello sommerso	'Submerged cap' method of maceration where cap is held below surface of must
Cascina	Farm
Ceppo	Trunk of vine

Colmatura	Topping up of casks with wine
Conca	'Shell'-shaped vineyard. Protected amphitheatre for vines
Concentrato	Concentrated grape must
Concimazione	Fertilization
Consorzio	Consortium of producers
Contadino	Peasant farmer, usually owning or renting a few vineyards
Cru storico	Historic cru with a tradition of producing superior grapes
Damigiana	Demijohn: glass bottle of about 50 litres
DOC	Denominazione di origine controllata. The official classification of Italian wines controlling origins, grape varieties, yields and methods of production
DOCG	Denominazione di origine controllata e garantita. A supposedly superior classification of wines that additionally have to pass a tasting panel. The category includes Barbaresco, Barolo, Brunello di Montalcino, Chianti, Vino Nobile di Montepulciano and Albana di Romagna (*sic*)
Enoteca	'Wine library' – specialized wine retailer
Fermentazione	Fermentation
Fermenti	Yeasts
Filare	Wire or trellis
Follatura	Breaking up the cap on the fermenting must
Fondo	Lees or sediment
Frazione	A small hamlet or village: usually a 'fraction' of a larger village
Frizzante	Slightly sparkling
Fusto	Small wooden cask of under 10 hectolitres
Gemma	Bud
Germoglio	New growth of vine (leaf or flower)
Giornata	2.66 *giornate* = 1 hectare. The origin of the measure (a day) was the amount of land one man could work in a day
Graspo	Grape stalk or stem
Hectare (ha)	About 2.5 acres
Hectolitre (hl)	100 litres
Innesto	Graft (of a vine)

Legatura	Tying up (vine canes)
Lieviti	Yeasts
Macerazione	Maceration (of grape skins)
Malolattica	Malolactic (e.g., fermentation: transformation of malic into lactic acid through action of lactic bacteria)
Metodo classico	Bottle fermentation of sparkling wine (cf. *méthode champenoise*)
Mezzadria	Feudal tenancy stystem under which the farmer gives half the crop to the landlord
Mezzogiorno	Literally 'midday' – the south facing exposition characterizing the top red grape vineyards
Mosto	Must (unfermented wine)
Muffa (grigia)	Rot (grey)
Negoziante	Negociant producer (purchaser of grapes and/or wine)
Normale	Often used to distinguish a producer's regular product as opposed to a cru or *riserva* version
Novello	New wine (usually red) made to be drunk very young (cf. *vin nouveau*)
Passito	Wine (usually sweet) made from partially dried (passiti) grapes
pH	The scale on which acidity is measured (n.b. high acidity = low pH and vice versa)
Pigiatura	Crushing (of grapes)
Polyphenols	Chemical name for tannins
Potatura	Pruning
Quintal	100 kilogrammes
Ragno rosso	Red spider
Resa	Yield. Also used to describe amount of wine that can legally be produced from a given weight of grapes (e.g., *resa in vino* 70 per cent)
Rimontaggio	Pumping fermenting wine from the bottom of the vat back over the top to assist fermentation and colour extraction
Riserva	Category of wine that has been given longer ageing (in practice often in cask) before

	release. Minumum age five years for Barolo, four for Barbaresco
Ritocchino	Vertically planted row of vines
Rovere	Oak
Sarmento	Branch of vine
Sfuso	Bulk (wine)
Sori'	Dialect word for vineyard with prized southern exposure
Sperone	Spur of vine (cane for subsequent year's fruit)
Svinatura	Racking of newly fermented wine off the mass of skins etc.
Terra/terreno	Soil, earth or land
Tino	Large upright cask (open-top versions were traditionally used as fermentation vessels)
Tipicità	Measure of a wine's truth to type
Tralcio	Shoot (of vine)
Uvaggio	Wine made from a blend of different grape varieties (cf. cépage)
Vigna/vigneto	Vineyard
Vignaiolo	Vine grower (cf. *vigneron)*
Vinacce	Mass of stalks and stems left after fermentation (used for Grappa production)
Vino da tavola	Literally table wine: theoretically the lowest quality denomination, but in practice including many of Italy's finest wines which fail to fit into any DOC pattern
Vite	Vine

SELECT BIBLIOGRAPHY

Anderson, Burton, *Vino*, London, 1982
Belfrage, Nicolas, *Life Beyond Lambrusco*, London, 1985
Camera di Commercio di Cuneo, *Albo vigneti, 1988, 1989*
Fregoni, M., *Carta dei vigneti di barolo, barbaresco e nebbiolo d'Alba*,
    Provincial Administration of Cuneo, 1975
Gianoglio, Domi, *Invito alle Langhe*, Turin, 1965
Gleave, David, *The Wines of Italy*, London, 1989
Goria, Giovanni and Verro, Claudia, *La cucina a quattro mani*, Turin,
    1985
Guida Turistica Enogastronomica delle Langhe e del Roero, Rome,
    1989
Massé, Domenico, *Il paese del Barolo*, 1945, reprinted Marchesi di
    Barolo, 1982
Massel, A., *Basic Viticulture*, Hindhead, 1976
Montaldo, Giancarlo, *Sulle strade dei vini d'Alba*, Turin, 1987
Morando, A., *Aspetti della viticoltura Albese*, Treviso, 1983
Peynaud, Emile, *Connaissance et travail du vin*, Paris, 1981
Peynaud, Emile, *The Taste of Wine*, London, 1987
Ratti, Renato, *Guida ai vini del Piemonte*, Turin, 1977
Vioglio, F. (ed), *La Scuola Enologica di Alba*, Alba, 1981

INDEX

The index lists names of people, companies, vineyards and unique wines; but not villages, towns, grape varieties or generic wine styles.

267